We Remember
DUNKIRK

We Remember
DUNKIRK

FRANK & JOAN SHAW

EBURY
PRESS

1 3 5 7 9 10 8 6 4 2

This edition published in 2013 by Ebury Press,
an imprint of Ebury Publishing
A Random House Group company
First published by Frank and Joan Shaw in 1990

Copyright © Frank and Joan Shaw 1990, 2013

Frank and Joan Shaw have asserted their right to be identified
as the authors of this Work in accordance with the Copyright,
Designs and Patents Act 1988

The Random House Group Limited Reg. No. 954009

Addresses for companies within the Random House Group can be
found at www.randomhouse.co.uk

A CIP catalogue record for this book is available
from the British Library

The Random House Group Limited supports the Forest Stewardship
Council® (FSC®), the leading international forest-certification
organisation. Our books carrying the FSC label are printed on
FSC®-certified paper. FSC is the only forest-certification scheme
supported by the leading environmental organisations, including
Greenpeace. Our paper procurement policy can be found at
www.randomhouse.co.uk/environment

Printed and bound by CPI Group (UK) Ltd, Croydon, CR0 4YY

ISBN 9780091941543

To buy books by your favourite authors and register for offers visit
www.randomhouse.co.uk

Contents

INTRODUCTION vii

DUNKERQUE xi

WE REMEMBER DUNKIRK 1

APPENDICES 335

ACKNOWLEDGEMENTS 349

INDEX 351

INDEX OF CONTRIBUTORS 369

Introduction

Dunkirk was the first great epic of the Second World War and the stories that appear in this book record only a very small part of it. That is inevitable – more than a million men of the Allied and German armies were involved. Yet their memories are the memories of hundreds, thousands of others. Personalised, perhaps, by individual incidents, in general terms they reflect the feelings and recollections not only of soldiers and sailors, but also civilians, nurses, voluntary workers and schoolchildren.

The British Expeditionary Force (BEF) had set out for France with high hopes. 'We're going to hang out the washing on the Siegfried Line' – the popular song of the time expressed both their confidence and their sense of being 'in the right'. The 'Phoney War' of 1939–1940 did nothing to dispel their feelings.

The explosion of the German armies into France, Belgium, Luxembourg and Holland without warning on 10 May 1940 took the Allies by surprise, but the High Command soon swung into action with operations to meet the main German thrusts that were confidently expected to come through Belgium and Holland. They didn't.

Instead, the main German armies burst out through the Ardennes Forest region of Luxembourg and France, bypassing the vaunted Maginot Line and swinging north to the coast.

Some considerable activity was certainly taking place in the Belgian/Dutch region, but it was largely a feint to ensure that the Allied High Command were confirmed in their belief that that was where the main attack would still come. In boxing parlance, it was a dummy right hook, followed rapidly by a left hook to the chin, with a vengeance.

In a matter of days the German army had covered the open rolling countryside to Abbeville that was ideal for their new concept of tank warfare. That move had two other advantages. It was an area that was largely unprotected and, once to the coast, the BEF and the French army were effectively cut off. It was only a matter of working steadily up the coast, capturing the ports – and the BEF and French army would be in the bag! It would then become just a simple mopping-up exercise.

The fact that this did not happen was due partly to orders being issued by the German High Command that slowed down the German advance when Calais and Dunkirk lay within their grasp. By the time those orders were corrected the BEF and French army had recognised the situation and taken measures to keep Dunkirk open. The heroic defence of Calais which is referred to by one of the writers in this book was a major factor in their being able to do that.

The Battle of Dunkirk was won by the German army. That was already inevitable once they had reached Abbeville on 20 May 1940, and before the Allied High Command had even realised the danger. But in a sense the battle was also won by the Allied soldiers and sailors, for although all equipment was lost, almost 340,000 men were brought out.

There have been different descriptions given to Dunkirk. Some saw it as a tragedy. Some as a miracle. There was, in fact, a national euphoria at the escape. There was also almost a sense of relief that at least Great Britain now stood alone – it concentrated the mind wonderfully.

But whatever celebrations there were of the escape from Dunkirk, Winston Churchill was quick to remind the House of Commons of the reality. On 4 June 1940 he said, 'We must be very careful not to assign to this deliverance the attributes of a victory. Wars are not won by evacuations.'

Nevertheless, in that way peculiar to the British, we rightly take enormous pride in what was achieved in those nine days of Dunkirk. To this day, to have been at

Dunkirk remains a signal honour. It was a time of immense courage and endurance, something which we should recall and remember. Do so by reading these letters. These people are writing as they recall events, and they are their own personal recollections. Allow for that when you read these stories and compare them with official histories. It doesn't alter the fundamental story of the defence of this country and, indeed, civilisation by these men against the Nazi terror that would otherwise surely have enslaved Europe, and possibly the world.

Anyone reading these letters will see there is no glory in war. But what there can be is pride in what you are doing, or why you are doing it. These people had both.

Frank and Joan Shaw

Dunkerque

1 June 1940

We fought our way like heroes, from Brussels to the
   coast
So they said, and let's believe them, a betrayed and
   battered host.
We didn't fight for victory, or for glory, but for life
In every march was discipline, there was coolness in
   the strife.
But, through all that bloody struggle, a star above us
   shone,
It was our nation's honour, upheld when hope was
   gone.
So after miles of hardship, 'twas in the dawn's grey
   murk
We battled through the shellfire, to the beaches of
   Dunkerque.
Before us stretched those beaches, bestrewn with kit
   and dead,
La Panne in flames behind us, Dunkerque ten miles
   ahead.
And in all that weary distance was no cover worth
   the name
And then like hordes of locusts, the German
   warplanes came.

Their guns aflame raked o'er us, we scattered 'neath
    their storm,
But 'ere the droning vanished the order came
    – 'Reform'.
Then on to face the bombers that 'pasted' Bray Les
    Dunes,
To see our shipping vanish to those missiles' spiteful
    tune.
But they didn't pass unchallenged, for as they
    zoomed o'erhead,
From desperate men with rifles, they met a storm of
    lead.
So up in threes we mustered, and on tired and
    blistered feet
We marched along the foreshore, asweat in the
    evening's heat.
'Twas thus we entered Dunkerque, our goal in ruins
    stood
We couldn't smell the glory, we could only smell the
    blood
Of those who'd gone before us, whose labours were
    in vain
For there in desolation, forsaken, lay the slain.
The final phase, the greatest test, before us lay the
    Mole
And down it weary warriors trudged towards the
    ships, their goal.
It lay just like a ribbon, just holding four abreast,
Without a scrap of cover we stood there on the crest.
As we stood and waited our turn to go aboard
Oh God, we made a target, our only Shield, the Lord.

God must have had compassion, as in the flame-lit
    dark
Although the Jerry shelled us he seldom made his
    mark.
And so by light of morning, we made the Dover roads
Set foot at last in England, the land of curious codes,
Which made others brand us madmen – but then
    they're blind,
For the battle had been won for us – by those we left
    behind.
We were just the lucky ones, we'd played a risky game
And fought a rearguard action, which bore unheard-
    of fame
For cut off, part surrounded, starving, weary, short
    of guns,
Of men and ammunition, we had left for our sons'
    sons
The story of a miracle – a truth we almost doubt
Of how by God's great mercy, the BEF fought out.
And now we rest in England, whose smiling acres
    roll
And the care of many thankful hearts, revives a
    shattered soul.

*This poem was written by Lieutenant Alan Tatlow of B
Company, 1/6th Battalion The East Surrey Regiment,
and was submitted by Ron Davison, whose own article
appears in this book.*

We Remember Dunkirk

I enclose a copy of a poem written by my husband. I don't think this is of any use in your books, but I thought it may give an insight into the hearts of some of our boys who, like Harry, were out there for four and a half years without seeing their loved ones. He was no Keats, and I could not bear scorn about it, but it may be of interest to you.

Far from those I love the best
England, home – and pastures green
Longing for a world at rest
And simple pleasures that have been.
To put aside all selfish thought
Strain nerve and sinew for one end
Be that my aim – no praises sought
The right to live at peace – defend.
And when this struggle dark and drear
Be ended once for all
May I remember things most dear
Regained by sweat and tears and gall.
Grant that I may at last be fit
Those blessings once again to know
May I myself so well acquit
No deed of mine our peace o'er throw.

My husband was with the RASC in Belgium at the time. They were in private billets and working in the factory through the day, making petrol cans to send fuel up to the troops.

I was working in a factory at home. We knew that things were bad out there. I was not receiving any mail and did not know just where Harry was but the news was brought to us from the office – they had a radio in there. I remember them coming up into the works and telling us that Leopold had let the Germans in through Belgium. This was the news we had dreaded hearing. I stopped my machine and put my head down on it and burst into tears. How kind people are to each other in times like that! My work mates tried to comfort me, the boss said would I like to go home, but was smartly answered by my friend, 'No, she wouldn't, she's better here with us, she will only brood if she goes home.' So there I stayed!

It was several days before I had any news, then I got a letter to say Harry was in England. He had been on the beach at St Malo with a group of his men for three days before they had managed to get a boat for England, and was now at Broadstairs being re-kitted. Everything they had was left behind in the billet. The lorries had gone to the factory and they had been driven straight to the beach.

We were both musical and when he was posted in 1940 he had taken his violin with him and they had formed a little orchestra in the company, and the violin was left behind at his billet with the rest of his belongings. This really upset him. He had had it from being a young boy. I believe it was passed on in the family and it was a good instrument, but at the time he had far more to worry him. He was not hurt physically but his nerves were in a poor state. He had terrible nightmares, but they were not given time to think about it. Six days leave then they were off again.

He bought a new violin later, which travelled half way round the world with him and the old one was never mentioned. But a short time after he was demobbed in 1945 he received a letter from the Royal Military School

of Music at Kneller Hall, saying that they had a violin there which they thought belonged to him and would he confirm the details in the enclosed letter.

It appeared that a Belgian lady with whom they had been billeted had gathered up all their belongings and hidden them, so that if the Germans came and searched, their things would be safe. When the war ended she had sent these things to England and the violin had found its way to Kneller Hall. He was overjoyed to have it back. We never found out the full story nor could he remember the name or address of the lady but whoever she was, I wish I could thank her for her kindness.

Lily Butterfield, Shipley, West Yorkshire

There have been a lot of books about Dunkirk, but from my personal experiences most of them miss quite a few things. The roads leading into Belgium from France were littered with dead civilians, mown down with machine guns from dive-bombers and bombed continuously from day to day starting at dawn and going on to dusk. Coupled with all that was the carnage of military columns of lorries, French horse-drawn artillery columns, blown and shattered horses lying dead, others kicking in pain, wounded and we, as an ambulance convoy, were trying to get to the front. In the process we were having to stack dead people on the side of the road.

One incidence of poignant memory was of a young mother dead with a baby still suckling her breast. We gave the baby to another young woman who had a child, to try to reach wherever they were trying to get to, but one never knew as the Germans encircled all these trapped people in the escarpment whether they ever got away.

We eventually lost our ambulances through bombing and running out of petrol. We then had to destroy the engines with sledge hammers and then make our way towards Dunkirk which was ablaze as the oil storage tanks had been bombed.

During our trek we were without food and water, occasionally getting a piece of rhubarb out of a garden or something similar. But I remember one day we found a truck with some tinned fruit in it which had been abandoned. But it didn't go far as it worked out at one tin between four of us! We found a lorry with whisky on board so we helped ourselves to a bottle apiece, which helped to keep us warm. Sleep was impossible except for occasional catnaps, as one was continuously on the move.

We were turned away from Dunkirk due to excess men trying to get away as the ships were being bombed on the quayside. I saw a hospital ship loaded with casualties blown apart. A destroyer was split apart when a bomb landed on it.

We were moved on to La Panne, and thousands of troops were on the sand dunes. A medical centre had been set up in a cafe, and surgeons were trying to cope with the wounded who were being brought in their hundreds, due to the continued bombing and strafing of the beaches. The padre on Sunday took holy communion on a makeshift altar on the sands, during a lull, but no sooner was the service over than the bombers returned and I didn't see me padre or his altar again.

Vehicles, including a whole lorry park of new vehicles, were systematically smashed with sledge hammers and fired. Canals around the perimeter were set on fire with drums of petrol poured on to the water to halt the advance but the bombing and strafing continued daily, screaming bombs being a speciality to put the fear of kingdom come into you.

Yes, we were scared. It could be seen on the faces of the men. No food didn't help. We stopped to suck pebbles during the day as our tongues began to swell through lack of water. Troops became separated and lost from their units, and officers were too few and far between to give any cohesive instructions. It seemed to me it was mostly the NCOs who tried to orga- nise the zigzag lines of men across the beaches to get to the small craft that began to arrive to take troops off to larger boats.

We had an order come through to us one day: every

man for himself. And then the soldiers, Belgian, French and British, were side by side in silent, sodden ranks in columns of three, zigzagged across the beaches. I still believe that this was done to minimise casualties. We had to wade out up to our necks in water to get on to a boat, ducking under the water when the Germans tried to mow us down. Eventually I managed to grab a chain hanging off a naval motorboat, and it was fully loaded, but I hung on even though they tried to push me off with a boat hook. After being dragged about a mile out to sea, we eventually pulled alongside the SS *Yewdale*. Somehow, tired and bedraggled, we clambered up nets which were thrown over the side. The decks were crowded with troops so we had to go into the hold which meant going down a ladder. I can remember hearing the continuous attacks by dive-bombers, and the Lewis gunner on the ship, as far as I am concerned, deserved the VC! He never stopped firing at the German planes.

About six o'clock in the evening some bombs struck the ship but somehow God spared us, and we didn't sink although a large hole was blown in the hold where I was. There was a blinding flash, and shrapnel flew all round and a terrible blast blew my trousers off and a wave of vibration went through my body. I knew I had been hit, but being momentarily blinded by the flash it wasn't until I felt blood trickling that I felt around me. I had a chunk of flesh torn from my thigh, and gashes under my chin, on my temple and cuts all over my face. The Frenchman next to me had been killed.

The water sprinklers came on, but someone shouted the boat was sinking. Panic followed for a few moments as men tried to get up the ladder, front, back and sides. At that time I just didn't care as I felt horrible, but a voice shouted down that the boat was not sinking and anyone who was wounded and could walk was to get on deck for treatment. I was bandaged up and put by the galley. The boat eventually got underway and went, I think, sideways across the Channel. I think by this time most troops were that weary that they fell asleep. Men lay on top of one another, as the boat was that packed.

I woke with someone hailing the boat in thick fog and asking the name of the ship. Somehow, I do not know how, I was sitting on the ship's handrail with my back against a lifeboat. I looked up and saw on the side SS *Yewdale*. I shouted back as they said they were pilots from Deal. They said they were coming aboard. They got on board and awoke the captain and he must have anchored. I presume that he had done that because of the shelling damage and had tried to offload at Deal, but was unable to do it. So we were taken to Ramsgate.

The wounded were taken off first. I was carried off and we were put in some huts where tea was being served by helpers. This was about 7.30am on 28 May. The wounded were then taken to Ramsgate station and at about 9am we moved off. Postcards were put through windows at various stations for us to write home. These were then collected and given in at the next station. Somehow, somewhere at some station, someone found me a pair of grey flannels to put on!

I was eventually taken off the train at Derby, and laid on a stretcher after documentation, and we were taken to Derby Royal Infirmary, to my unit at Bullford.

However, I was taken off the train at Salisbury and ended up at Salisbury Royal Infirmary, with delayed-action shell shock. After a week I was transferred to Tidworth Military Hospital, and after another week taken all the way to Sutton Emergency Hospital in Surrey for treatment for shell shock. I spent a further seventeen weeks there and was finally discharged as unfit for further military service.

Arthur Thomas Gunn, Aldridge, Walsall

My birthday is on 28 May and it had become a family tradition that I would have strawberries and cream for tea that day. However, on 26 May 1940 I had more important matters to think about, for I was on active service with the British Expeditionary Force in Northern France where we were given orders to abandon our Signal Office and head for the English Channel.

Everyone in the billet had two minutes to decide what they should take with them and what they should abandon. I chose my shoulder pack, gas mask and cape, rifle and about thirty rounds of ammunition and we all piled into the back of three company lorries and set off in convoy, with our commanding officer leading the way in his car.

The main road was already cluttered with a non-stop stream of refugees. The wealthier were in their cars with a mattress or two on the roof in case of air attack. The poor had a selection of prams and handcarts containing their most prized possessions, and our convoy crept its way through them, young and old, men and women and crying and frightened children. Now and then the sound of an approaching plane was a signal for everyone to stop and take shelter, with many civilians huddling in the ditch while the bombs were dropped and the road was strafed with bullets, causing many casualties.

I lay under our Bedford lorry with my comrades until the danger was passed then we would resume our journey until the whole thing was repeated a few miles further on. During one such attack our commanding officer's car was hit and we carried on under the command of our captain. We were eventually stopped by Military Police who told our drivers to smash the lorry engines before pushing them into a nearby canal. Amongst the lorries already pushed into the canal was a NAAFI convoy

carrying supplies and its crates of foodstuffs had already been smashed open earlier by hungry soldiers. I took a packet of cream crackers and a pot of marmalade from the first truck and while in the second truck came across one small tin of cream, which I also quickly pocketed! Somehow I knew there and then that there would be a tin of canned strawberries somewhere in the third and last lorry and I searched and searched until I found it!

I then had to hurry to catch up with my mates who were stepping out for the coast but nightfall eventually made us all call a halt and I had a cream cracker and marmalade supper before eventually curling up in a barn for a rather apprehensive night's sleep.

In the morning we resumed our trek and by afternoon had reached La Panne. Here there was a solitary Military Policeman directing us along the sand dunes towards Dunkirk over which hung a large black cloud of oily smoke. The nearer we got to the port the more various sergeants ordered us to make ourselves as inconspicuous as possible by crawling crab-like towards the quayside where we might, if we were lucky, get taken off by a boat of one sort or another. It was during this time that I became detached from my comrades but I eventually, several hours later, climbed down a quayside ladder on to a lovely filthy coal barge which was chock-a-block with weary soldiers, but heading back towards England and home.

And so the beautiful morning of the 28th found me on deck watching, through misty eyes, as the white cliffs of Dover came nearer and nearer and then I ate a very non-traditional breakfast of strawberries and cream on a very memorable twenty-fourth birthday and I thanked the Lord for my deliverance and wept with joy.

So my family tradition was maintained against all the odds!

Ken Bamford, Wollaton Park, Nottingham

Dunkirk! It came as no surprise when we in the SS *Paris* hospital carrier received the orders to assist in the evacuation of Dunkirk. Calais had fallen about three hours after we had left with wounded from the port, and so we sailed again from Newhaven up the coastline of the English Channel to the Strait of Dover and on our way to Dunkirk. As we got nearer to the French coast, guns from one part of the coastline opened up, but the shells fell short. Then we saw the telltale smoke from the large oil containers which had been bombed. The smoke was billowing out for miles around.

But what a sight met our eyes as we sailed into the port. Ships of all shapes and sizes were plying to and from the docks and farther along the sands, taking away as many troops as they could carry. Some ships were partly submerged in the water, having been sunk. One, its guns pointing upwards, firing to the last. We eventually wended our way to a jetty to tie up, the main landing place having been destroyed.

Our orders were to evacuate as many wounded from the beaches as possible. Stretcher parties made their way down the jetty avoiding the holes which had been caused by shrapnel. The ship's crew in their civilian clothing, including the cook with his white apron on, hurrying down as well to give a hand to the wounded. What amazed me was the number of dogs which in terror had left the town of Dunkirk and were crowding on the jetty getting in the way.

After taking as many wounded as possible on board we gladly left Dunkirk on our way to Newhaven and England. Hot tea, soup and food were given to those who could take them. The seriously wounded were attended to and everyone made as comfortable as possible. Having reached our port in England, RAMC personnel were waiting to take the wounded off and transfer them to ambulance trains to hospitals in England. Fresh supplies were taken on board the SS *Paris* and again we sailed off on route to Dunkirk. The time on the way was taken up

with cleaning up our hospital wards and making up the beds for more to occupy when we landed, but the peculiar smell of gas gangrene from the wounds of men who had not received adequate attention was with us all the time, on our clothes and other material. Again as we neared the French port we saw the familiar sights of burning oil tanks and ships crowded with tired and war-scarred men.

Another hospital ship was leaving the port, signalling to us that the port area was being shelled. The Germans were closing in on the town. Once more we tied up alongside the jetty. Shells were dropping dangerously near, and some Nazi planes appeared from behind the smoke from the oil containers which was still pouring out. Every available gun from the ships around started to fire but the planes dived and machine-gunned the troops in the boats who replied with fire from their rifles. Having crammed every suitable place on our ship with wounded men we again left the port unscathed. The decks were packed, the wounded lay on stretchers, and our sleeping quarters were made into temporary hospital wards on our way to England again.

Here the same procedure was carried out, wounded transferred to hospital trains, supplies taken on board, on our way again up the coast of England to the Strait of Dover where we anchored. The evacuation of Dunkirk was coming to a close. We were told this would probably be our last journey across before the Nazis occupied the port. Another hospital carrier, the SS *Worthing*, was on her way across but to our surprise we saw the ship half an hour afterwards on her way back again. She had been attacked in the Channel by Nazi planes and so was returning. We did not know what damage had been caused.

After a short time a message was signalled to us to set sail on our way to Dunkirk. On board orders were given to put on our life jackets and tin hats. It was a lovely June evening and the sea was very calm, yet there was that eerie stillness about it all. Not a ship in sight as we sailed on our own. Pieces of timber floated by from some vessel which had been sunk. About six miles from Dunkirk I had just gone down below and was talking to two of my friends when one of the chaps on deck came down and quietly said, 'They're here.'

Three enemy planes had spotted us and begun to dive down on to the ship. We heard the roar of the planes and the screech of the bombs as they carried out their attack. A tremendous explosion shook the hospital ship as the bombs exploded in the water very near to us. The few of us who were talking together were thrown on our backs. A fire extinguisher was shaken off the wall and shed its substance amongst us. One of the men lost his nerve, thinking the ship was sinking, and ran about shouting the word 'Mother'.

A sergeant came up and very wisely, but roughly, quietened him. The ship was by now leaning at a peculiar angle. I decided to go on deck, and on my way there in one of the wards I noticed the empty hospital beds which were by now in a tangled mess. I remember thinking what a blessing it was that we weren't carrying any wounded. The liquids from bottles broken in the dispensary were flowing together to the side of the ship.

On deck everything was in a cloud of steam and smoke. The main steam pipe had burst from the explosion. One of the engineers had been badly scalded. However, his injuries were carefully attended to and he was carried to one of the lifeboats hanging out of the davits. The nursing sisters of the Queen Alexandra's nursing service, who were with us, were asked to get into the lifeboats. As I passed the wireless operator's cabin the officer told me that he had received a message from a place near Dover saying that help was on the way.

Distress signals were fired off when it was found impossible to sail the ship under its own power. Yet it seemed that the distress signals were an indication that another attack was imminent, for more Nazi planes were seen heading for us. Those of us who were fortunate dashed for cover. More bombs dropped on the helpers' ship in spite of the clear marking on the decks and sides of the large red crosses. It seemed that the Geneva Convention agreement meant nothing to these pilots.

With no opposition at all they came down and raked the decks and lifeboats with machine-gun fire and then left us to our fate. What a sight met our eyes when we got on deck. Many lifeboats, including those with our own personnel in them, had been hit and were floundering in the sea. Some were lying on deck having been hit with machine-gun bullets and shrapnel. These were helped into the lifeboats which remained and an order was given to abandon ship. When our lifeboat was lowered into the sea we helped into our boat some who had been in the water after a second attack. Other of our lifeboats picked up the remaining survivors. Amongst those who were wounded, one of the nursing sisters received severe head injuries and another had an arm badly shattered.

Two of the men died, one from extensive scalds and another from a machine-gun bullet which had penetrated a large artery in his leg. Our small boats kept together as far as possible although it meant baling out the water with our tin hats because of the bullet holes in the bottom of the boats from the air attack. We were glad to see, some time later, a trawler some distance away. As it came nearer someone on board shouted to us if we would care to come on board, but they were going to Dunkirk. We replied, 'We will come on board if you take us to England'! We eventually were taken on the trawler and arrived at Dover in the early hours of the next day.

Frank Lee, Bolton, Lancashire

It was on Tuesday, 28 May, 1940, when we were at Ypres that we were told that we had to retreat rapidly towards the coast. We were getting used to retreating by then. Since 16 May, when we had moved into Belgium, we had retreated from Belgium, moved down to Arras, retreated from Arras and again from Vimy and back into Belgium. We managed to drive to about six miles from the coast and then we had to abandon our transport. All the roads were blocked with vehicles that had been abandoned by troops as they neared the coast and so we walked the last few miles to the beach, machine-gunned and dive-bombed most of the way.

It was the Friday afternoon of 31 May when we reached the beach and it was already crowded with troops who had to keep diving for cover as the German planes strafed along the beach. We did not know what to do or where to go. Someone said that boats were coming to pick us up but there were none visible at the time. The lieutenant quartermaster in my unit suggested that we walk into Dunkirk and so six of us set off with him and I was thinking that at least we would have some cover from the buildings instead of having to lie out on the open beach. It was a hard slog through the sand for some miles, keeping our eyes on the planes and lying down when the strafing came too near, and it was getting dark by the time we  reached the town. In the confusion we had lost the officer and three of the lads, so the remaining three of us slept in a dance hall that night despite the noise outside.

The next morning, 1 June, we headed back to the seafront and we were roped in by a naval officer to carry wounded on stretchers alongside the mole to the ships tied alongside. The mole had been bombed in several places and across the gaps gangplanks had been placed. It was difficult carrying stretchers along it and then having to lift them shoulder height across the gangplanks. On our second trip the mole was strafed by planes and lying down beside the stretcher wasn't any protection at all. Just as we were moving on an officer examined our stretcher case and said, 'He's dead, tip him out and fetch another.' That's the horror of war. Late that afternoon we were loading a stretcher on to a paddle steamer with the help of a naval officer and suddenly he said 'Jump aboard, this is your last chance.' So we scrambled aboard.

The ship was dive-bombed and machine-gunned on the way across. It was so overcrowded that we could hardly move without scrambling over stretchers and other troops. When we were attacked for the first few times everyone rushed to one side or to the other side when the planes were approaching. Then someone on the bridge bellowed over a megaphone, 'Sit down and keep still.'

We docked at Dover near to the rail terminus and it was nearly midnight when we landed. I was one of the first off the ship and headed towards the trains and it was then that I noticed that the name of the paddle steamer was the *Medway Queen*. Standing at the entrance to the platform was a young girl aged about sixteen years with a big tray of sandwiches. I asked if I could have one and she just nodded her head. Looking back I must have been a frightful sight to her, unwashed, unshaven, uniform torn, blood and dirt everywhere.

I took the sandwich and walked on and when I looked back the girl couldn't be seen, only the soldiers surrounding her and grabbing sandwiches.

Brian Bishop, Lockerbie, Scotland

I joined the South Eastern and Chatham Railway in 1917, during the First World War, at the age of fifteen. By the Second World War I was driving steam engines.

I remember 'Dunkirk Week', as it was called by all those who worked in the thick of it. It was the most vivid week in my railway career. The South Eastern and Chatham Railway was the only railway to serve the south-east ports of Dover, Folkestone and Ramsgate, so all the Dunkirk evacuation had to travel via that railway. As it was too dangerous to go via London, all the trains went via Tonbridge, Redhill, Guildford and Reading. As Redhill was at one end of a triangle this was indeed a difficult operation, as all trains had to pull into the station for the train engine to be detached, and for another engine, facing the right way, to be attached to the rear of the train to go to Reading.

As the men from Redhill, Guildford and Reading depots were the only men who had knowledge of the Reading branch it was the lot of these depots to work all the trains from the south-east ports and to work the empty trains back. The first thing that took place was to cancel all rostered duties and all booked trains. As each pair of men signed off duty, it was book on again after nine hours off. This was the earliest time one could be brought back on duty. It was marvellous how the men dealt with the situation. The trains were moving continuously day and night.

I shall never forget the troop trains. Out of every compartment the soldiers' clothes were hanging from

the windows to dry, for many
of the men had to walk in the
sea to the small boats which
brought them back to England.
Another thing I remember
well is the number of people
on each station platform and
beside the track, to see if they
could spot their relatives and

friends. When the trains stopped at Guildford the
soldiers were given tea etc by many willing helpers.

Another interesting thing happened to me. I was
standing on the footplate of an engine in a siding at Ash
Station in Surrey, waiting to work a train forward to
Reading, when a train came in to the down platform
loaded with Moroccan soldiers who had come from
Dunkirk. As it stopped an officer beckoned me over and
asked if they were near Reading. I told him it was about
eighteen miles away. He then asked me if I was going to
Reading. I said, 'Yes, it is where I live.' He then asked me
if I knew a shop called Jackson's. I said, 'Yes, Jackson's
Corner is a well-known landmark in Reading.'

He then gave me a card to take to a Mr Edward
Jackson who owned the shop, and to tell him the train
was going to Southampton via Aldershot, and to ask if it
would be possible for Mr Jackson to go to Southampton
to see him. Of course I said, 'Yes, on my way home from

work.' When I looked at the card it was in the name of a French Count! On my way home I called in at Jackson's shop and asked for Mr Jackson. The assistant tried to put me off; I suppose I didn't look fit to see his boss – I was rather dirty, after a long day at work. Of course I said I must see Mr Jackson at once. Mr Jackson came into the shop and I gave him the card. He said he would go at once and said how grateful he was. The Count had married his au pair girl some time before. I felt all I had done was worthwhile!

Jack Hewett, Earley, Berkshire

I was in the 50th (Northumbrian) Division, and a driver in the 12 Troop carrying company, using three-ton Bedford vehicles. We were, of course, in the Royal Army Service Corps. I first became aware that something was going wrong when we were in Lille where we were ordered to park our vehicles and, after a brew-up, 'await further orders'. It was during darkness that Lille then presented itself to me as a place of another sort of darkness and lifelessness. I don't recall seeing a single light.

Explosions from shellfire were happening everywhere and, quite frankly, were too close for comfort. Buildings were being damaged but I don't remember any other casualties. Eventually we were ordered to 'reform convoy' and move off. The truth of the state of the war, if we needed it, was soon to become very clear. Lille again came under further bombardment as we received orders to remove camouflage nets (for the last time) and in convoy proceed towards, as we later learned, Armentières.

A short distance out of town our convoy was slowed to walking pace because the road was blocked by civilians. I wasn't aware of orders, but soon our 'troop carrying' role changed to 'civilian carrying' as we were all moving in the same direction, west. Homes and shops were deserted, the owners having fled. All the doors were wide open and, of course, inviting theft. This fact was brought home to us (during a halt) by our passengers who had jumped down from the vehicles, entered the shops and emerged with their arms full of all manner of food in boxes and tins. It goes without saying that these people were hungry and anyway, by now, it was realised that everything that was left behind would be possessed by the German army.

We didn't realise it, but our brew in Lille on the previous night was to become the last 'government' issue to our company, at least during our service in the British Expeditionary Force. In retrospect, we realised that the civilians already knew something that we didn't – that the Germans were coming and the Allies were retreating.

Very soon now the civilians were ordered to get out

of our vehicles and the military convoy proceeded empty westward. Around midday we arrived at the village of St Sylvestre-Cappel. Parking our lorries beyond the village, orders were given of a defensive nature. I found myself pointing a .303 rifle along the road from which we had arrived. Nothing happened for a while and then we were instructed by our officer to 'stand down' and my recollections tell me that we were then told, 'Every man for himself.' Vaguely I remember the church tower was used by us as a good observation point from which, within a very short time, we could see, as well as hear, the approach of the German tracked vehicles and tanks. They positioned themselves in a copse outside the village.

It appeared we were a group of ten or twelve left in the village by now and I remember a cafe owner had provided for us since we had arrived. Frank Morris, Mark Law

and I still found time to accept their kindness. Suddenly a French lady present shouted 'Boche'. Walking in single file at the lower end of the village were the German soldiers. We three were ushered out of the back door of the cafe by an elderly lady. Keeping as low as we could, we crossed a field towards a road which approached the village from the south. We had seen a small convoy approaching and I always remember my pleasure to find that it was British!

We stopped the leading vehicle and warned the officers of the occupation of the Germans of the village. 'It's the only avenue of escape,' said the officer who, with the company sergeant major, went to reconnoitre. Turning the corner of a building they were met with machine-gun fire. Thankfully the two officers returned, but the company sergeant major had been wounded. He had lost part of his chin. We were impressed with his courage and coolness. The commissioned officer said we would have to 'run the gauntlet' and invited those of us remaining to board the lorries, lie on the floor and speed through the village and take the road signposted to Dunkirk. Above the noise of the speeding engine we could hear the machine-gun fire but to my knowledge no one else was injured. We were also aware of the enemy aircraft threatening so much that our vehicle at last ended up in a ditch! We had travelled by then probably six miles or so.

We then walked, in twos or threes, in the direction of the coast and Dunkirk still a few miles away. It was covered by a black pall of smoke. On the road we, and other units, met up at an area where all vehicles were immobilised. Dunkirk had been bombed and shelled and was now in ruins. Embarkation, which was the theme, from the mole and docks was impossible and our army was now directed along the sands towards La Panne.

We settled on the sands until darkness came, and within an hour or so we saw flashes of lights at points out to sea. In turn we were to wade out to sea, then swim and clamber aboard the waiting ships whose crew I remember warned us to 'keep quiet or else'. We lost a few poor souls that night alone, because they could not swim. Each of us survivors had just enough energy, I feel sure, to save themselves.

We were all presented with a tot of rum and settled down somewhere to sleep, thankfully. We were awakened in daylight and entering a port, in our case Ramsgate. Though we were even then urged to move quickly as the ship had to make a return trip to La Panne.

After writing to you I remembered that at St Sylvestre a particularly sad thing happened. In between the arrival of the German tanks in the copse and their troops marching into the village a civilian (French) car sped through the bottom road towards the oncoming Germans. It was impossible to warn the people in this car as we were at the upper end of the square and I recall it seemed to come from nowhere. I also recall one of our lads saying, 'Wait for it.'

We understood this remark and following the distinct noise of a gun turret revolving there were two almighty explosions. One came from the gun, and the other from the destruction of the car, with all its occupants.

George Bowers, Stoke-on-Trent, Staffordshire

I suppose the first realisation of what war meant was the day that I was asked to be a cashier on the counter at the bank where I worked as, one by one, the men were being called up for service. I guess I was among the first women to be given this 'honour' as before the war women on the counter were not generally encouraged! Incidentally, the most pay I ever received was £2.90 per week. In the evenings and Sundays I worked as a Red Cross nurse at the hospitals in Birmingham. I worked at the Queen Elizabeth, the General and the burns unit at the Accident Hospital.

When Dunkirk took place, my next realisation was when our 'boys' were shipped home to Southampton.

One of my neighbour's relations took his cabin cruiser over and helped bring some of them back. Dozens of private boat owners risked their lives doing this. From Southampton, some of the wounded were transferred to a train up to Birmingham and along a local line which doesn't exist now, right up to the Queen Elizabeth Hospital. We had to cut off their uniforms, some still wet with seawater and full of sand and dirt, and stow them under their beds.

Every ward was crowded and, funnily enough, I remember that the latest pop record at that time was 'Sand in My Shoes'! Although I had worked on surgery I had never witnessed such appalling wounds as I did then. Some had legs or arms off and many had those awful shrapnel wounds which I will never forget. Sister always seemed to ask me to be the one to help her do the dressings and one day I asked her why this was, as I was only a voluntary nurse, and she told me that it was because my eyes above my mask were always smiling; I never never showed the man lying there the horror of what I was looking at.

Funnily enough, Vaseline was our godsend then. We sprinkled powder on to the wounds and then packed the large shrapnel wounds with bandages coated with Vaseline on both sides.

Our best enjoyment was on Sunday nights when we went to the Warley Odeon where they had live bands: Geraldo, Sid Lawrence, Billy Cotton etc. My lifelong friend and I sometimes went to the Odeon after church on Sundays. Our parents would have been horrified had they known! On Saturday nights we held the church socials in the church hall, table tennis, concerts and general fun and games. But I had two boyfriends from there killed, one on his first flying mission, and the other starved as a Japanese prisoner of war.

So many boys from our social club never returned.

I remember two who were conscientious objectors but still went into the Medical Corps and served on the front line.

A happier memory of the war is that my brother, who was in the navy, survived his ship being torpedoed by a U-boat. He was picked up at sea and taken to Florida. He lost his speech for days but after a month of good food and care he came back to us on another ship. I clearly remember that he brought back for each of us a banana, but for me, particularly, my first pair of nylons. What a thrill!

I hope people will always remember to buy their poppies on Remembrance Day. All those lads I saw without arms and legs, or with badly scarred faces from burns, still desperately need our help.

Mary Cope, Norton, Stourbridge

I landed in France in January, 1940 with 271 Battalion of the 68th Field Regiment, Royal Artillery, being called up from the Territorials. A fortnight before that I had been working on the farm. The guns we had were eighteen-pounders with wooden wheels, straight from the

1914–18 War. Our transport was confiscated furniture vans, coal wagons and many other associated vehicles. This, to fight the might of the German army!

We arrived at Amiens, Northern France, myself and two mates a day later because of an accident we had which, to me, was very funny at the time but not to the Frenchman who was driving the other vehicle! In those days a lot of French trucks were driven by steam. They had a boiler at the front which was fed with wood or whatever. However, it came out of the side road a bit too far and my wagon caught his boiler and sent it flying with steam, flames and sparks everywhere. Soon we had a Frenchman jumping up and down in anger and a crowd gathered round and at the finish the gendarme arrested him for striking him in his anger and we all moved off sharply!

On a lovely May day we heard news that the Germans had invaded Belgium and Holland and we set off and entered Belgium with lilac leaves and flowers being given to us from the civilians packing the roadside. Little did we know that within three weeks we would be overrun. We proceeded to just outside Brussels but this was after many harrowing hours clearing the roads of the dead and wounded refugees who were fleeing their homes, leaving everything bar what they could carry. They were machine-gunned by the German fighter planes to block the roads by causing confusion and so hold up our tanks and guns.

The task of clearing the roads was a task I shall never forget. Children and babies, old and young, some so badly injured that the French 'medics' were putting them out of their agony with half their bodies blown away and with terrible injuries. As a twenty-year-old who had never up to then seen a dead person this has stuck in my memory and will do to the end of my days. Within two days my unit had been scattered by the incessant dive-bombing of the German Stukas, as many as three hundred in the air at any one time. Having lost all our equipment, we were formed into an infantry battalion using rifles of our dead comrades. Food was not a problem. There were many NAAFI store vans and army store trucks abandoned and, as we pulled back to Tournai, there wasn't a house or shop occupied. In the houses people had left the tables with half-eaten meals and shops were abandoned.

In the afternoon a formation of German bombers arrived. We were now down to three men and a truck. They bombarded the town for two hours and we were under the truck and there wasn't a building left standing when they departed. The task of the police and rescue services must have been enormous. We made our way out of the town and finished up with a hundred or so lads from the 51st Highland Division. Then we got the news that the Belgian army had surrendered. That left one flank wide open, but a ring was formed around the town of Dunkirk itself with orders to be captured or to lose your life but no retreat as the BEF was being taken off by sea. We were surrounded, but there were still some units fighting it out at Calais. Then an officer came to us, said that we had done our stint, we were being replaced and to make our way to Dunkirk.

This we did, arriving in the town. It wasn't badly damaged and we made for the centre, and then they came over and the sky was black with planes. We made for a small brick shelter which had been built above ground and the whole place shook for about an hour and a half. I was petrified! I never expected to come out of there alive but, by the grace of God, I did and the devastation was horrendous at the harbour area, in ships and hotels, everywhere people were trapped and wounded and we spent a day and a half helping the rescue services. Then we were ordered back to the beach. On the beach there were thousands of troops, French and Dutch and, of course, the British. Hundreds of wounded laid out on the sand waiting to be taken off. The columns of troops were orderly until the planes came then [they] dispersed, firing with the only thing we had left, that was the rifle, and it was to no avail. The Germans came in as low as they possibly could, strafing everyone including the wounded as they laid helpless. I remember the bellies of the planes seemed to be nearly skimming the sand!

The situation looked hopeless so I and my mates

decided to get off the dunes and wait to see what happened. As I made my way up the slope I recognised my sergeant from my unit on a motorbike. He came round the corner and I think he had had too much French wine and went straight into the harbour, bike and all! Some fishermen fished him out. I remember the hundreds of trucks of all types of equipment. We set fire to everything we could lay our hands on. We had to destroy or damage everything beyond repair.

I remember those days of the sea mists which stopped, for some short time, the German fighters seeing the beaches and it was at that time that most of the troops were taken off. However, I was not one of them! But when the mist cleared and the little boats and the navy came in they suffered severe losses. I saw about twenty ships sunk, including a hospital ship and two destroyers full of Guardsmen, and many of the brave little ships were victims as well. But they came back in again despite all that. The night before I got away, a handful of French nuns came down on to the beaches and they gave to as many of us as they could some coffee and rolls with no thought for themselves. I will remember them, as I will remember many a brave act from kids of eighteen or nineteen who lost their lives and whose heroism was never honoured.

I got on a small boat. I don't remember its name but I remember it was from Ramsgate and I thought my ordeal was over, but a returning German bomber looking for anything he could drop a bomb on, came out of the sunlight and I was on the siderail of the boat and they all shouted 'it's a Spitfire'. We all jumped to cheer and then we saw the markings on the  wings and I crouched down by the side of the boat and I felt the crush of the other troops against me. I saw the bomb drop and it missed the side of the boat but only by a few feet and I felt that if I had put my hand out I would just have been able to touch it.

Yes, I remember Dunkirk. To round off that day, Dover was under heavy bombing as we entered the harbour but what a wonderful feeling to be back on English soil again and what a wonderful reception the WVS, Salvation Army and all the other organisations gave to us and that helped to ease the horror of the past few weeks.

But I will also remember this. To send an army out there against the might of the German army, armed with First World War weapons and tanks straight from the training centres that broke down after a few miles, and 1914 Lee-Enfield rifles against their automatic weapons, and with an air force outnumbered by at least twenty to

one and a Maginot Line which was useless ... then somebody had to be responsible. And where our MI5 or
whatever it is called got the idea that the German forces
weren't so good I don't know! But I do know that
everyone who took part in that Dunkirk episode was a
hero, whether they were in the armed forces or in the
little boats or in the Women's Services and, of course, I
will never forget the wonderful nurses and the people
who looked after the wounded.

Thomas William Jones, Clayton, Bradford

I was sent to France with the 44th Home Counties
Division. We went through France up to the Belgian
border, having little to do other than training. When,
unexpectedly, the Germans broke through Belgium we
had our first encounter with them at Oudenaarde. The
Germans were far superior in weapons, training etc, so
we were really outmatched from the start and almost
immediately started retreating, coming back via Ypres.

At Zonnebeke they asked for butchers with slaugh-
tering experience. I and eleven others volunteered and
our job was to go up forward to kill cattle and pigs to
supply our division. We took a breakdown truck with a
crane to hoist up the cattle and we then gutted them and
halved them and loaded them on lorries to take back to
the supply depot, which was a brick factory at Zonnebeke.

The problem was that we had no hot water to scald the pigs, and so we had to skin them, which was a difficult job to carry out in a brickworks! Each time the Stukas came over we rushed into the brick kilns, often knocking over the skinless pigs into the sand. Certainly I should imagine they would be an experience for some poor soldier to eat.

At the end of our work we were sent back to join our company, but on arriving at our headquarters we found that it had gone and at the rail track opposite our billet the rail carriages had been turned over, blocking the crossing.

We took a side road not knowing where it would lead us, but luckily we met up with a few chaps and an officer whom we knew. He told us to make for the frontier, so twelve of us set off.

We arrived there and we were then told to dump our trucks in a field with hundreds of others and immobilise them. We were then told to make for Dunkirk where we might stand a chance of being evacuated.

Having arrived there, the whole place was a shambles with troops lying about everywhere. There were fires and thick black smoke from the docks.

I finally met up with three chaps that I knew and we made our way along the beach and then decided to have a try to find something afloat. After what seemed days we saw a small light signalling out at sea so two of us decided to investigate.

We threw away all our equipment and also our rifle, after removing the bolt, and I and a chap named Curly Taylor swam until we came to what looked like a coal ship with a net slung over the side, and quite a number of soldiers hanging on.

There was an officer pointing out who was to climb up, telling us whoever came up without his orders would be shot! It's quite an experience being told that, and then, when your turn comes, trying to climb a net after having been soaked to the skin!

After everyone was aboard we set off, taking over seventeen hours to reach Ramsgate. Then we went by train, not knowing our destination but which turned out to be Reading.

I am now seventy-one and have not seen Curly Taylor since, but I would love to meet him again.

Bob Raynsford, Reading, Berkshire

It all began for me when I was detached from my own section to work with another who had lost a vehicle and men. All through the campaign I may say there were humorous and grim times.

This is one of the latter. We were moving to a new location on a fairly long, straight length of road in the usual clutter of French refugees. As soon as the dive-bombers appeared everyone dived for the roadside. Out of the vehicle in front of me one Len Draper took a flying jump into a ditch, but it had about six feet of water in it. He was not a happy man!

My pal and I were all right. Right near us was a farm cottage behind which we had sheltered when they released the bombs. They made a few return sweeps with their guns, but all we had to do was walk from end to end of the cottage. Soon they cleared off and we could carry on. As well as we could that is, with dead and wounded all over the place. Nothing we could do to help and we had to reach a point to 'open up' a communication link. By a miracle, men and vehicles were untouched.

We reached this point, a great château where we stayed three or four days. It was outside Armentières, maybe about twelve or thirteen miles. The shelling and bombing was very heavy. We were in the cellars and I didn't fancy it coming down on top of me, so I went for a walk in the grounds. The whole building was rocking. At some stage I asked the lieutenant when we were going to move. 'God knows,' he said. 'I suppose when we get told where to go.'

At last we did close down and packed up to move.

Down a long drive to the main gates, where would you believe it, there were two Military Police on motorcycles. The conversation went like this. Military Police, 'Where are you going?' Lieutenant, 'So and so.' MP, 'Not now.' Lieutenant, 'Why not?' MP, 'Pull forward so you can see.'

Away out to our right the whole town was in flames. MP, 'All bridges are blown and the town is going up in flames.' Lieutenant, 'So which way can we go?' MP, 'Turn left, first turn left, and go like hell, you haven't any time.'

In the event we made it. After a few miles' hard drive we saw, in a field, a whole line of French 88s [anti-tank guns], wheel to wheel, gun barrels level, maybe twenty in all, all blazing away and when an 88 lets go it makes a most fearful crack, so imagine the noise from that lot.

Anyway, they had a short ceasefire until we got clear and then started up again. At last we pulled into a field where some more of the unit were. By now it was early evening. They rustled up some food and drink and then we got our heads down. Next morning breakfast, whatever there was, but at least the good old standby, a mug of tea. Soon enough the German air force arrived. Heavy bombers. We must have been small fry, because they ignored us. I had been counting them and one of the blokes said, 'How many, Hawkeye?'

'Don't know,' I said. 'I got to seventy-nine then I

gave up. Somebody's getting an awful bashing.' Little did we know.

A while later the major called us together. 'I have to tell you carry what you can, leave the rest, move out and head north for Dunkirk.' 'Where is it?' 'Never heard of it.' 'Where's north?' 'I can't tell you any more. Just go. Follow the crowd. You'll get there and good luck.' 'How far?' said one. 'Oh, maybe sixty or eighty miles.' 'Do we set fire to vehicles and gear first?' I said. 'God no, don't do that, they might find our position!'

'Well,' I said, 'I thought they knew that ever since we arrived in France. What a damn disgrace. Less than a month and we're kicked out.'

'Page, I'll tell you something. We have nothing to be ashamed of. This last five days we've held twenty miles of front. Our quota is five miles.'

So we left all and went. Why did we leave those vehicles and signal equipment? I have always wondered.

So the trek began. Carrying only small pack, gas mask and arms. No food, there wasn't any, only water bottles. Lovely weather for a walk through the country. Like the major said, we found the crowd. A real mix-up. There were five of us together. A second lieutenant, corporal and three men. Mostly cross-country, and at one stage uphill across a very large field. That was when the first trouble hit us. An artillery barrage and Stukas. So it was a few steps, flat on your face, all the way. Going on yard by yard.

Suddenly I saw one of our men coming back again. 'Look,' I yelled, 'He's lost his way.' But he hadn't. He went to the lieutenant and said, 'Sir, look what them buggers has done.'

He held his small pack up and a big hole was torn through it. A few inches to the right and it would have been him. 'I'm telling you now, sir, because I don't want to be on a charge when I get back. Damaging my gear, you see.' 'Yes, right ho, Jackson. I'll make a note of it. Meantime press on with us.' It took all our time to move for laughing. But not aloud! I never did see him again.

All the time the shells were landing and Stukas up above. Suddenly a yell went up. They only had their 'screamers' going. They had no bombs or ammunition. They were pinning us down. So off we went again and soon got clear of the barrage. Then we found a road which made going easier, but a real dog's dinner. Men from all units, transport of all sorts. If it moved it carried men. I even saw one man riding a white farm horse!

So we trudged on and, despite the heat and discomfort, a lot of banter to and fro. On through the day and into the night. During the dark hours we heard a shout. 'Signals.' 'Yeah.' 'Over here.' There was R. G. 'Pip' Steele, Corporal Page, and a few more with dixies of hot tea. They slapped a 'doorstop' of bread and marge with a slice of corned beef and a mug of tea into our hands. 'Get that down you,' said Pip.

That was the first food and drink since breakfast the previous day. After a relax we moved off again with calls of 'good luck' from each side. I never saw them again. On into the night again and soon daybreak, with the shambles now worse than ever. On the way we saw some chap talking to some women outside a house. They called us over and it seemed that a young woman there with a baby was English. Her husband had been a waiter in London, and was in the French army. The baby was five days old and saw daylight for the first time then. They had all been down in the cellar. We tried to persuade her to come home with us but she refused. She was going to wait for her husband. Anyway I took her name and address to write to her mother to say she had a granddaughter, and both were safe and well.

So on we went and the worse it all got. Vehicles, motorcycles, guns, everything into the dykes each side of the road. It looked like a scrapyard. By then we could see we were near to the town. On the way across the docks some men were looking at what looked to be a large lump of coke. We decided it was either a man or a woman, and completely incinerated.

On for the last few hundred yards and up to a breakwater,

and there were ships of all shapes and sizes. My first thought was 'thank God we've got a navy'.

It was on the way in, by the way, some way back, that we met a body going the wrong way. It appeared they were a TA Unit going in. They had their guns, but no ammo. We told them theirs was a lost cause. Turn round and come home. Another load of gear wasted!

On the beach were hundreds of men, sitting, lying, wondering, sleeping. It was then that the full scale of the disaster hit me.

On the groynes was a navy petty officer, drunk as a lord, yelling at us to sing. 'If you don't sing, you won't bloody well go home.' We sang! Then he held his right arm out. 'All on my right stand up. You're not on my right. All of you sit down. Now we'll try again.' We started to move along to a small jetty, and then the first ranging shots came in, just before we reached the jetty. 'Leave your side arms here, you're not taking them on board.' An enormous heap, another waste!

The four of us, still together, went on to a small open motor boat. Four men, two crew and we were full. About a hundred yards offshore and the jetty exploded. We were lucky, for that was when they had to start fetching them off the beaches. From that, a mile or so out, we transferred to some sort of a large open boat, taking about two hundred men. Further on some of us transferred to a destroyer. I was still on deck when one of the ratings told me to move out of the way. 'If we fire, when the case comes out it'll sweep you overboard. Look up there.'

'There' was the *Dunkerque* [French battleship] firing broadsides inland from the port side. Then she slowly manoeuvered round, and fired from the starboard side. It seemed that the Germans had set up some shore batteries and the *Dunkerque* had wiped them out for us.

We had a peaceful run home to Sheerness. On the other side of the river I could see my home town of Southend. So near, yet so far. On to the station, where the ladies handed out meat pies, sandwiches and cups of tea. Then on to Devizes, where a hot meal and bed waited for us. Our first meal and sleep in three days. There for five days and then to Halifax, where we reformed. We were so depleted we absorbed the 51st Lowland Division.

In that week, I must say, those people were so good to us. All in civvy billets, but nothing was too good for us. They opened their homes and also their hearts.

Frederick Page, Ipswich, Suffolk

I was working at Grantham, at MARCO's munitions factory, and it was during this period when the evacuation of our soldiers from Dunkirk began. We knew from reports of the difficult and dangerous conditions in which they were returning and that all trains at Dover

were struggling to get the men away from the coast. Grantham was a stop for the steam trains to take on water and so some of us girls were going to Grantham railway station in our dinner hour to collect anything we could muster from the canteen, whether cigarettes, chocolate or whatever. As the trains came in we, together with the Red Cross, would try to cheer the chaps up.

But what sad and heartbreaking sights we saw on those trains. The faces of those brave lads I will never forget. Packed like sardines they were dirty, eyes red from lack of sleep, bloody bandages roughly tied on to wounds, clothes dishevelled, and all in a total state of exhaustion.

But at the same time you could almost sense the relief that they felt in knowing that they were safe after such a terrifying and horrific experience.

Gladys Brown, Melton Mowbray, Leicestershire

When the German army invaded the Low Countries on 10 May 1940, the 98th Surrey and Sussex Yeomanry, of which I was a member, moved into Belgium. During the following eighteen days we were constantly in action or on the move, losing most of our guns by enemy action. The last of our guns was knocked out by German tanks some miles from Dunkirk and the remaining members of the regiment were then told to make their own way to Dunkirk.

Arriving on the beach area our eyes were greeted by long lines of battle-weary troops slowly, oh so slowly, wending their way towards the mole, which was a concrete structure like a pier going into the sea.

A very large black smoke-screen from a burning oil refinery covered the whole of the area. We were under fire from shells, bombs and machine-gun bullets more or less continuously, or so it seemed. Food and water was very scarce, the little we were able to scrounge did not go very far. But it was meticulously shared as everyone was in the same situation. After some days and nights spent moving from one shallow trench to the next we finally came to the head of the queue at the shore end of the mole. A naval

officer very calmly controlled the number of people moving at any one time. He sent batches of about thirty men on to the mole at one time, with instructions to move as quickly as possible down the walkway to where the ships were being loaded. As

we reached about halfway we were shelled, and I found myself in the sea. Being a reasonably good swimmer I headed out to sea where more ships were waiting. On my way I saw two men making slow, hard work and little progress, and realised then that one of them was just about all in. His mate was in little better condition. I swam over, and between us we managed to reach a ship with a rope ladder hanging down its side. With a great deal of pushing and shoving we managed to get the third man out of the water and on to the ladder.

At this moment German dive-bombers arrived. Deciding that I would make a smaller target in the open sea, I swam away.

Eventually I was picked up by a naval cutter and was conveyed to HMS *Vanquisher*, which was a destroyer. Here I was given my first satisfying meal for days. It consisted of a thick bully-beef sandwich, and a mug of hot scalding tea.

James A. Bambury, Stone, Staffordshire

After landing in France with the BEF soon after war started, very little activity took place until May 1940. Although I have to say that one of my 'nostalgic memories' is of being put in an isolation camp as one of the first British soldiers to catch German measles in France!

My section was stationed for nearly six months on a

gun site close to Vitry [Vitry-en-Artois] aerodrome, and when allowed out we became friendly with many local villagers but it was with great remorse that we then unexpectedly, at short notice, moved off without even having a chance to say 'au revoir' to anyone.

When I think of Dunkirk I ask 'Was I really there? Did it really happen? How did so many survive? Perhaps I have watched too many films!' Seriously, nearly fifty years after, it still seems like a dream, but I know in my own mind that it really did happen.

Due to very poor briefings and lack of communications we arrived at the perimeter of Dunkirk under the impression that our heavy anti-aircraft unit was there to give cover to reinforcements which were shortly to be landed prior to a big push through Belgium. It was not until we had used up all our available ammunition in action and were ordered to immobilise our guns that the truth suddenly dawned on us.

Later, being instructed to proceed to the beaches at La Panne, it was heartbreaking to pass so many abandoned vehicles and spiked guns. Upon pausing to examine one of these guns I came across a small blue triangular pennant marked IAA in red lettering which I salvaged and later took back to Normandy and on to Germany, which gave me an enormous amount of pride.

There is no doubt that the most anxious times whilst queuing on the beaches were when the Stukas made such screaming noises as they dive-bombed, and it felt as if they were all aimed directly at you. Thankfully, the fact that we were surrounded by soft sand saved many lives. Many of us took refuge in old bomb craters in the long-held belief that it was a 'million to one'  chance that a bomb would land in exactly the same place twice!

Probably one of my most significant memories is of peering over the edge of one of these craters and watching helplessly as dozens of ships were being targetted by the dive-bombers. It was horrific to feel what they were going through without us being able to do anything to help. Several of the ships were soon, alas, to disappear from view.

During a period when the mole was damaged, embarkation was postponed and it was at that time that one of our gunners produced a pair of hair clippers. Believe it or not he gave a few of us a haircut while waiting in the sand dunes, but priority was given to anyone able to reward him with a cigarette left over from their last ration issue.

Eventually, when the mole was partially repaired, we were able to board a small vessel which soon afterwards was damaged, luckily with no casualties. Fortunately a larger Royal Navy vessel came to our rescue. The crew were wonderful and before you could say 'Jack Robinson' they had brewed up and we had our first drink for many days.

The journey back was not without incident as a floating mine passed too close for comfort, but we survived and reached Dover to be welcomed with another 'cuppa' and sandwiches from the WVS before entraining to proceed to Yeovil. Sadly I'll never forget that on the way I passed my home without being able to let my parents know I was safe. On arrival at our destination first priorities were a shower and change of clothing, but four days later, after complete rest and medical check-up we were allowed home on a weekend leave and I shall never forget the look on the face of my sister who was on leave from the ATS, when she opened the front door and saw me. They had not received my card informing them of my safe return home.

Douglas Hellings, Richmond, London

Some years ago I wrote to General Sir Brian Horrocks, who was at Dunkirk, asking him why he had never claimed his Dunkirk medal which was given to all the British troops who were there.

You will see from the reply that I received that there

is a reason why he did not claim his medal and that reason is, basically, that he was a very modest man as anybody who knew him will tell you. He was what is called 'a soldier's general'. He knew very many of the troops who served under him by their first names and he cared for all the ranks from the top downwards. He was the only person I knew who could live up to that old saying, 'an officer and a gentleman'. He was a perfect gentleman.

The letter describes his part at Dunkirk and his arrival back in the United Kingdom. When I met him at his home at Shepton Mallet some years ago he again related this little story to me and with a smile he said to me, 'Fancy going through all that and then finishing up in Darlington instead of Reading.' He was a lovely man to know and it was a very sad day when I attended his memorial service in Westminster Abbey a few years ago. Not many generals would take orders from a naval lieutenant.

The letter from General Sir Brian Horrocks reads as follows:

'You pose a very interesting question: why did I never claim my Dunkirk medal? The answer is that I feel it is wrong to claim a decoration which was not earned. I had practically nothing to do with the evacuation at Dunkirk. When Lord Alanbrooke had to go back to England and Monty took over our corps, I was given command of an infantry brigade holding the left flank of the bridgehead, as the brigadier was to take Monty's place as divisional commander.

'I went round the line, but never actually saw the brigade concentrated.

'They then passed through a checkpoint to the village of La Panne, where they were due to embark in small craft for England. After the last of them had passed through my checkpoint I went to the beaches expecting them to be empty. Unfortunately the tide was out and none of them could reach the craft, which we could see in the distance. I then called on General Johnson, commander of the 4th Division, and he told me to search the cellars and to clear the beaches, as the evacuation was to take place from Dunkirk. I did this calling out loudly, "No evacuation from La Panne, move to Dunkirk." When they had all gone I walked along behind them. On arrival at Dunkirk the jetty was practically empty, so I joined General Johnson on a destroyer. On the way over we were constantly bombed and eventually there was a resounding crash. We heeled over, and all jumped clear of the destroyer into the sea just before it sank.

'I was picked up by a small Dutch coastal steamer which was packed with troops, and the young British naval lieutenant called out, "Can anyone fire a Lewis gun?" I said, "Yes," so I was told to man the gun on the poop, which was engaging the German bombers who were constantly attacking us. There was nobody from the brigade on my boat and as far as I can remember, I never succeeded in hitting any of the German aircraft.

'Eventually, very tired and wet, we landed at Ramsgate. I walked across the town to the station where a train was waiting. They told me it was going to Reading and as my family were quite near there and I had no troops under my command I got in and settled down in the corner, wet and very tired, and went to sleep. I woke up as somebody shook me and I said, "Have we arrived in Reading?" and a voice said, "Reading? Certainly not. You're in Darlington!"

'I have told you this rather silly little story in detail to explain that, in my humble opinion, nothing that I did in the evacuation of Dunkirk was worthy of a medal, so I have never claimed my Dunkirk decoration.

'Signed,

'General Sir Brian Horrocks'

Roy H. Smart, Kirkby la Thorpe, Lincolnshire

Having been posted as a surveyor in the Royal Artillery to 2 Survey Regiment, I eventually caught up with them outside Lille. Bad news travels fast, but after being told that Lille was 'in flames' we were pleasantly surprised to find no suggestion of a fire when we drove through the following day.

The regiment was already 'out of action' and after daily moves we arrived at a place thirty miles from Dunkirk. Here we enjoyed what was to be our last good meal before Dunkirk. It consisted of a small pig which our cook had acquired because already the food chain had broken down!

When we moved on we were told to park our vehicles in a field and here we were then told to destroy the equipment and immobilise the trucks as best as possible. That consisted of deflating and slashing the tyres and puncturing the petrol tanks with pick axes and smashing the engines.

Rumours were rife. It was said that all non-combatant units were to be withdrawn as a 'big push' was about to go ahead. Then it was rumoured that the regiment was to be disbanded and the members posted to infantry and gun regiments.

Having completed the destruction exercise we mounted the three vehicles that we had spared. A staff car, one three-ton truck and a thirty-hundredweight Bedford truck. Some fifteen miles further on, driving towards the coast and crossing the Franco/Belgian frontier a time or two, we finally abandoned the vehicles and proceeded on foot. I can remember seeing a road sign *Dunkerque 20 kilometres* which was at the time of no great significance.

We arrived in the dark at a place on the coast well east of Dunkirk and walked and marched and clambered up the dunes, not an easy task with army equipment on your back. It was very dark and the only signs of life was of the phosphorescent sand being disturbed by movement of troops. This made us decidedly uneasy because we thought it could easily be picked up by enemy aircraft.

It would appear that we had arrived at a wrong section of the coast and we were told to move back away from the dunes and rest until called. Consequently my colleague and I found an abandoned truck and we sat in the cab, screening the dashboard light by newspapers and groundsheets over the side and windscreens and settling in for rest and many smokes! Some hours later we were called – by whispers I remember. Nobody shouted – maybe we thought the enemy was so near we might give our position away! In retrospect I find this very strange and can only put it down to a psychological reaction to the situation at the time.

Several miles along the coast near La Panne we again

arrived at the top of the dunes to be presented with an extraordinary sight. The dunes were plastered with troops. On the beach two small columns were formed up in order to feed the two small boats which were being rowed to and fro to a vessel of some 3,000 tons. It was a sort of cross-Channel steamer. Alongside were several military policemen armed with rifles to deter anyone from rushing to the boats when they arrived back on the beach.

During the day a heavy thunderstorm took place which gave us a fair soaking. Happily, as the weather was very warm, we dried out and as dusk approached we were told to get some sleep as we would not be getting off the beach that day.

My friend and I noticed what I could only describe as a hen house in which, as luck would have it, inside there were some dry blankets which had obviously been abandoned by soldiers who had been there previously. Tired and hungry we bedded down and enjoyed the 'sleep of the gods'.

Then at about 6am we woke and emerged not to find any of our comrades, who had obviously left earlier, nor even any British troops but a crowd of French soldiers who were lining up for their mug of coffee. Naturally we partook of this nectar and decided that there was only one course for us to pursue and that was to return to the beach. Here we spied a high-ranking officer who appeared to be in charge. He was in fact the beach master and he told us to join party No.30! This was a motley crew including some members of a Scottish machine-gun battalion.

This was by now 29 May, and by way of the beach and following the railway track, we finally arrived at Dunkirk. Here, for about twelve hours we were subject to the bombing by Heinkels and Stuka dive-bombers. Out offshore were one or two destroyers or corvettes making a zigzag course and belting out smoke in order to reduce the accuracy of the bombing. Near the mole was a hospital ship painted in white with an enormous red cross on its side and listing badly having been hit.

There was an incredible amount of noise from explosions, planes and ships' anti-aircraft guns. Half a day I think I spent lying on my stomach. Then I noticed a man in uniform standing by the corner of a building taking moving pictures of the dive-bombers, and I assumed him to be a war/press photographer. Cool courage, no less!

At around 1.30am, on what was by now the morning of 30 May, I and twenty others finally got on board a small boat and left for Ramsgate. The boat was a drifter and the skipper had corned beef, bread and water.

There was then little else to tell. Train at Ramsgate. Eight to a compartment. Eight apples. Eight buns. Next stop, sandwiches, cards on which to write a few words, address and hand back. It was all a great organisation, with all the Red Cross girlies helping the WVS.

A band greeted us all at the little station near Worcester and played us to Norton Barracks. The rest, as they say, is history. What we learned on catching up with the regiment finally in Wiltshire was that because of our heavy sleep we had missed them sailing on 29 May on HMS *Grafton*. But shortly after she sailed, HMS *Grafton* was torpedoed with many casualties. So our heavy sleep perhaps did us a power of good after all.

I think one of the extraordinary things about all this was the fact that we had no idea of the enormity of the operation until we read in the press, the day after arrival in England, all about it. We imagined that this was just a 'one-off', as they say, and confined to a small area. But the fact that the whole of the British Expeditionary Force was being evacuated never entered our heads.

We were, of course, treated as heroes. At least that was the idea. It was quite ridiculous, of course. There were certainly many heroes but I was not to be included in that category. I had no option but to be there. But that was it. For a week it was everything free for the 'Heroes of Dunkirk'. Then some wag said to me, 'Make the most of it while it lasts. You'll soon be back to normal.' He was right.

Cyril L. Beard, Bushey Heath, Watford

I was seven years old when war was declared, and evacuated to Norfolk with my sister who was twelve. War didn't mean a lot to me at the time except that it meant my father leaving home and going into the army. After six months my mother brought my sister and I home because nothing much seemed to be happening, and we were very homesick. We still had no news of my father and I kept asking when he would be coming home, and my mother kept saying 'soon', but I missed him very much.

At the beginning of April 1940 my sister became very ill and was admitted to hospital. My mother and a good neighbour were at the hospital day and night but my sister grew worse. My mother tried to contact my father through the police and the War Office, but they couldn't help at all and we didn't even know if my father was still alive as the news from France was very bad. My sister died of meningitis in May 1940, two days after her thirteenth birthday.

My mother was ill and I had to be quiet in the house. I was a little scared because my sister's coffin was in the front room, but life was much the same with still no news of my father. Then, the day before my sister's funeral, I was swinging on the front gate when I looked up the road and saw a soldier coming towards me. It was sometime before I recognised my dear dad. This man looked old, scruffy, and very tired, and needed a shave. I ran towards him shouting 'Dad, Dad', and he lifted me up in his arms and kissed me all over my face.

By this time my mother had run to him and they put their arms around each other very tightly. Then we went indoors and my mum told me to run along to my grandmother who lived a few doors away, and tell her that Dad was home!

My grandmother kept me at her house for a while and later, when we went home, Dad's eyes were red and I knew Mum had told him about my sister Joyce. As I went to sleep that night I felt very sad, as I could hear them both sobbing quietly. I grew up that night and knew I would never be the same again.

The funeral took place next day, and it was only as I grew older that I realised what a terrible time it must have been for my parents, especially my father. He went back to the war but sadly he was later killed in North Africa and is buried there. He was Sergeant Clifford

Spackman in the Loyal Regiment (North Lancashires). He was only thirty-four when he was killed, and although I am a woman approaching sixty my love for him is stronger than ever and every day I think of him and remember in my heart I am still his 'little girl'.

Pauline Jewiss, Gravesend, Kent

I remember Dunkirk well because I arrived there during a heavy thunderstorm on the evening of Wednesday, 29 May 1940. I was a member of the RAOC Light Aid Detachment, called 'The LADS'. We were a unit of a dozen men in the charge of an officer, Lieutenant Warner, which was attached to 145 Brigade of the 48th Infantry Division. The LADS last billet before the final retreat to Dunkirk began was a hay barn at a farm near Houtkerque, a few miles north of Steenvoorde, where a couple of days earlier we had witnessed at close range a German plane dropping bombs on the town square and the church.

We left the farm in the early afternoon of 29 May with orders to proceed to Dunkirk from which, on the horizon, a dense column of black smoke was already rising high into the sky.

As we neared our destination the roads were becoming more and more choked with vehicles and we were obliged to abandon ours and make the rest of the way on foot.

With one hand I was carrying my rifle and in the other a suitcase containing our officer's personal belongings.

On our way through Dunkirk – it was along what I now know was the Rue des Fusiliers Marins – we came upon an air-raid shelter and we took refuge there from the pouring rain. But not for long, because we were ordered to evacuate at pistol point by a French officer! This curiously, is the incident I remember most clearly of that eventful day.

We continued on foot to the shore at Malo-les-Bains, where we spent an uncomfortable night on the sands. We were tired, hungry and wet and at the mercy of periodic raids by enemy dive-bombers.

Some of our unit, including our officer, had become separated from the rest, whereas about half a dozen of us who had kept together were embarked the following day on the destroyer HMS *Wolsey*, which had come in along-side the already damaged mole. As we jumped aboard we were instructed to dump our rifles on deck, but I managed

to cling on to the officer's suit-case, having carried it that far!

We made a rapid crossing of the Strait and disembarked at, I believe, Dover, where a welcome cup of tea was provided while we were herded into a waiting train. The long, winding journey by rail took us eventually to Exeter, but during the stop at Salisbury I managed to divest myself of the suitcase which a kind-hearted member of the WVS undertook to send to Lieutenant Warner's home at Ramsgate. I think his wife must have been very surprised to receive it in this way!

Our brigade was reformed in Devon, but soon afterwards I was posted away from the LADS and lost contact with them.

Since the war ended I have tried to retrace Mr Warner but without success. If he happens to read this I hope he will get in touch again with his former driver, because we certainly should have plenty to talk about!

George Critchell, Purley on Thames, Reading

I was in the Royal Engineers, attached to the Royal Army Service Corps in France in 1940 when we proceeded, as a whole company, a few miles across the Belgian border into a wooded area and the next few weeks passed by without any particularly memorable incidents. Suddenly everything seemed to happen and we heard that the Belgians had surrendered and we were cut off, and next came the orders to head for Dunkirk with our equipment.

I remember the roads being filled with people and carts and with both French and British soldiers and the drainage ditches on each side of the road still had water in them. I remember on our journey a Stuka came very low, and we managed to fire a .303 at the Stuka, but the only result, for me, was that I slid down the bank and got my feet wet! We reached La Panne and the dunes and I remember the beach was filled with masses of troops, mostly under no command, with equipment of all kinds strewn everywhere.

Dunkirk in the distance was covered with an enormous black cloud of smoke which was too dense to disperse, and we slept on the dunes and ate mostly biscuits. The German shelling seemed to be mostly directed at the off-lying ships and warships but occasionally the shells fell on shallow water and I remember one shout of 'gas' but this was the fine mist caused by shallow shell explosion. I clearly remember a gun crew on the beach whose dedication and fire power kept the planes fairly high until suddenly an almost direct hit silenced it. Then I remember an order came for our Royal Engineers section, with others, to unload our bridging girders, lashings and planks from the lorries into the sea and improvise a pier. I believe it was partly successful, but the power of the tide restricted its use.

Shortly afterwards we received instructions to march to Dunkirk, which was about eight miles away, to the mole for possible evacuation. All that was left of our Engineers Section was one officer (Captain Munro),

*Ernest Foard, left, receiving his Military Medal from
Field Marshal Montgomery*

Sergeant Chant and a total of about forty-five sappers. That would be on or about 31 May or 1 June. We did march in good order, some but not all of us retaining our rifles. On reaching the outskirts of Dunkirk my first sight was of a line of French soldiers who had been killed by the roadside. We passed them by and joined a queue at the mole which was being shelled and received a hit whilst we were there, but our section was not affected. Eventually we reached a ship which had a rope ladder down by its side. I remember being told the ship was a NAAFI supply ship but I'm not sure, but I do know that tins of peaches and milk were handed round and I found a shelter by the anchor and we sailed during the night.

On arrival at Dover trains were waiting for us and I managed to clean up a bit and we were sent to Manorbier in Wales. After many stops, where on each occasion we were showered with gifts of food etc from the local people, we eventually arrived in Manorbier about 2 June. I remember that the ATS girls at Manorbier, many of whom were off duty, still remained on duty to provide everyone on the troop train with a meal.

Our Royal Engineers section remained together and after the risk of invasion had ended our company was reformed and went to Egypt. I was then in Italy and brought back just after D-Day, where I landed with the 7th Armoured Division and went right on through to Berlin.

Ernest Foard, MM, Aldershot, Hampshire

On 10 May 1940 the German offensive began. As dawn was breaking, planes were bombing northern France. The French civilians were in the streets and above the droning of the planes could be heard the shrill cries of the women and the continuous barking of the dogs.

Some twelve days had passed and now no one knew the day, or the date. It was of no importance. The BEF had been cheered by the populace as their trucks sped over the opened frontier, deep into Belgium. Now we had completed our rearguard action from Waterloo back to France. The troops were weary and the battalion had suffered losses. The refugees who had once treated us as heroes now competed with us for road space and we were no longer popular. Wherever we put down our defences it was certain that death and destruction would follow. Again and again we had escaped being overrun by withdrawing, through the night, some fifteen or twenty miles to new positions.

It was about 22 May that some two thousand men were drafted to Cassel to protect the way to Dunkirk. There, situated on the highest point for miles around, we could see history in the making. A blazing Dunkirk was just ten miles away down a very straight road. For a week we saw the bombers on their way to the beaches to drop their bombs and witnessed the Stukas dive-bombing our convoys passing northward up that straight road. Now the German tanks had cut the road from the east and from the west and a plane had dropped map pamphlets on the hill. 'British soldiers – lay down your arms! This is your true position.' Looking across the plain at night was similar to bonfire night as the Germans kept their troops in contact by lighting straw fires.

Cassel was a fine old town but with the small-arms fire and shelling it was breaking up. Food and ammunition were in short supply and it was obvious that time was running out. It was probably 29 May when the offensive against Cassel increased and the battalion headquarters (the gendarmerie) received a direct hit and a gaping hole was knocked in the building. The shell failed to explode and although the major was killed instantly, casualties were comparatively light. The choking dust had not settled before the adjutant said that all equipment apart from rifles and Bren guns were to be destroyed.

'We shall be making for the coast tonight,' he said – just as if it was to be a trip to the sea on a bank holiday.

'And what is to happen,' a soldier asked, 'when we reach the coast?'

'There should be boats to pick us up,' he said, 'so we can be landed westwards to take up new positions.'

'Put a bayonet through the canvas of my camp bed,' he added.

This bed had been transported all the way down into Belgium and back again and because of the continuing withdrawals had hardly been used. The destruction of the camp bed seemed to emphasise the hopelessness of our position!

In our harassed state everything appeared unreal. Pickaxes were being used on carriers and trucks but as the evening approached the shelling died down and we were able to have the best meal for three weeks. Surplus tins of food were buried and no one knew when it would be possible to eat again. We left Cassel as soon as it was dusk, in a long line with instructions to keep in contact with the man in front.

The pace was brisk and there was no noise. There were mines about so care was necessary. Our way lay southwards at first along lanes and cart tracks and for some three hours we made good progress but we were in enemy territory so it came as no surprise when in the early hours we were halted by small-arms fire. Conflict, if possible, had to be avoided so immediately we divided left and right and our half headed over fields of long dewy corn.

The nights are short at the end of May and our scout in front could just discern the early signs of dawn. As he swung right into a lane, he became aware of a vehicle in front. The column was immediately halted and all took any cover available. An officer came forward to investigate. Screams and shots disturbed the silence. As the advance party quickly withdrew it seemed impossible that all would get away unscathed. A few minutes later a German plane tore over our heads but by the time we had thrown ourselves into a ditch it was already past.

Clearly the hunt was now on, and it was not long before enemy fire ahead caused us, abruptly, to change direction and to plod on over more wet fields. Shortly we were being fired at from the right and from in front, causing men to lie low. Mortar shells burst on us from the left. A group found themselves in a small farmyard with a farmhouse and buildings some hundred yards away. The Bren gun being fired by the soldiers was

Rowland Young at Stalag VIII B. Top right, with pipe

sluggish and the gas setting had to be adjusted. Suddenly the thatched roof of the barn caught fire. The heat was intense. A few moments later three pigs, squealing in terror, rushed past. There was a smell of cooked pork!

Casualties were mounting and the adjutant was severely wounded but he remained calm. A stretcher was called for but, with the confusion and noise, it was a hard task to locate a bearer. Suddenly some six enemy tanks wheeled round into position. They were about five hundred yards ahead and moving towards us. Surprisingly, and to our relief, their guns remained silent. The leading tank commander, a brave man surely, stood up in the turret and our colonel ordered us to surrender. In the silence that followed, we were conscious of a deep depression.

We had all known that we might be wounded or killed, but few, at that early stage in the war, seemed to have contemplated the possibility of being taken prisoner. We certainly did not expect sympathy.

Now there seemed to be Germans everywhere. They were tall and many were manning the defences that the BEF had constructed during the previous cold winter. They gave us scant attention and doubtless we were nothing to look at. There was a little banter – 'So Tommy, you hang out your washing on the Siegfried Line, yes?' 'England Kaput!' But our spirit still lived and we had the usual army replies ready!

The search was thorough and not without drama and then we were marched into a church with a machine gun pointing down the aisle. It is not surprising that within a few moments many of us were asleep. We quickly learned that we would not be left alone for long and were disturbed by much shouting – 'RAUS! RAUS! RAUS!' Officers were parted from the men.

We were taken to a town square, where we had to stand, whilst three or four tanks drove round the perimeter. We took little interest, indeed the noise, fumes and dust only served to confuse our weary minds. The main road westward ran through the top end of the square and it was clear that enemy convoy reinforcements were moving up. The Germans were singing lustily. It seemed almost like a carnival. Many had cameras. One pretended to be Chamberlain with umbrella and top hat, whilst some vehicles had banners reading BERLIN, THE HAGUE, BRUSSELS, PARIS, LONDON.

Within an hour (it was still quite early in the morning and becoming very warm) we began the line of march and began to learn just how hard life can become without a proper supply of water and food. It might be thought that, in modern parlance, the British were 'very angry' or 'extremely bitter' but many felt a wave of patriotism and began singing. This was not at all popular with our captors who had plenty of ways of defusing our spirits until all we could manage was to trudge along.

Frenchmen who joined the line seemed to suffer more than the British. We had the minimum of clothing but many Frenchmen tried to take greatcoats, blankets and other impedimenta into captivity and consequently suffered in the heat. As we rested in fields at night – the nightingales sang!

The routes to Stalags in Upper Silesia and Poland were hard and varied. From dawn to dusk we marched. A piece of rhubarb was a luxury. Then came forty-eight hours in rail trucks. We knew little of the evacuation from Dunkirk and we only heard about bombing raids on Britain, the fall of France and the sinking of our ships. With so many prisoners the Germans certainly had problems. As the cold weather approached efforts were made to improve our conditions but it was the Red Cross that came to our aid and raised our morale so that during 1941 we were able to replace our lice-ridden clothes. There were cheerful letters from home, too, and the unforgettable Red Cross food parcels. These parcels confused our captors whose own rationing was severe and who were told that Britain was on the brink of starvation. This may, at times, have been true and we were very grateful to those at home for their sacrifices.

Rowland J. S. Young

The above account was written by my husband, Rowland J. S. Young who died in 1987. It does seem right to remember the civilians, sailors, soldiers and airmen of many nationalities who lost their lives or who were wounded. Those, too, who made the trek to Lamsdorf and other camps in the east should also not be forgotten, particularly those who failed to make the journey home.

Joan M. Young, Newbury, Berkshire

At the time of Dunkirk I was nineteen years old, a regular soldier, having joined the army at the age of fourteen years as a boy entrant. In May 1940, the day and date I do not recall, but I know I was at the battery command post when I heard that the Germans had broken through the French and Belgian fronts and were circling our positions and that we were to retreat forthwith. All was confusion and disbelief, but we pulled out in an orderly column and headed northwards in the general direction of the coast. We travelled for some distance and then poured into an orchard under cover of the trees as German aircraft were in the sky above. There we were ordered to cannibalise our vehicles and guns, making sure they were useless for the Germans.

After that we set off marching on foot towards Dunkirk, where we had been told evacuation ships and boats would be waiting for us. I managed to fill my haversack with cigarettes, chocolate and several tins of beans! As we proceeded along the roads we were constantly machine-gunned from the air by the Luftwaffe, having to dive into nearby ditches to escape the bullets. It was, to put it mildly, extremely frightening! We passed endless streams of French and Belgian refugees, making their way across country towards Paris to escape the Germans We spent nights in farm buildings and had to feed off the land, plus any food we had managed to carry with us.

By the time we were halfway to the coast, our regiment had stretched out for miles in little isolated groups, all heading for Dunkirk. We were extremely tired and disillusioned by now and we had lost all recollection of time and days. What I do remember is the roadsides being littered with vehicles and equipment.

Eventually we were informed that we were to head for La Panne, just over the border from Dunkirk, where a boat was to pick us up. On arrival at La Panne those of the regiments who had managed to keep together flopped out on the road and paths while

waiting to embark. Night-time came and still no word of our boat. The next morning we were told that our boat had been sunk and that we had to proceed to Dunkirk. I managed to open a tin of beans and eat them before we started our trek towards Dunkirk. My feet were sore and filthy, my socks stank to high heaven, and I had had no change of clothing and smelt like a sewer rat.

Some of our chaps who had gone ahead had managed to start a discarded French coach and a Leyland pontoon-carrier lorry. They had dumped the pontoons and made room for many of the lads to climb aboard and hang on to the pontoon stanchions. The last I saw of these two vehicles was that they were still busy running back and forth, ferrying in our lads to the Dunkirk beach area.

The beach area leading up to the mole, where most of the evacuation by boat and ship was taking place, was crowded with troops both British and French. I could see the masts of sunken ships all over the harbour. Some had been blasted on to the beach, and there was evidence of aircraft dogfights, with parts of shot-down planes of both sides littering the sands. There were hastily prepared slit trenches dug by those who had preceded us and in quite a lot of these trenches were dead bodies of those who had been killed by enemy action. It was a terrible gruesome sight.

The harbour master and his assistants were trying desperately hard to organise the embarking of troops into any boat or ship that had managed to reach the side of the mole. When my turn came I remember having to balance across a gangplank that had been put across a part of the mole that had received a direct hit. That hit had left a wide gap between the two sections. I remember seeing the bodies of several Guardsmen who had been caught in the bombing and they were lying along the edge of the mole. Whether they were ever shipped back for burial I'll never know. In the dock area of the town black smoke was pouring from the fuel tanks that had been set on fire, adding to the devastation around us.

I was ushered out on to a paddle steamer called the *Medway Queen*. Some sailors with mugs of tea were busy handing them out to us and then telling us which part of the ship to go to. I was sent to the stern end, where I quickly undressed down to my PT shorts and vest, ready to dive overboard in case of attack or sinking. Almost before I had finished undressing we were underway, heading out into the English Channel. Enemy aircraft were overhead but, lucky for us, being a small paddle steamer they were concentrating on bigger ships and left us alone.

We eventually landed at Margate pier. I dressed myself again as land came into view. Of course everyone wanted to get off quickly and in consequence with so many of us scrambling on to the nearside of the steamer, it caused the opposite side paddle to almost come out of the sea and threaten to capsize the vessel.

I remember the picture as I walked along the pier up to the main road. At the end of the pier was a huge pile of small arms, rifles and bayonets which were taken off anyone who possessed them. Across the main road the dear old British public were queueing for the cinema, as though nothing had happened. It was just wonderful to be back in Blighty, alive and in one piece.

Ernest G. Long, Amesbury, Wiltshire

At the time of Dunkirk I travelled daily from Salisbury to Tisbury. As trains came into the station – locked – full of soldiers, they were being fed and given postcards (later collected and posted by the WVS).

I was late for school, but my excuse was accepted. 'Thank God they are getting them out!'

About that time, too, I heard my name called as I left the station. There was my brother, hatless, his uniform very dirty, he was on his way to see his wife and son who had been evacuated to a nearby village, and who had been informed that he was 'missing'.

He had left his lorry at the docks and got on the last boat to England. Needless to say he was disobeying orders to report to Bulford; 'not till have seen Kath and David and Mother!'

Veronica Harfitt, Salisbury, Wiltshire

I was in Belgium in May 1940 when the Germans broke through the Maginot line, and we were ordered to destroy all stores of petrol and ammunition and to make our way to Dunkirk, where we would be taken over to Blighty by boat. Whilst crossing the barbed wire on the frontier, I got caught up in the barbed wire and could only be released by being pulled off and losing the seat of my pants. A few days later we arrived at a village where people were collecting together for the evacuation, and I walked through with a groundsheet round me like a skirt!

Getting further on, we got down for the night in a wrecked house when all of a sudden shells started dropping all around us and a big oak tree, about six feet in diameter, just outside got a direct hit and all that was left was the roots in a gaping hole. We continued on, badly in need of food and water and sleep, until we got to another village which was desolate and wrecked. We saw a hole beside a villa which had been an inspection pit for a garage so we just got down into this for a sleep.

All of a sudden we heard the drone of an aeroplane and it flew low over us and then came back and started to machine-gun us. I was slightly wounded in the left side but we decided to get on to the road and get to our destination as best we could. By this time we were fatigued in a bad way. Eventually we got to Dunkirk which seemed to us hell. Everything was alight and bombs were dropping everywhere and our thoughts were 'what chance have we of ever seeing dear old England again?'

But the navy had things in hand. Men were lined up in an orderly manner, being put aboard the ships as they came in, the sick and wounded being given special attention. I know because I was one of them.

By now I was partially blind, wounded in the left side, unable to walk owing to badly blistered feet, and still minus the seat of my pants! Eventually we were put aboard an Irish steam packet and steamed for Dover. We left at about four o'clock in the afternoon and they told us we would arrive at Dover at about eight o'clock but the Germans decided otherwise.

Again, a new aerial attack was mounted and one of those attacks hit us amidship with a bomb and another one hit us at the aft and knocked off a blade of the propellor. That put us down to half speed but with no further incidents we arrived at Dover at twelve o'clock at night where I was put aboard a hospital train for Dorset.

After several months' treatment and rest I was sent to Pwllheli in Wales for convalescence and the people who took me in gave me every care and attention, waiting on me hand and foot. As a result of my injuries I was transferred to the reserves and I went back to my job at the power station in Essex. However, that was not to be the end. I reported for fire-watching with the ARP wardens and it was on one of those nights, during a bad raid, when we had put out a load of fire bombs and I stood outside a shelter which held about thirty people who included my mother, twin sisters, brothers, sisters-in-law and nephews.

At about midnight, at the height of the raid, I heard a terrific roar. I threw myself to the ground and from then onwards I don't remember anything until I woke up on a stretcher in hospital where I lay minus my clothes. My body was as black as charcoal. They told me they had found me at five o'clock in the morning a couple of hundred feet away from where the bomb had fallen. I was covered in debris.

But worse was to come. The shelter which my people had slept in had had a direct hit and my brother, mother and father, and brothers and sisters were badly injured. My twin sisters and brother, his wife and my nephews were missing. Where the shelter stood there was now just a huge crater.

I escaped with only a slight injury to my back and thigh. I had to keep going back and forth to the mortuary to identify the remains of my dear ones as they were found. My father is dead but my mother and sisters and brothers still bear the scars of that terrible ordeal and the graves of our dear departed ones are in the local cemetery and I still thank God for my providence.

J. W. Porter, Dagenham, Essex

This is the story that my late father-in-law, Thomas Selwyn Edwards, told me many times about Dunkirk. He was born in Abercynon in South Wales and he was married in 1939 and by then lived in Chester, where he was employed as a lorry driver. It was in that year that the Cheshire Territorial Army was scheduled to hold its summer camp in Abercynon. Not having been to his old town since his youth and there being, in those days, no such thing as 'summer holidays' he joined the Territorials in order to see again the place of his childhood. Unfortunately at that time Hitler's armed forces were beginning to pose a threat to Europe, and so the summer camp of the Territorial Army was never held in south Wales and it was not until after the war was over that he visited his old home town again! In fact, as a result of what he did he was in Paris, three days before war was declared, as a British soldier.

He spent many days on the beaches of Dunkirk, his company being moved repeatedly from one point of the twelve miles of beach to another. Finally his platoon, now reduced to just six men, were ordered to wade out to a minesweeper which was anchored off the shore. On his  way through the water that was chest-deep he saw another ship nearby named *Hilda* which was the same name as his wife. He saw that as some sort of omen and so he did not go to the minesweeper but in the direction of *Hilda* and was eventually hauled aboard that ship by waiting seamen. It was whilst he was on the *Hilda* that he saw the mine-sweeper that he should have been on blown up and when he got back to England learned that it had taken a bomb down its funnel and every one of his mates were killed.

When he returned to England he was put on a train and taken to Dorchester where the first order that all the troops received was to parade before some 'fresh' officer who had not seen active service. These survivors being very dirty and extremely tired, not having slept for weeks, one by one threw down their rifles on to the ground 'having had enough'.

My father-in-law saw a sergeant major come across the parade ground and speak into the ear of the officer and the parade was immediately dismissed and immediately afterwards allocated new quarters.

He remembers sleeping heavily for forty-eight hours and, after having been issued with new gear, went with some other soldiers to a local cinema. They were still in no mood to be messed about with and at the cinema, apparently, some argument developed over what was considered to be the 'high price of admission'. It was their state of mind at that time that one of the soldiers immediately pushed a 'round' of ammunition into the breech of his rifle and apparently everyone then went in straightaway for nothing!

He had an eventful life during the war and having survived Dunkirk he returned to France two days after D-Day.

Ivor Davies, Wrexham, Clwyd

I was in the Royal Army Ordnance Corps, which together with the Royal Army Service Corps had moved into Belgium from Arras. When King Leopold abdicated, and all the Belgian forces surrendered, the British army was driven back through Belgium and the fighting began, so far as I was concerned, at a little place called Aalst, and the retreat route was to Lille.

However the refugees packed all roads, and it took the trucks, carrying assorted ammunition, guns and maintenance equipment, over two days to do an equivalent of an hour's journey.

The Germans bombed and machine-gunned the roads. There were refugees heading westwards for Paris. Horses, carts, prams. Dutch, Flemish, Belgian and French. All subjected, together with the British army, to non-stop attack.

The weather on 10 May and onwards made the German attacks very easy from then until the evacuation date early in June. There seemed to be no real darkness to provide any cover or respite.

Everyone scrounged what food they could. We came to a farm where a herd of cows were frantic with pain, as their udders were so full. No one knew how to milk a cow, and they tried with two men holding the cow's head whilst two more tried the 'milking'! In fact the animals went berserk, and had to be shot.

There was no 'army organisation', and eventually we took cross-country routes as the roads were too easy a target. I know that eventually all vehicles were abandoned as they ran out of fuel.

During those four days it was a case of digging a hole or hiding in the large sand dunes, and watching the occasional dogfights between the RAF and Germans. We had become shell-shocked and deafened by the noise of the shells hitting the concrete roads etc. We cheered when, occasionally, a German plane fell to earth. We helped one

another as best we could, standing for hours in water up to our chests. We were cold, wet, hungry, and tired. My rifle was tied round my neck and my tin hat never left my head.

A Royal Navy destroyer picked us up, using scramble nets. We just thumped down on deck and stood in warm corridors, anywhere one could stand. Though tired, if you heard a plane you moved! Always move, move, move. Don't be a sitting target. This was army discipline absorbed in our training days, and it paid off in my case.

The noise made by the Royal Navy guns was terrific, and we became numb, so that we moved mechanically. We travelled very slowly all night and came ashore at daylight at Dover in the early hours of the morning. We were met by the press and photographers.

The reward for all this was that nine months later I was shipped off to Malaya, where I fought the Japanese and was taken a prisoner of war at Singapore. I was a prisoner of war for three years and eight months, and suffered many hardships, indignities, slave labour in coalmines and cement works in Hokaido, in northern Japan.

When we were released I returned via America crossing to Halifax, Canada, and arrived back home at Southampton on 5 November 1945. Never again!

Frank Shearman, Kettering, Northamptonshire

You will understand as the years roll by a lot of things fade away in our minds but one story always stays with me. On getting to Dunkirk I had one thing on my mind and that was to get out!

I was a gunner in an anti-aircraft battery. We were mobile 3.7-inch guns. On reaching the beaches, as all this turmoil was going on I got detached from my own unit and as you may know you can always find a mate in the army. So there were about six of us teamed up together. I remember getting to the water's edge not noticing to worry about time, day or what have you. I don't know if I was ordered to go out to this little boat or volunteered, but I know I was dragged in the boat by someone remembering I could not swim! Anyway we set off and thinking of home sweet home, we had not gone very far when this other boat came alongside and as it was on its way to England we soon boarded her and she set off.

I recall it was a French drifter and we found out we were the only British on board and to make things worse nobody could speak French and the French could not speak English so we were kept in the dark whatever happened. Well wet and weary, chins up and all that we didn't care because we knew it wouldn't be long before we would get to England. I remember checking my pockets for items. I had my pay book, my army Bible which I got from the soldiers' home in Camberley before we went over to France and I had the map Jerry had dropped, telling us to surrender. I still have it now, ageing, like me.

Our fully laden little drifter chugged along and at last the white cliffs of Dover came into sight. Everyone was feeling good as we had made it. Anyway, after some time we laid off the port as there were ships everywhere. I don't recall how long we laid off there, then all of a sudden we were sailing again but alas not into the port. We thought 'Ah, well with too many ships in Dover we were going to some other port'. But to our dismay we were going out to sea again! Horror and disappointment came quickly. What had we to do? We could get no understanding from anyone on board! Dumbfounded! Land! Yes we sailed into France again, Le Havre!

On land we were shunted around, some to other regiments. We finally came out of France at St Nazaire so I did get back after all to England. But then we found out that we would still not be going home for some time, so we decided we must get some contact with home and each of us started off for our home towns. One fellow was

from Scotland, some from the Midlands, London etc. I was up north. On the way I sloped off where I got a lift and a very good couple took me in their house. I had a shave and a good meal and they gave me ten shillings (50p) to help me get home. God bless them. I never did see them good people again. Pity.

Now you will understand all Britain was in a turmoil. I bluffed my way from Kingston upon Thames by lorry and train. I must say I was questioned a few times on the way and when I look back I must have been a bit crafty and to think I only had my battledress on and a tin hat! I arrived in Darlington station, got a United bus to Billingham, not one penny in my pocket, and 'home'! My mother was in shock for three days. Unknown to me someone had come from Dunkirk and told her I was dead.

Just a quicky! When in France I remember being friendly with a girl. One day I visited her people and grandma and she showed me some photos of 1914, of two Germans standing round the bell of their church. 'Oh,' we said, 'don't worry, Grandma, it won't happen this time.' A week later Jerry chased us out! I often wonder what grandma said about us!

Jim Walker, Billingham, Cleveland

I was born and brought up in a little village, in the heart of Kent, called Headcorn and at the time of Dunkirk I was thirteen years old and attending the County School for Girls at Ashford. That was just fourteen miles down the railway line. As the men started returning from the coast the train service inevitably became disrupted, as most of the railwaymen and trains were diverted to the rescue. Consequently my brother and I were unable to get to school. I was waiting one morning for a train (that never came) when one of the trains carrying survivors stopped on the opposite platform, because Headcorn was one of the stations supplying food and drink to the weary troops. At Headcorn station a long bed of flowering shrubs was on the down platform and a soldier leaned out and shouted to me to get him a bunch of flowers.

I was amazed, a man, and a soldier at that. What did he want with flowers? In any case I was under the eye of the stationmaster's house and too scared! Several more asked for flowers and then I did pick a few branches of mock orange and Weigela. One of the soldiers jumped out of the train, came across and took them and passed them amongst the others. I was much older before I realised that the sight of an English schoolgirl, complete with Panama hat and blazer, and the lovely summer flowers, must have made them feel wonderful after all the horror that they had been through.

As Headcorn was supplying food to troops passing through on the trains, I did not go to school for several days and helped with the preparation of food in a large barn near the centre of the village. I do not know who organised this but the whole village joined in, everyone giving what time they could spare. The local bakeries made bread non-stop and each person did the task best suited to their capabilities. The older women sliced bread, no pre-sliced bread in those days, others buttered it whilst men sliced meat and boys ran messages and took handcarts of food down to the station. Big girls looked after babies while their mums did a stint, and men would do a couple of hours after work at night. At thirteen I was allowed to grate cheese and butter bread but only after being watched to see if I could do it right! One day I had the job of peeling a bathful of hard-boiled eggs! Shells went into a bucket and eggs into a big bowl. As fast as it was filled women took them for sandwiches. I tell you, I couldn't eat a hard boiled egg for years after that!

As the flow of trains eased I was allowed down to the station one morning to help hand out food and drinks. Trestle tables stood on the platform with tea urns, boxes of sandwiches, buns etc and the women moved along passing into each carriage a ration for each man. They were very mixed. Some cheerful, some so sound asleep we didn't rouse them, other just sitting with blank staring faces. Poor men. Various nationalities too. I remember I spoke to Frenchmen, one who insisted '*Je suis Belgique*,' and one coloured man in baggy white cotton trousers, red waistcoat and a strange hat who came from heaven knows where. I often wonder what happened to him – he looked so exotic. Some were only wrapped in blankets. Others looked quite spruce but all had the strained look around the eyes that shows when anyone has been through a hard time.

But when I look back, as a girl of thirteen at that time, I have to say that it was a great time to have lived through.

Joan Launders, Mexborough, Yorkshire

I am now eighty-one years of age but I remember that we went to France in September 1939 and I was a lance corporal in the Military Police. We had our headquarters at a large villa near to Arras.

I remember that the Germans had been moving quickly in our direction for some time when I, together with my friend Bill Semple, were doing a patrol of the arms dumps in the Arras area. We were some way out of Arras and so we had our packs of 'bully' sandwiches and a flask of 'char' and around one o'clock we moved to a small thicket on a hill some two or three hundred yards off the road. It was quite a hot day and we parked our Norton motorcycles in the shade and settled down for our lunch.

We could hear a lot of gunfire to the east and we saw large columns of smoke across towards Douai. Heavy Stuka raids were going on in the same area.

Having finished our lunch we laid back and enjoyed a 'fag'. For several days we had seen convoys moving up to the Belgian border but suddenly we were surpised to see a large convoy moving *westwards* along the road which we had just left. We were somewhat puzzled but not too bothered. We decided to let the convoy pass before we returned to the road. Then came the sound of heavy small-arms fire from the area of the Royal Engineers unit to our west, followed by huge explosions which obviously meant that the ammunition dumps were being blown up. Naturally by now we were confused and decided we'd best get back to Arras and report. Deciding that discretion was also the better part of valour, I took the side road back 'just in case'.

We entered Arras and found not a soldier in sight!

When we arrived at the headquarters there was no one there. Everyone had gone. We went along to the Welsh Guards unit at the canal bridge to find them on 'stand to'. We learned then that the headquarters had left and gone north and we were advised to do the same. Off we went over Vimy Ridge and arrived eventually at Hazebrouck to find various soldiers from different companies. There were no officers and I was put in charge and promoted to staff sergeant. It was then we found out that the convoy we had seen was part of the German troops heading for the coast via Abbeville. What a shaker!

We eventually reached Bergues about five miles from Dunkirk, with no orders, no officers and no rations. We could by now hear heavy gunfire and small-arms fire from all around us. Thousands of vehicles had been abandoned and we had no information of evacuation and no orders. I decided, therefore, on my own initiative to patrol the road south as it was obvious that a heavy battle was going on at Cassel some few miles away. Ambulances would need a clear road. Unfortunately no ambulances came through. They were in a convoy which I understand was wiped out by Stukas. I lost Bill Semple on this patrol. He died of wounds in Dover. On one raid on Bergues a sergeant and I dived under a truck on the town square. When the raid ended we looked in the truck and we found it was loaded with high-explosive shells. Our lucky day! In this raid one of my corporals was hit by flying debris but recovered in England.

On one patrol my mate, Lance Corporal Wright, and I were coming back to Bergues on our Nortons. As we approached the hump-backed bridge on the south we came under machine-gun fire from a Messerschmitt. Jack dived off to the right and I to the left, both of us into the ditches. Both sides contained nettle beds but eventually we surfaced and we were both indeed very 'nettled'.

On the south ridge there was a 3.7 'ack-ack' gun with a young Royal Artillery officer and a few men. They had the road covered and they were there to repel tanks or anything else that came along it. One night he sent a runner to say a tank was approaching. Just as we arrived a gun fired two shots. A tank had been hit and gone into the ditch. We rushed down as the turret opened to disgorge the crew. Four very scared French soldiers, shaken but otherwise unhurt, climbed out!

The following night a very fierce fight was going on some three miles south-east of us and red and green lights were going up at intervals. A young Royal Artillery officer asked me to go out and investigate what was going on. Since I was armed with just three rounds of amunition and a .38 Enfield pistol, I refused to go as ordered. It was obvious that a rearguard action was taking place. Then the firing ceased and all was quiet. Long afterwards we learned that this was the unhappy event when, after a brave fight, our lads had laid down their arms and some 100 or so unarmed men were slaughtered by the SS.

By this time we were under continuous shellfire both

day and night. Since we were now alone in Bergues I decided we should all get to Dunkirk as quickly as possible. All the bridges were under constant shellfire but we mustered in the square and considered what to do. Some wanted to go out via the Ypres bridge but the rest preferred the Dunkirk bridge. There were now forty-three of us, including myself, three sergeants and one corporal.

It was decided that all my section would follow me, plus a few others, and the rest would go with the sergeants via the Ypres bridge. We all got away and we were later at Crookham in Hampshire.

Reginald Blackburn, Newport, Gwent

My most lasting memory of Dunkirk can even now bring tears to my eyes. I wasn't at Dunkirk, I was walking along the promenade in Blackpool, enjoying the sunshine with my children. However, I can remember the hush that went over the promenade and suddenly people were standing still and even the traffic slowed to a halt.

I turned to see what was happening and out of the station came a column of soldiers. That was not an uncommon sight in Blackpool, because the town was then full of troops but these were different. They were dressed in an assortment of odd uniforms, some had no caps and I remember clearly that some had no boots and their faces were drawn and tired. But I remember quite clearly that they still marched in line with their heads erect.

I stood to watch them pass with tears streaming down my face and I knew even then that whatever the coming years might bring, I would never forget those brave men.

Anne Hine, Wisbech, Cambridgeshire

As a regular serviceman of the Royal Corps of Signals, I was stationed in Armentières, manning a telephone exchange along with a few others. We were not alone in doing this for there were also French tele-phonists – *mademoiselles* – manning exchanges as well which needless to say, we didn't object to! Alas, it came to a dramatic end one day when a young officer came speeding along in a jeep, out of the blue, with orders for us to pack up what possessions we had, and leave at once for Dunkirk, preferably in small groups.

We had previously suspected something was in the wind, so to speak, but totally surprised with such orders at such short notice, but orders were orders and ours not to reason why, but to do or die, as the saying goes. We hastily got our belongings loaded on to what transport we had, and said fond *au revoirs* to our friends whom we were leaving behind, and set off on our way.

Quite a few miles from Dunkirk we had to abandon our vehicles. We were told that another unit would follow up and destroy them before the Germans got their hands on them. So off we trekked, kitbags over our shoulders, and rifle of course. The kitbag we had to eventually dump by the wayside. We were continually being strafed by enemy aircraft, Messerschmitts and Stukas. One of our chaps was killed, so we stripped him of his name and number tag, and personal possessions and dug a shallow grave by the roadside and buried him, erecting a rough wooden cross with his helmet on the top and continued on our way.

During that time we lived off the land. We passed through abandoned farmyards, so there was never any shortage of eggs and poultry and sometimes, if farmers and their families were preparing to leave their farm, they gave us permission to help ourselves rather than leave food for the Germans. Roads were cluttered with refugees and their belongings making it an easy target for the dive-bombers. So we kept clear of the roads but we were still scared out of our wits by the continuous strafing. Our rifles were of little avail against such odds. Fortunately the rest of us made it, finally, to the beaches a few miles from Dunkirk town itself. By then Dunkirk was just a blazing inferno, with gasometers

blowing up etc. We settled in amid the dunes as best we could, every so often firing our rifles in a group in the hope of hitting a vulnerable spot on the low-flying enemy aircraft. We never saw any of ours. Must have been busy elsewhere!

Anyway we spent four days and five nights before finally we got the chance to wade out to a boat, helping a wounded comrade who had got shrapnel in his leg. We were then rowed out to a larger boat and taken aboard and given blankets and hot cocoa and finally made it to Southampton.

There we disembarked where we were given plenty of cups of tea and sandwiches by the WVS, of which in grateful remembrance at the age of seventy-nine I am a member, along with my wife who is a district organiser.

From Southampton we were sent off to various units for re-kitting out and given two weeks' leave.

Looking back over the years it seems like a nightmare now. I was in the north-west frontier of India from 1938–39 and I thought that was bad. That was my first taste of active service. But Dunkirk...!!

William B. Vincent, Whitley Bay, Tyne and Wear

My memory of Dunkirk is of dawn breaking and in a misty atmosphere seeing the white cliffs of Dover from my minesweeper. We were on our way to a mustering point to join up with other convoys and I remember when I saw the ships together how magnificent they looked, because I had only been in the navy for five months.

It was only then that the word 'Dunkirk' was mentioned and I heard other bits of information like BEF, retreat, beaches, soldiers, and only slowly did the story come out that we were all heading for Dunkirk where our troops were waiting to be evacuated.

I was just twenty-one years old at the time and when we arrived offshore at Dunkirk we saw that there were hundreds of other ships there as well and as one looked towards the beaches it just looked like a huge sandy desert filled with ants, but these were our troops coming in, dossing down anywhere that they could, weary and simply exhausted.

Two hours had passed before we started loading but we were a shallow draught ship drawing just nine feet of water so we could get in a little closer than the others. The lads came waist-deep out to us and then had to finally swim to us before we could get them aboard. Everything was going well and then we heard the drone of a plane and saw Stukas with their yellow nose dropping bombs and machine-gunning the troops and I remember thinking that these poor lads had nowhere to hide or to go to. They seemed at the mercy of the German planes but as the planes vanished we loaded more troops and casualties aboard until we were loaded beyond belief with human bodies.

The lads on the boat dished out tea to them as best they could and then we heard the planes coming again but somehow we got under way. But still we were bombed, until the ship seemed to lift out of the water and everyone I remember was in a crouched position.

The bombing knocked out our compass but I remember the skipper giving orders to steer by buoys in the Channel and that's how we arrived home. But worse was to come when we started unloading.

As we unloaded a number of men dropped to the floor because they had been killed by the shrapnel from the enemy planes. The shrapnel travelled through the iron casings and walls of the ship, killing the men as they stood crushed together, poor things. There were some other men from our crew killed as well that day, and others injured.

That was my first baptism of fire but I remember that our skipper, Commander Watson, who had brought us back from Dunkirk without any compass, transferred to another ship a few days later but three weeks after that was killed in action

My ship was the HMS *Pangbourne* and she survived the war after taking part in the Normandy landings. I was proud to have served aboard her, but she was scrapped in 1945 at Swansea.

However, I still keep a photo of her on the wall, where I also keep my Dunkirk medal and certificate.

I am seventy-one years old now but that event remains – and always will remain – vivid in my memory.

Robert Brown, Oldham, Lancashire

I am enclosing a letter orginally written by my late brother, Sapper Allan Greenwood, who went through Dunkirk and afterwards survived the Greece and Italian campaigns. He died in 1972 after being involved in an accident. He was a wonderful brother and I still miss him.

'Dear Mum, Dad and Verna,

Well I suppose you received my telegram last night and now know that I am safe in England. I have never been so glad in all my life to get back here after what we have been through the past week. I think it must have been Granny's lucky shilling which pulled me through. We have been bombed and machine-gunned constantly for days on end and how I escaped being hit I don't know. I am at a big camp at Lark Hill near Salisbury and am the only one of our unit here. Where the others are God only knows. But I suppose the best thing to do is to start my story from the beginning.

I was working on a boring job at Doullens when the trouble first started. A fortnight ago today, Captain Watson came on the job to pay us out in the afternoon and told us to dismantle the rig and return to HQ. That was four o'clock and we were worked through until 9.30 getting the stuff loaded etc. We got back to HQ and the whole unit moved off in a convoy at 2am on Saturday morning to some unknown destination. We travelled all night and arrived at St Pol at six o'clock. We stayed for dinner there and moved again up towards the coast. We were on the move like this for seven days, sleeping in the open fields, anywhere we could find. We eventually got to a village about fifteen miles from Dunkirk and stopped there until last Monday. There had been air raids all round us but not until Monday was there one on our village. We had just finished breakfast and were ready to move off

when they came. All of a sudden four big bombers dived on the village, bombing and machine-gunning for all they were worth. They were so low I could see the pilots in the cockpits. I dived for a hedge and got underneath, a bomb burst on the church about twenty yards away and machine-gun bullets kicked up the ground six inches away. I thought that I was finished. The second attack they made I had my rifle out and fired like mad at them but it was no use they still came on. I kept on firing until they went away. It was all over in about ten minutes but what damage they did in that time. The church was wrecked, houses and shops blown to bits. Luckily none of our chaps were hurt, but fourteen of No. 1 Section who were travelling with us were killed and several injured. When everything had subsided we left all our lorries etc and prepared to march to Dunkirk. I dumped my overcoat and kitbag and just took my pack. We then marched without a stop to Dunkirk, with a lot more troops, a matter of about eight to ten miles, being bombed and machine-gunned most of the way. By the time we reached the outskirts of Dunkirk I had dumped my bag and got only my rifle and equipment. We lay all afternoon in a ditch alongside the roadside and every half hour the German bombers were coming over and bombing the city. Dunkirk is an absolute shambles, fires are burning in every part and at night it lights up the district for miles. We slept in the sand dunes Monday night and on Tuesday morning marched down to the beach to try to get on a boat.

Myself and twenty others waded out into the sea to try to get on a launch. I waded up to my chest but the boat was too far away for me to swim for it so I came back. One of our chaps tried and drowned. The beach was packed with dumped kits so I managed to get a towel and dry underwear and had a change. In the meantime the unit had moved to another part of the beach so I had lost them. I joined another party and lined up for an hour without any luck. Then an officer told us that if we would care to march up the beach to Dunkirk docks we were certain of getting away. It was a five-mile walk but I saw a motorbike unattended so I jumped on it and rode along the beach as far as I could until it got stuck in the mud, then I walked the rest of the way. I got on a boat about three o'clock Wednesday morning and was I glad to be on it. I was as happy as a king when we left. The Germans were shelling the town, you could hear the shells whistling. We arrived in Dover about 6am and then got on a train to this place. I hope to be coming home for forty-eight hours soon, so you can expect me in a day or two. But I close now, hoping to see you soon. Your loving son Allan, Royal Engineers.'

Verna Grant, Ashford, Kent

In May, 1940 I was twenty-one years old and had been in the Royal Army Service Corp since being conscripted for six months military training in July, 1939. At about four o'clock on 26 May, 1940 'somewhere in France' we

were suddenly told to evacuate our billets and parade thirty minutes later with our small pack, rifle and water bottle. All other kit was to be left behind. At the time I was working in the company office as a pay sergeant and all papers had to be burnt before we left. The cash box was left behind, but not before the commanding officer had filled his pockets with the large value notes!

On this parade all five hundred members of our unit were 'herded' on to the backs of a few Bedford lorries. After about an hour of very slow progress we stopped and were told to dismount. We then had to walk or semi-march. We had not the faintest idea where we were heading, or indeed why this was happening. We did notice, however, that the only transport to be seen was a couple of our motorcyclists who rode beside our commanding officer who was walking at the head of our unit.

We continued to walk throughout the night, always on roads flanked by ditches and fields. When it started to get light these ditches proved useful places to dive into when the enemy planes came over. At about 7am we arrived at the coast. There was very little activity and very few military people about. We still had no idea where we were. All I knew was that my feet were badly blistered and seemed on fire. After all, we had been walking for over twelve hours. The thought of taking off my boots and having a paddle in the sea proved irresistible! But I had enjoyed the feel of the sea water for barely a minute when an officer barked, 'What the hell do you think that you are doing – get back to the dunes at once.' It was just as well that I did as I was ordered, because an enemy plane suddenly swooped in and started machine-gunning the beach!

By now very many more troops were arriving on the beach, which I was to learn much later was Dunkirk. The next thing I noticed was a very small armada of boats had anchored about 150 yards from the water's edge, and when I saw small boats being launched and coming towards the shore, I had to assume that they were coming to pick us up. The only way to get one of these boats was to join one of the queues at the water's edge. This I did but each time I got anywhere near the head of a queue it seemed an enemy plane warning would be given which caused a mad two-hundred yard dash back to the sand dunes, and so I lost my position in the queue! After several attempts I realised the hopelessness of it all and returned to the relative safety of the sand dunes.

By now, due to the large number of troops on the beach, there was total confusion and I had become completely detached from my own unit. I realised I was 'on my own' and could no longer just await orders. I just sat for some time, looking at the sea, and wondering how on earth I was to get across that stretch of water back to England. Or indeed if ever I would. I was quite young and I recall being pleased with myself for feeling quite calm and fatalistic about the whole thing.

After several hours of just sitting and waiting, I overheard someone say that about a mile or so to our left there was a jetty where some small navy craft were tied up. I decided to walk in that direction. I still had my rifle and, although it was probably useless because of the sand which had got into the barrel, I could not bring myself to throw it away, like so many others had!

I was very disappointed at the large amount of army equipment, lorries etc which had just been dumped. One of the lorries had been looted by the troops and a case of sultanas had split open, leaving a heap on the ground. I bent down, picked up several handfuls, and ate them quickly, realising suddenly that they were the first things I had eaten for at least twenty-four hours. After walking some distance I was very pleased to see a small jetty with two navy boats alongside. I also saw a long winding queue of troops awaiting to get on to the jetty.

I joined the queue and after what seemed an age I reached the jetty itself. I then found, halfway along, a bomb had blown a hole in the jetty. This gap was about five or six yards across and it had been temporarily 'repaired', but even so one had to walk on two very narrow planks across the 'opening'. I achieved this very success-fully and found that the two navy corvettes were laying side by side at the end of the jetty. To get on board the vessel furthest away, to which I was directed, I had to cock my leg over. Unfortunately when I had one leg on each, the swell of the sea caused the two ships to drift apart but somehow I just managed to avoid a nasty accident!

Once aboard I was surprised at the small number of troops to be seen but I was so relieved that I merely followed a few other soldiers and found a corner out of the wind and settled on deck with my gas cape over me for protection. We soon set sail. Again I had no idea exactly where we were going but I felt so relieved to be on the way home. When we did eventually arrive safely at Southampton, it transpired that whilst the few of us were freezing and starving on the open deck, very many hundreds of troops had been *below* deck being wined and dined by the navy!

Percy W. McDonald, Chelmsford, Essex

What dreadful anxiety when we heard of the retreat to Dunkirk! My brother had got home on the Wednesday but I then had to wait for news of my husband.

Early on the Saturday morning my brother-in-law came to the house with a message. He had had a phone call from a customer where he delivered newspapers. She was a member of the WVS and had been on duty on Salisbury station during the

night where several troop trains had passed through. A soldier had heard the name 'Salisbury' and had asked her if she could get a message to his wife. She said she was not allowed to take a letter but would try to phone my brother-in-law.

What relief and excitement for me and our little daughter. I knew that my husband would come or contact me as soon as he could. The day passed so slowly but early evening we walked along to the shops and I said to Carrol that Daddy would probably come on a bus from Salisbury. As we looked towards the bus station there he was, coming towards us!

He looked very weary and only half dressed, the rust marks on his khaki shirt were from his braces where he had been wet and dry so many times trying to swim out to a ship or boat.

He told us of coming through Salisbury on the train and the tea and jam sandwiches given to them. But as the train pulled out a girl pushed a ten-shilling note into his hand. His one regret was that he didn't thank her!

They didn't know where they were going but he ended up in Borden. There were thousands of them and there were four sittings for breakfast. They were disgusted that, as it was Saturday, the NAAFI was closed and they couldn't get any washing kit. He and one or two others decided to take a taxi to Salisbury and from there he got the bus to Amesbury.

An embarrassing journey, as he felt so conspicuous, looking so dirty and unshaven. His ten shillings came in very useful for his fare.

As soon as he was clean and changed we went out to buy some extra food. We bumped into the kind lady who had phoned the message about his safe return and he was able to thank her. She said that it was the nicest thing she had been able to do during the war!

I know there are many stories of those awful days on the Dunkirk beach but I was one of the lucky ones to have my husband safely home. Sadly, he died in 1980.

Mrs P. Greenhow, Salisbury, Wiltshire

My story starts in Belgium when orders came to withdraw and the sky was full of Stukas and bombs caused havoc and then they machine-gunned everything that moved.

It was our first action and afterwards, when we who were safe found our mates who were dead or wounded, it was then we realised what war was all about. We were told to head for Dunkirk, 'somewhere in that direction', and so in small groups we started out.

We walked over fields for days, and the roads were getting more and more dangerous. We were always dodging enemy planes that took delight in firing at anything that moved.

That night, tired and hungry, my mate and I crawled in a ditch and lay against a log to sleep and wait for morning. At dawn we woke up to find our log was in fact a dead horse. We moved off very fast!

It was on our sixth day when we saw Dunkirk for the first time and we then spent the next three days in the sand dunes.

Whilst some of us were trying to float a small boat that was floating offshore an officer called us to help carry some wounded to the hospital ship that was at the end of the mole. After making many trips we were about to go back for more then he told us to stay as the ship was leaving.

As I looked at the beaches and the thousands of men there I thought how lucky I was. Ten minutes later a Stuka dropped a bomb and it hit the ship and I found myself in the sea. The most heartbreaking thing was those chaps on and below decks who were crying for help as the ship went down and I and many others could only look and help where and when we could. But it is something I will never forget.

I spent another four days on the beaches and was taken off on 1 June and landed at Ramsgate the next day.

While on the beaches many terrible things happened, but the worse was when my mate was killed beside me whilst I was not touched. Les is buried in the small churchyard in Malo-les-Bains. I have been to his grave when on the pilgrimage and this year I laid a Royal Artillery wreath on it.

It must be realised that what happened on the beaches can never be shown, because if it was and people saw what had really happened they would be too shocked and upset. I know that many people who were on the beaches, even fifty years later on, still have bad dreams about it all.

Albert 'Bunny' Burrow, Maidenhead, Berkshire

The war in France seemed very far away and nothing much was happening when, one night in April 1940, we were paraded to the Midland station in Leicester and sent by train to Portsmouth. There we boarded a transport ship and sailed off to Cherbourg. The weather was good and we were tanned and fit when, on 10 May, Hitler decided to invade the Low Countries, which was largely a confidence trick as his main effort was to come further south, near Sedan. The British Expeditionary Force was on the Franco/Belgian border and so we set off to join them.

Our mode of travel was by '*40 Hommes – 8 Chevaux*' (forty men or eight horses) – NOT a recommended way to travel! Barely enough room to sit down on the floor.

Sleep was almost impossible, what with being trod on by people going to the door etc. We had about two days of travel and what a wonderful sight it must have been for the French as we struggled to perform our natural functions out of the sliding door! Every time the train stopped there was a rush to the driver to get some hot water from the engine to boil some tea. Bread was out of the question – biscuits (hard things), bully beef and Maconochie stew were to be our main diet from now on. Eventually we came to a place called Seclin where the railway had been bombed, so it was with some relief that we got off the train.

The British army had by then moved into Belgium so we started to march after them along straight French roads where the cobbles were hard on our feet. We marched on into Belgium till we came to a small town called Nederbrakel, not far from Brussels and there we met the refugees – thousands of them, all going west and our first job was to herd these unfortunate people off the roads. That was the last thing they wanted to do as the Germans were near to Brussels and, with Stukas bombing indiscriminately, they naturally wanted to get as far away as possible.

The British army was by now retreating from Belgium and we went with them, sleeping in the open and short of food, and we found ourselves back in France, lying in ditches, firing at Stukas with our rifles! On we went marching till we came to a small town called Carvin and there we came under shellfire. This place was right at the bottom of the British sector, with only rifles, a few Bren guns, obsolete anti-tank rifles, no divisional artillery and only a few bits of signalling equipment. If we had any tanks I didn't see any. The defeated French army was going the wrong way, bombs coming down, shells galore, our rifle companies met the Panzers and everything was chaos. I have read since that sixty girls at a convent school were killed by bombs at Carvin.

I was at battalion headquarters, or what was left of it. Our signals sergeant and some of my friends were killed on a patrol, and some of our companies overrun. Those of our company who could ride on the little transport that we had were ordered to fall back. We had to walk, so with two corporals and five signallers, we kept together and eventually we reached a farmhouse where we found an RASC unit. As it was getting dark we asked if they could tell us where our HQ had gone – they couldn't, so we bedded down in the barn. During the night they pulled out and said that we could go with them as the British army was going further back. With no radio or news of any kind we had very little idea of what was happening – only that we were very tired, hungry and scruffy, although we did manage to shave occasionally. But at least the weather was good!

Travelling by lorry, mostly at night, we eventually reached the outskirts of Dunkirk. I had never heard of the place previously. I know we passed through Poperinge and Armentières – all heavily bombed. Large oil tanks at Dunkirk were ablaze, planes were bombing and there were fires all round. The lorries were put out of action and we went into the town, picking our way through the rubble with telephone lines dangling everywhere. We managed to get into a cellar, where we stayed throughout the day. At night we were told to get down to the mole where we might get a ship. I remember passing a NAAFI store where we were told to help ourselves to cigarettes – everyone smoked in those days and I brought four hundred Gold Flake back with me! We managed to get on a ship called the *Mona's Isle* – an Isle of Man ferry. We crowded on and it was standing-room only and no life jackets. I remember a sailor giving me some fried tomatoes which tasted lovely and we set sail from Dunkirk just before dawn.

The ship went along the coast towards Calais which, unbeknown to the captain, was already in German hands. Suddenly shells from the shore began to hit the ship and quite a lot found their target. Luckily we were down below – don't know if we could have got out. Then the planes came – they strafed the ship with cannon shells. Twenty-two men were killed and dozens wounded. There was nowhere to dodge to as it was so crowded, and when we eventually reached Dover it had taken over ten hours to cross as the shells had damaged the steering. We saw that the ship's funnels were riddled with cannon shell holes – a good job they didn't have bombs! A hospital ship was already awaiting our arrival and we, the lucky ones, were put on a train to a tented camp at Tweseldown, near Ascot, where we were sorted out.

It was hard to believe we were home, where only a few miles away our friends were still striving to get off the beaches. We were eventually sent to the well-known Belle Vue Amusement Park at Manchester, where we met up with some of our friends. Most of the others were captured – we couldn't do much with rifles against tanks.

We then went to Rochdale, nearby, where we were put into civilian billets. I don't think they had had many soldiers before, for we were treated like heroes – free bus rides, free cinemas, strangers giving us cigarettes – all this on fourteen bob a week, all in! (Seventy pence these days.) We certainly grew up quickly in those days!

Dick Cobley, Warwick

My most vivid memory of the early years of the war was the day that our soldiers were brought back from Dunkirk. I was living in Yeovil at the time, a town where there were army camps on the outskirts, and the word went round that a troop train was approaching Pen Mill station carrying lads from Dunkirk and that the army trucks were going to the station.

The road from the station to the town quickly became lined with people and I do not think that there was a dry eye amongst the watching women as the trucks went by filled with young soldiers dressed in the most motley assortment of clothes, uniforms and jackets and the like that you ever saw.

It was a sight never to be forgotten and our lads were cheered on their way whilst cigarettes, sweets, choco-lates and fruit were thrown into the trucks as they passed. I am now seventy-eight years of age but the memory of those boys is still quite clear and I can still see their faces expressing elation, relief and exhaustion. I remember that we all thanked God that they had been saved.

When they had had time to settle down and receive check-ups they were kitted out again and allowed to come into Yeovil. Most of them were city lads and, of course, as you know Somerset is a cider county and naturally the majority of the lads made for the public houses. Having tasted the cider they thought there was nothing to it and continued drinking it as if it was lemonade. That was all right until they came out into the fresh air and then wham, they fell about all over the place! However, they soon learnt.

We didn't have them long in Yeovil because they were sent to other units ready to carry on with the war, but I never fail to thank the 'little boats' that brought them back from the hell of Dunkirk.

Mary Collins, Weymouth, Dorset

It was in the Christmas mail of 1939 that I received my reporting papers to tell me that I had been conscripted into the British army. Little did I realise at that point in time that it would turn out to be a six-year term and that it would take me all over England and Scotland and into France, Belgium, Persia, Egypt, Tunisia, Italy and Germany.

Departing from Southampton in 1940 we sailed for France and eventually landed in Cherbourg. Once having settled into camp, our main function was building a railroad into the centre of France and it was during this time that the Belgian line came under threat and began to crumble. So we were packed up and sent post-haste to try and stem the crumbling Belgian, French and British forces. Unfortunately we did not arrive in time, finding ourselves three-quarters of the way there when the forces in Belgium collapsed completely and so we turned around and retraced our steps in the direction of Dunkirk, as we were ordered.

We had to footslog it all the way back because trucks and every type of transport were burning all along the roadside. Buildings, too, were blazing away as a result of all the bombing by the Germans, but steadily we made our way and I, accompanied by our company sergeant major, plodded on, eating corned beef from a seven-pound tin salvaged from one of the supply trucks.

Going through the streets of Dunkirk, heading for the beaches, we found supplies were strewn everywhere. Everyone by now was too weary to stop and gather up anything, even bottles of spirits were left. Arriving at the Dunkirk beaches the scene was one of utter chaos. Again, burning transport by the score, with hundreds of men on the beach, none very happy at the turn of events!

Marshals on the beaches were trying to sort the men out into regiments and grouping them together but during this time the German aircraft time after time strafed the beaches, leaving large numbers of men wounded or dead.

When the ships arrived the marshals directed us to a jetty being used to get aboard the ships. We made our way, some one hundred or so of us, along the long jetty to board a ship that had tied up waiting to take us on. About halfway along we had to dive over the jetty sides for cover from the German bombers. When everything went quiet we climbed back up on to the jetty only to find a big hole in it as a result of a direct hit from one of the bombs.

We had to wait until half a dozen engineers bridged the gap with planks before we could move forward again. It didn't take long to fill up the waiting ship to capacity and then we cast off and moved out.

I remember the ship had old tyres along its sides, used as bumpers, and it was at this point as we pulled out that those tyres scraping along the jetty side caught fire from the explosions and the ship's crew did a marvellous job in getting them put

out and so we sailed into open water, leaving behind Dunkirk beaches and thousands of men still waiting to be picked up.

I remember once we were out to sea some of the crew coming round with a ration of corned beef and 'hard tack' biscuit. It was only at this point that we learned the ship was a merchantman carrying a consignment of corned beef destined for England, and so there was plenty for everyone!

After the Channel crossing we landed at Dover. Here, home troops were waiting for us to disembark, forming us up into single file ranks. They then asked for, or searched for, packs of ammunition etc. After what we had been through we were too exhausted to be even bothered to find and hand over what ammunition we had.

We were then transported away from Dover in different directions. Our group was loaded into a three-ton lorry and transferred to Blandford in Dorset for rehabilitation and eventually returned to our own units, or what was left of them.

Wilfred Wright, Newcastle-under-Lyme, Staffordshire

When the German attack came through Holland and Belgium we packed our belongings and our armaments and marched into Belgium. I was in the 5th Battalion of the Royal West Kent Regiment.

The first night after marching all day we slept in a wood on our groundsheets and had no supper or anything else to eat or drink, so we drank the rain off the leaves, as it had been raining. We were told that our convoy of food had been ambushed. Then we were marched again to a place called Oudenaarde. Here we took up a position and dug ourselves in because German soldiers were in a derelict house across the river, which was opposite to our position.

About a week later we pulled out to go back to the north of France around Armentières. We were round there for a couple of weeks until one day, marching through some wooded countryside, we suddenly fell to the ground as a shell landed near to us.

Many men near to me were injured and in particular a sergeant of our platoon had half his face blown away.

On 29 May we took up a position in some woods, when suddenly there was a thunderstorm and we got drenched. As a result of being drenched to the skin we went into some evacuated cottages and lit some fires to dry out our army clothes and took some women's clothing from some drawers, which had been left behind by the civilians. We wore those whilst our army clothes were drying!

Then at about 9pm we had orders to get out on the street, in no particular formation, as apparently our area had been surrounded by the Germans. I remember

that we rode in convoys, even including the night-time, and that at other times we were machine-gunned by German aircraft.

I remember once when some mates and I and some other soldiers had great fears and started to pray in earnest for God to protect us at this time. I can particularly remember thinking like that when we were in a ditch taking shelter! Then we got to Poperinge where we had a little sleep on some duck-boards that had been laid in some trenches by some other regiments.

So after tramping about forty miles we finished near the coast at a place called Bray-Dunes. This was a little way from Dunkirk, towards Belgium.

We had some more sleep in the sand dunes until about 5pm when we scrambled for a small boat offshore. We waded up to our necks to reach the boat. As we got to it about forty soldiers tried to get in at once. You can imagine the result. We were all soaked to the skin again!

We returned to the beach when the Germans started another bombardment, at about 10pm but we were taken off the beaches shortly afterwards on a paddle steamer called the *Royal Eagle* and arrived at Sheerness the next morning.

I would add that when we were told to get out of those cottages in France, I kept on a lot of the women's clothing under my battledress, and so I don't know what would have happened had I been captured!

Harold J. Chalker, Weymouth, Dorset

Our last encounter that led to our final retreat to Dunkirk was when the South Lancs gave us covering fire at Lille. We marched all that afternoon and into the night, and at about midnight we arrived at a place where there was a big square. It was full of soldiers. They were British, French and French colonial troops. They had pieces of artillery with exceptionally long barrels drawn by mules. They looked like very ancient pieces to me.

We stayed there about half an hour while the company commander went somewhere to receive further orders and eventually we set off again. We marched all through the night and about eleven o'clock the next morning we halted and had a meal. Then the company commander called us all together. Everyone's pack, that contained a change of underclothes and one blanket, was put on a heap and set on fire.

Then seven men and one NCO was allotted to a fifteen-hundredweight truck, along with any ammunition that we had, and then the company commander said that we had to make our way to a place called Dunkirk. We were told that we were all on our own, and we were not to take orders off anyone who we did not know. He wished us the best of luck and I remember he said, 'I hope that you can keep together and we'll meet on the other side of the water.' After being strafed on three separate occasions, we finally made it to the town of Dunkirk, which needless to say looked the worse for wear! However, the driver was told to leave his vehicle and immobilise it.

Before going down to the beach we looked around the lorries to see if there was anything worth picking up. There was. There were ration wagons full of tinned food and clothing, a water wagon and so we had a wash and change of clothes and then made a meal. Then the corporal said that we were to go down to catch the ferry!

As we got near to the bridge there were three Scotch soldiers walking towards us. 'Don't go down there yet, Jock, it's murder.' We could see and hear the planes diving. So our corporal told us to stay where we were for another hour and then we would go down when it would be getting dusk. As we went on to the beach it looked like a sea of khaki. We settled down along with the other chaps and got chatting, and they said they had been there four days and had hardly anything to eat. So we gave them the bully and hard biscuits and tins of fruit that we had.

Though the days were hot it was very cold at night with the mist. There seemed to be quite a lot of fires in

Fred Mutch, far left

and beyond the town and you could hear the artillery close to. As it began to get light and the mist began to disperse it was then you could see the sunken ships at sea. The men who had been there before us said, 'It doesn't look as though there'll be any ships this morning.' So our corporal said to us, 'Come on, we'll go back and make a meal. We don't mind getting blown up, but we're not going to starve to death.' He told me to go and get food from the truck and ask Thorpe to get a fire going and 'us three will go and see what we can scrounge. We will meet under the avenue of trees.'

While Alf and I were walking back we came across a BSA motorbike. Alf said, 'It's hardly run in. I wish I could get this back home.' He rode off, and I made my way to the trucks. On the way there I met a Belgian soldier and he said something and pointed to his boots, which were just about worn out. I beckoned to him to follow me and I took him to the truck that had boots in it, and he seemed chuffed and we shook hands and he left. I went on to get the food for the meal and returned to the avenue.

On the way I was passing four French soldiers when one of them pointed to a wagon and as our driver had immobilised our truck, I took it that other drivers had done the same. So I made a noise like a motorbike. He shook his head and I beckoned him to follow me which he did until I got to the narrow avenue of trees. He wouldn't come any further, so I motioned to him to stay there and I ran to where I knew Alf would be.

I shouted to him, 'Don't wreck that bike.' He hadn't. I told him that there was a 'froggy' wanting to get home. So Alf rode it down to him and off went the French soldier!

Our corporal and the two men returned before we had finished the cooked meal. They bought Alf and myself three china souvenirs, each with 'Dunkirk' written on. After we had finished the meal we set off once more for the beach. By now the Stukas were busy again, but we managed to keep together until there was an extra barrage of bombs came down and when I stood up I couldn't see any of the other four.

So I went walking around to see if I could find them, when suddenly a sergeant with a sheet of paper asked me where I was going. I told him I was looking for my mates.

He said, 'Stay here and make this group of fifty up!' Eventually I was taken off the mole.

At Dover we were taken up to a platform and told to get into the next train that came in. I threw my rifle and ammunition on to the rack along with my souvenirs. There were facilities for sending a telegram home, so I asked the porter how long it would be before the train left. He said half an hour. So I nipped out to send a telegram, and when I came out the train had gone, along with all my few treasured possessions and my one souvenir of Dunkirk!

Fred Mutch, Paignton, Devon

Amidst all the carnage and chaos, and the bitter memories, and the sad memories of losing pals, I find it easier to remember some humorous moments; two in particular.

During the retreat to the coast, German planes came down to strafe the roads, killing troops and civilians. Everybody dived into the ditches alongside the roads. Then someone started laughing and cheering and as I looked up along the road I saw a British soldier, sitting astride a French cavalry horse, and wearing a French helmet. He was trotting

on the horse down the road, acknowledging the cheers by doffing his helmet to left and right. He must have been 'bomb happy' but he certainly restored morale that day!

The second incident occurred at the beach at La Panne.

We were the last remnants and a British naval boat was ferrying from the shore to a merchant ship. We tumbled in, hardly aware of what we were doing. We started rowing, making little progress, until the petty officer said, 'I think lads, that if you turn round the other way to row we will get somewhere.' Weary, tired and desperate, we were all facing out to sea rowing a beached boat!

Bill Flaherty, Merthyr Tydfil, Glamorgan

I arrived in Dunkirk as a straggler, having got separated from my unit, the 6th Green Howards, so I had no option but to join the back of one of the queues waiting for the small boats to take them out to the bigger boats.

For some time a boat, which we later found out was a coal hopper, had been stood off the beach and none of the small boats had approached it. Around 4.30pm some of the 'stragglers' decided to swim out to it, walking out as far as possible. They walked until the water reached their chins, but then the water got shallower so that when they reached the boat the water was only up to the waist! A scramble net was lowered over the side and they climbed aboard. When I realised the water got shallower I decided to make the trip.

About sixty of us got aboard when the naval officer, possibly a petty officer, ordered the rest of his crew (two lads who could not have been more than sixteen years old) to pull up the net. Then he explained that we were on a land bank and the high tide wasn't until five past six! Even then he was not certain he'd be able to get clear, especially with our weight.

Of course we were all below deck in the hopper hold. Up above the crew sounded as though they were working with chains. Suddenly we heard a German plane coming down strafing and one of the lads came diving through the hatch on to the top of us. He stood up, looked around and straightened his uniform. Then he pulled his tin hat firmly back on his head and climbed the ladder on to the deck and through the hatch I saw him giving a reverse 'V' sign!

The time got around to 5.45pm, and the petty officer came down and said, 'Sorry lads, it's a bad job. You'd be better off trying somewhere else.'

A sergeant major asked, 'Is there anything we can do to help? If we could get a rock on the boat it might help?'

For some reason best known to the navy, the engine was still running while he was talking. So the sergeant major lined us all up along the seaward side of the boat and shouted 'Run' and we all ran towards the shore and 'Back' and we ran back.

We kept this up for some time and the petty officer, I remember, shouted, 'You're wasting your time lads, the tide has turned.' The sergeant major said, 'Keep it up, we have nothing to lose.'

Two minutes later as we ran shorewards for about the hundredth time, a wave must have hit us and knocked us into the deeper water, because we shot forward like a speed boat for ten yards, and then set off, 'chug chug chug' across the Channel!

At about eight o'clock the petty officer told us it was brewing time, and by taking it in turns and with what mugs we had, we all had some of the 'cup that cheers'. Twelve hours later we arrived in Dover.

I suppose I have thought of this experience many times, and over the years and even as I write it, I have become filled with pride over the behaviour of those two lads and their skipper. Maybe they learned how we felt when we gave them 'three cheers' when we got off at Dover.

Arthur Davies, Middlesbrough, North Yorkshire

Our retreat to Dunkirk, although we did not know it at the time, was from a small village near Péronne in May, 1940. Nearing Dunkirk, myself and a notorious reservist nicknamed 'Curly' were detailed to drop off with a Boys anti-tank rifle which we set up at the side of the road and await fifteen enemy tanks purported to be coming down the road! Luckily we were recalled before they arrived – I didn't relish firing a 'peashooter' at an enemy tank but was prepared to 'if and when'.

I was nineteen at the time and had joined our local light ack-ack battery at Paignton in Devon some twelve months before and here we were en route for Dunkirk docks, through the perimeter, where rearguard actions would be fought in due course.

Our Bofors gun was sited inside the docks. Waves of German bombers came over – every gun of the light and heavy ack-ack regiments opened up a terrific barrage. The whole wave of attackers turned away – mighty cheers from all around us!

That did not happen again. Next time they came over out of range of our guns and plastered the place. All hell broke loose, bombs dropping and guns banging away. I noticed our troop sergeant major with a Lewis gun on stands, one at each shoulder, firing at the Stukas for all he was worth. In the lull between raids a hospital ship was being boarded by the wounded and there were fires everywhere. Eventually we were withdrawn from

the docks and brought into action on the perimeter of the beach until it all became untenable. The last official order I remember was an unbelievable 'every man for himself'.

In the dunes we were waiting and wondering, strafed and bombed, men killed and wounded all around. Three of us were crouched down behind the other during one attack. The first man bought it with shrapnel through his side – I know because his blood spattered over us. In the same raid one of our officers had his foot blown off. He was carried off. His foot, still in the boot, lay in the sand. Gory details, I know, but this is the sort of thing one remembers.

Long queues formed in the water; seemed like suicide to me with the Jerries coming over with monotonous regularity. So a few of us made for the docks, I recall jumping on an overloaded truck which was making its way through falling buildings, some alight. I got off and made for the mole and joined the queue.

This was another unforgettable experience. Our goal was a destroyer at the end of the mole – slowly, slowly edging our way along, jumping across where it was breached, ducking when the planes came over strafing, some men going over the side.

After an eternity it was my turn to be pulled on to the deck of what I think was HMS *Codrington*, by a sailor who said, and I well remember, 'Come on Tommy, you have had enough for one day.' Below deck, nice thick steel above – hot cocoa – packed like sardines but wonderful. Ship's guns banging away as we moved out for home.

Norman Hammond, Bath, Avon

In 1940 I was twenty years old, a PBI [Poor Bloody Infantry] territorial soldier in the Queen's Royal Regiment. We went to France on 1 April, 1940 and after a short lull we crossed the border into Belgium on 10 May. From then on such names as Armentières, Lille, Courtrai, Oudenaarde and others took on a reality somewhat different than my father, one of the Old Contemptibles, used to tell me concerning the First World War. Then, in the hell of that month, May to early June, my story starts.

It seemed to me that the whole world had suddenly gone mad. We had been bombed, shelled, marched off our feet, been in action umpteen times, I cannot remember when we had last eaten. Then with chin on the ground we heard General Gort giving the order 'every man back to Dunkirk'. It seemed then that the orderly withdrawal was no longer orderly! I crossed the border into France at Armentières which was being bombed, and on the outskirts of that town an old French lady suddenly came up to me, running to keep up with us, and carrying a jug of hot water, a cup, into which she put a cube of French sugar. She mixed it with the hot water and gave it to me, saying in broken English, which she had obviously learnt during the First World War, 'Drink it son, it will keep you going, I did it for your fathers in the first war.' I shall never forget her, her white hair, and pinned to her dress was a small paper Union Jack like we have on flag days. I am certain the good Lord has given her a rather special place in heaven because she was a woman of his making. God bless her.

Some days later I found myself, after three days of hell, on the beach at Dunkirk, sitting next to a young lieutenant in the signals. We had shared all we had, which was a bottle of wine plus one army biscuit! There was no water. Suddenly a Lysander plane was flashing a signal but it didn't mean anything to me. The lieutenant shouted to me to get the nearest lot of men to prop up a deserted fifteen-hundredweight truck by the front so that he could signal with the headlights to the plane. This he did, at the same time shouting 'the navy is coming, the bloody navy is coming' and the news of that went across the beach like wildfire.

At about 4pm that afternoon smoke on the horizon was seen and the big boats lay out in the deep water and I saw those big guns on the boats turn and lift and then they fired and somehow we felt safe.

I remember I was bleeding from the mouth because in all the excitement I had bitten my tongue, but I knew with all those little boats coming in that, with a little luck, somehow we were going home. That was a fateful year in the life of a twenty-one-year-old. It was an appalling time, but as I looked back I am glad I didn't miss that experience of Dunkirk.

Ronald H. W. Mott, Godalming, Surrey

I was a telegraphist at the time of Dunkirk on board HMS *Brighton Queen*, a rather elderly paddle minesweeper, her peacetime role being that of a cross-Channel pleasure boat. I can recall the vast number of ships of all descriptions berthed all over the harbour at Dover including destroyers, pleasure boats, yachts, trawlers, lifeboats and others and these ships didn't include the rescue ships on the way in or out for the evacuation.

The evacuation had already been in progress for some while when we received our sailing orders and we were on our way to La Panne near Dunkirk with some other paddle sweepers of the tenth flotilla. At dusk we were attacked by some enemy aircraft flying fairly high who dropped bombs well wide but we opened fire with our popgun, which was a twelve-pounder, and I think that we missed them by as much as they missed us! That was my initiation to being under fire.

On arrival at La Panne we dropped our hook near the shore before dawn and then lowered the boats and our crew went off to review the situation. They were away for ages but returned with whatever 'pongoes' they picked up from the beach and then they transferred them to our ship.

Daylight arrived and then the fireworks started. We were not under continuous attack but it seemed like it and then the boats soon began their shuttle between the beach and the ship. Any boat to any ship seemed to be the plan and I shall never forget the orderly queues of 'pongoes' up to their chests in water waiting for a lift, ducking as the bombs exploded in the water or on the beach. Those who were wounded were being lifted aboard but they were well looked after by their mates.

I myself found, apart from helping the lads aboard from the small boats, that I spent a lot of my time rearming a Lewis gun which was mounted on deck outside the radio cabin. I don't recall being fed at all, but I do remember the cox'n coming round with our tots possibly more than once, so we must have more than 'spliced the mainbrace'! Anyway the evacuation continued for some hours and the bombing and machine-gunning seemed to get heavier.

When we had got our maximum number of troops on board we set off for Dover, leaving behind thousands of troops, and I remember seeing ships hit off La Panne and there were more than a few half-submerged off the beaches. I had only one signal to make on the way back, which was to give the number of soldiers lifted off, which was about six hundred, and the number of casualties. I had six soldiers sleeping on the deck of the radio cabin and two on my bunk and they had been dug in at La Panne for three days. We were attacked and 'near missed' on the way back, but no damage was caused to us. The sea was wonderfully smooth and we made good time to Dover, had a quick turn-round and were soon back on our way to Dunkirk.

This time we set off in the forenoon in beautiful weather. I think it was 1 June. We made a good rate of knots and it wasn't long before we reached Dunkirk with its oil tanks burning and we were attacked on the way in but, again, no damage was caused to us. Dunkirk was protected by two moles, east and west, and we berthed this time on the east mole and immediately the troops began to board ship. All the time the harbour was under attack from the air and from inland, and alongside our berth was the wreck of a British armed trawler with the ensign still flying and ahead was a wrecked French destroyer. She had already been badly savaged by bombing. It was about this time that both moles were attacked by dive-bombers and this is something I still remember with a shudder.

I was helping the troops aboard when I heard this screaming noise. I couldn't pin it down at the time but, my God, I soon realised what it was when the bombs started exploding. I had heard about these screaming Stukas from other crews but this was our first experience and it scared me stiff. The planes were aiming for both moles and were having some success. We carried on loading the troops, which included French and Moroccans, and as they were coming aboard we were trying to indicate that they should remove their great-coats and packs. Some of them did and I think that they were the lucky ones.

When we got a full load, about seven hundred this time, we cast off and made our way out of the holocaust through the flotsam, including a lot of the poor lads who did not make it. I was making my way to the bridge to see if there was any signal to send and we must have been four or five miles away from the mole when a major air attack developed. I actually saw three aircraft plummeting down and the next thing was an almighty crash astern. I ducked and when I looked up I saw bits of wreckage and bodies coming down. I didn't see anything going up. The bomb or bombs must have gone through the deck and exploded below the waterline because the ship began to sink immediately and I went into the radio cabin to switch on the transmitter. However, the water was rapidly waist-deep and I got out pretty damn smartish and by the time I had fully inflated my lifebelt and kicked off my boots I was afloat and swimming away from the ship. Suddenly I had thoughts about the boilers exploding, and the result was that I made my own rapid rate of knots away from the ship!

Lots of the soldiers were drowned and killed by machine guns. Some, I think, would have lived if they had removed their greatcoats and packs. After swimming for a while I lay on my back and looked at the beautiful sky. At that time I had suddenly got to the point where I wasn't particularly worried about not being picked up but I did hope that it would be a ship on the way home rather than one going to Dunkirk! After about thirty minutes the Royal Navy frigate HMS *Saltash* came alongside with scrambling nets down and lifelines over the side and I grabbed a lifeline and was up and over pretty smartish and once again I found myself helping survivors aboard.

Whilst aboard I saw SS *Scotia*, a naval transport, hit

by a stick of bombs. She was in serious trouble and very soon sank and I watched while men were walking down the ship's side into the water to be picked up by other ships. Soon after that we set off for Blighty and after a few hours berthed at Margate pier. I had taken off my clothes and put them in the boiler room for a quick dry after I was picked up but they had disappeared when I went to collect them so a friendly matelot gave me a towel and so my return to England was walking down Margate pier, dressed in a towel, but with my moneybelt still around my waist and VERY thankful to be out of it.

Arthur Blakeburn, Sunderland, Tyne and Wear

I was in the 11th battalion of the Durham Light Infantry when we were sent to France, and as far as I am concerned we were sent out to France with generals that were still fighting a 1940 war with 1914 tactics. The weapons we had against German tanks were a two-pound anti-tank gun and an anti-tank rifle, and I can tell you that wouldn't have put a hole in a tin can, never mind a tank. Our personal weapons were a .303 rifle and an eighteen-inch bayonet. The general in charge of operations at this period was Lord Gort who, apparently, was heading for the coast days before we made it to Dunkirk. I think he was sent to be the governor of Malta shortly after, as a cushy number.

In early May the Germans struck and we didn't know what hit us. Their armour plus their airforce just swept us towards the coast so that there was no organised front and each unit fought its own battles when the Germans caught up with them. Officers from each unit tried to make their own way to Dunkirk with their own unit's survivors, and I remember that the roads were chocked full of refugees and military. As vehicles ran out of petrol they were vandalised, with tyres being slashed and petrol tanks punctured so that the Germans couldn't use them and then they were pushed off the road.

At Dunkirk there were thousands of troops, French, British and Belgian, but we all wondered where we could go from here with nothing but the sea in front and the Germans behind.

Then, for me, it was the miracle of Dunkirk when the German armour stopped moving forward when it could have taken a lot of us prisoners, and shortly afterwards there was another miracle when boats of all descriptions appeared on the horizon. There was the navy, motorboats, pleasure boats, hundreds manned by ordinary people with the small boats taking the tired hungry troops out to the larger boats for shipping back home to England.

But not all of them made it. Bodies were washed up on to the beaches with each wave as boats large and small were dive-bombed and machine-gunned by the planes.

Troops that could not get on to the boats were in the sand dunes near the beach waiting their turn for the boats. I was one of the lucky ones who made it.

Four years later I was on the beaches again, but at least this time we were going in the right direction. Berlin!

Mr L. Handley, Nether Kellet, Lancashire

I have a few memories of Dunkirk. I was serving with the British Expeditionary Force with the King's Own Scottish Borderers, looking after the spare parts for the vehicles of the transport section.

I remember having one narrow escape. I was machine-gunned whilst driving an ammunition wagon, but was either half asleep or so unaware of what was happening that I could not understand why those in the front of the column of vehicles were diving for the ditch. I slowly got out of my truck to see what they were doing and was amazed when they told me and then I saw the plane. He missed the lot of us, but I don't think he could have tried very hard!

During the journey back I remember that we stayed at a farm near Poperinge, and I remember an old lady who cursed and raved at us when we tried to park our vehicles on her land and near to her buildings. Of course, because of what was happening at that time we ignored her, but

I remember she called us English pigs in both French and English, and made no bones about who she supported! I remember this place in particular because my father had been wounded here in the 1914–18 war.

Further on, having put all our vehicles out of action on the outskirts of La Panne, as soon as it was dark on the evening of Friday 31 May we marched to the beach with the idea that we were going to be taken off in boats from a jetty made of RASC lorries. We never saw this construction because some distance from it the Germans started shelling us and we laid up against the sea wall under the promenade for about three hours. So we decided to make for Dunkirk and set off 'in good marching order' but kept being held up by something at the front of the column.

It was the officer in charge, one Major S. . . . .N as apparently he was drunk and kept falling down! By now there was little discipline left in any case and this officer was a regular and near the end of his career and he must have heard remarks addressed about him and to him he had never heard in the whole of his army life!

'You drunken old sod', 'Stand up you old git' etc etc. Finally, one of the NCOs said, 'Let's leave the old bastard.'

And we did! His servant was one Charlie Flint, and he stayed with him and brought him home safely. Flint stayed on with us, but I never saw the major again. We were told he had had a nervous breakdown.

Halfway between La Panne and Dunkirk I saw four soldiers, one to each corner of a blanket, carrying a lad who was wounded and appeared semi-conscious. They were trying to cheer him up and nodding towards the jetty at Dunkirk now becoming visible in the early morning light. 'Not far to go now, so and so.' I am sure they had carried him from La Panne which was three miles back but still [had] some distance to go. It doesn't require much imagination to realise how cumbersome this burden must have been, especially for the two on the two back corners of the stretcher which they were trying to keep as even as possible all the time.

About a mile from the jetty at Dunkirk I ran into a Lancashire lad from our unit called Ellis. He asked if I was thirsty and when I said that I was he handed me what looked like a bottle of water. I started to drink it greedily. It tasted vile, and I think it was 'eau-de-vie' or something. He roared with laughter when I spat it out and shouted, 'You rotten bugger, I suppose you think that's funny.' He said, 'I'm going for a kip up there,' pointing to the houses on the front. 'There's plenty of cellars we can get down in. Are you coming?' Because of what he had done I refused, but I never saw him again.

About two miles from the jetty at Dunkirk I had tried to wade out to some rowing boats manned by civilians. A wave swept me off my feet, and as I fell I shouted to one of our unit wading near me in panic, 'I can't swim'. He pulled me to my feet and went on his way. I returned to the beach soaked and having lost my rifle. A few minutes later in a light reconnaissance vehicle which had been abandoned I found a pair of dry battledress trousers and, much to my relief, a rifle. I changed into the trousers and took the rifle. The reason for the relief was because I had already started to worry about losing my own rifle with visions of a court martial!

When we started to reform at Shepton Mallet in Somerset we were allowed a seventy-two hours' leave, and I left this rifle in the gents toilet of that station en route home. Plenty of others had come back without their rifles and no questions had been asked. I was always getting into trouble for a dirty barrel, and this one was in a very dirty state and I didn't fancy trying to have to get it clean again!

Two things stand out in my mind from that time. I never ever saw civilian refugees on the roads being machine-gunned, though there were plenty of rumours about it at the time and some of the films I have seen since and books I have read implied that it was done. In fact I never saw a dead civilian.

However, there was bitterness towards the RAF. We did not know how short we were of planes and thought their absence was because they were frightened to come out and fight. I am sure I read somewhere shortly after coming home that some of those who had been evacuated and were waiting near an aerodrome in the south to rejoin their units went into the RAF quarters one evening and had a free for all with the RAF personnel because they thought they had been let down. Perhaps they were drunk, but it was all rather sad.

E. Newbould, Leeds, West Yorkshire

I was at a loss when asked to contribute a recipe, as my cooking expertise is restricted to boiled eggs, scrambled eggs, poached eggs and toast. (Aren't you lucky! cries out my wife of fifty years). However, I have remembered a complete recipe for a whole meal, which was served up to me forty-nine years ago by two very good friends.

I was a sergeant stretcher-bearer at the time with the 141 Field Ambulance attached to the 5th Infantry Division. We were being chased out of France and Belgium by Hitler's 'blitzkrieg' in June 1940. Chaos reigned, our transport had been taken from us and my company, A Company, was ordered to find our way towards Dunkirk on foot.

After two days' march, I found myself with about thirty others in a pine wood approximately five miles from the beach, completely exhausted and very, very hungry indeed. The whole supply system had broken down and we had not seen a sign of any rations for the last two days. We were unarmed, with a Red Cross armlet and no use to anyone.

Imagine my joy when my two friends, Corporal Percy Goldsack and Lieutenant Baker appeared in this wood, driving their 'impressed' vehicle on which could be clearly seen through the hastily painted camouflage 'Bentall's of Kingston'!! (*Dad's Army* indeed).

These two were the quartermaster and his corporal. If anyone was going to find us some food they were our best bet. Lieutenant Baker was a First World War soldier, charming and very efficient. Percy Goldsack sold Bibles in civvy street and was the most wonderful scrounger for the unit. He had a great sense of cockney humour, always coupled with more than enough of the appropriate swear words. (He assured us he didn't use them when selling Bibles.)

True to form, on their retreat to the coast, these two had found a bombed French goods train in a siding, with one of the wagons containing NAAFI goods, blown open. These were shared out amongst my Merry Men and myself and consisted simply of tins of pilchards and tins of sliced peaches.

After nearly fifty years I now offer that recipe for a first class meal, as it was the best meal I have ever had and it was our last meal until we got back to England.

Ingredients:
Tins of pilchards
Tins of peaches
A group of very hungry friends
A pine wood far from home

Sad to relate, Percy and Lieutenant Baker were both killed on the beaches forty-eight hours later.

Graham Castle, MC, MM, Redhill, Surrey

My story starts a day or two previous to the evacuation. I was the wireless operator of a forward observation party in a battery of 18/25-pounder field guns. The officer in charge was a Canadian, Lieutenant Ross, and we got left behind when the orders to withdraw failed to reach us.

We drove off towards the coast till the engine of our truck seized up. Then we walked and I got separated and got badly blistered feet; I remember it was on a hot June day. In the confusion and utter chaos which existed, I came across a field with French cavalry horses in it and saddles and bridles dumped there also. I caught a chestnut horse, saddled up, mounted and continued my way,

following the crowded road. I was part of a mass exodus. However, being a competent rider of the Royal Horse artillery tradition, pre-war, I soon overtook my erstwhile comrades along the way!

Inevitably, of course I was ordered by an officer to dismount, but in view of the state of my feet and the fact that we only had one horse between us, I ignored his order and promptly trotted off in the direction of Dunkirk.

As I arrived in Dunkirk I saw that it was under fire from heavy enemy shelling. The port was full of ships and troops of different nationalities. Sizing the situation up, I turned away and went along the coast a few miles further down. There I unsaddled the horse and turned it loose into a field.

I was at La Panne, near a large building like a hospital on the seafront. I was both very hungry and very thirsty. I joined other troops, dug a slit trench in the sand dunes and settled down.

All around were dead bodies, the result of the German fighters strafing and machine-gunning that day. Whilst we were there we saw the motley of ships leaving and entering the port, all of them being bombed and I remember one being hit and sinking.

My next recollection, after spending the night in the sand dunes, was walking near the water's edge next morning and noticing a destroyer lowering boats over the side and coming towards the beach. In a leading boat was a big sailor waving and shouting,

'Come on, do you want to f. . . . . .g go home?'

Divesting myself of equipment, rifle etc, I plunged into the sea, half swimming and half wading, till I was pulled aboard with many others.

We were taken aboard the war ship – a motley collection of soldiers of all descriptions, and sent below deck where the hatches were battened down. Getting under way the ship went towards Dunkirk jetty, to take on more troops. Whilst we were there German dive-bombers dropped bombs on us, narrowly missing us, and rocking the ship and frightening all of us into silence.

Having had only half a bottle of dry champagne to drink and nothing to eat, I inevitably was sick that night crossing the Channel!

I landed at Dover, being billeted at Dover Castle.

Charles Williams, Blackburn, Lancashire

I suppose the first time I realised that the BEF was in fact surrounded, happened after the battle of Oudenaarde where I, together with several members of the B Company, 5th Northamptonshire, were surrounded by the Germans.

We fought our way out and retreated towards the Belgian/ French border somewhere near Tourcoing. I remember much relief on seeing the lines of pillboxes. We helped to build them during the winter of 1939!

It was then that we were told that the Germans had broken through, and were in fact behind us, in France. We then began the long trek back towards Dunkirk. I myself was driving the company commander's pick-up. The remainder of the company, together with lots more troops, were in a variety of vehicles along roads choked with refugees. All of them were fleeing. They didn't know where. We were continually subject to air attacks, Stukas and fighter planes strafing us and we suffered terrible losses. Eventually we arrived somewhere east of Dunkirk, and took up positions in the sand dunes. I was told to drive my truck into a ditch and leave it as it was, but not to wreck it.

After a while an officer of the company came to me, and I had to recover my truck to take him on a mission. He left me parked behind a battery of field guns (not a very healthy place) and off he went. I stayed in the truck and, being very tired, fell asleep. Later I was awakened by a sergeant of the gun troop who said, 'Come on laddie, you had better be moving, we have used up all our ammunition and we are going to blow up our guns.' He directed me which way to go and I caught up with some of my regiment marching back towards the beaches.

I was next detailed, together with four more truck drivers, to proceed towards the front line to convey some of the troops fighting the rearguard action back to the coast. This was from an area inland of Nieuwpoort. We took them to Nieuwpoort, and then had to disable all but one of the trucks, which we used to head for the beaches just west of the town. It was whilst driving along this road and quite near to the coast, that we saw a Stuka diving on us. We all baled out and dived into a ditch. The truck was completely destroyed but we all escaped injury, except that I got some bomb splinters in my lower left leg.

I stopped to put a field dressing on it, and by this time the others were out of sight so I started to make my way to a field dressing station which was just along the road from me. I did not get there. It received a direct hit just before I arrived. By now I was getting pretty desperate. At last I got to the beach amongst a lot of stragglers, and there I was given a tin of bully beef with nothing to open it but my bayonet!

There was, close by, some roped-off areas and this is the only piece of news at this time that I can still laugh at. I thought the men standing in them were to be taken out to some boats, so I ducked under the rope and stood behind the rest, just in time to hear a sergeant say, 'Right you men. You will row boatloads of men out to the ship there.' I can tell you I quickly ducked out again, as I didn't fancy that job!

I then rejoined the party of stragglers from various regiments and we were told to move along the coast westwards and get back to the dunes and wait for night-fall. All the time there was this screaming of shells and aircraft overhead.

After dark we were mustered and told that we had to march along the coast to La Panne. We started off by walking at the edge of the water, as the sand was firmer there, but after a while we began to get shelled and realised that our footprints glowed fluorescent in the wet sand, and there must be a spotter plane overhead directing gunfire. So it was back to the soft sand and really hard going. After marching some eight or ten miles we arrived at La Panne and were told, 'There is your boat and you have to try and get to it.'

We started wading out, but it wasn't long before we were out of our depth and we had to swim for it. I am afraid quite a number didn't make it. The boat turned out to be a Thames corn barge, and we were helped aboard so that when we were all on there were about eighty of us.

When they went to move off they realised that we

were stuck on a sand bank! So they put us all down below and shut the hatches to make it look as though the boat was deserted. We were all so dog-tired that I suppose we all fell asleep. However, the Lord must have watched over us, for we were untouched, and some time the next day we were refloated and I woke up to find that I was back in England at Margate. It was 2 June.

We disembarked and as we filed off the boat we were given a lovely cup of tea and a cigarette by those wonderful ladies of the WVS. We then boarded a train and next morning arrived at Manchester, where we were billeted at the Royal Manchester's depot.

After a lovely breakfast I had the bomb splinters removed from my leg, and next went outside in lovely sunshine where I fell asleep and slept soundly for twenty-four hours!

Bill Burbidge, Market Harborough, Leicestershire

I remember events in May 1940 while trying to reach Dunkirk from Lille in France. We were travelling in convoy when we were ambushed by German tanks, and some of our colleagues were killed, some were wounded and some were taken prisoner. At the time of the attack I was sat on an ammunition box and as soon as I heard machine-gun fire I moved quicker than Seb Coe ever did in his prime!

Anyway, luckily in France they did have some nice deep ditches by the sides of the roads, and it was into one of these that I dived after tossing my rifle beforehand. Then I found I couldn't move as the road was being sprayed with machine-gun fire and one false move and my head would have been full of holes. The driver and the co-driver of the water truck were shot dead before they could move.

The vehicle behind us went up in flames and some of the crew were wounded. After a short time I managed to crawl out of the ditch into a farmyard and went into a brick-built barn which had big iron doors. There were three of us stood in the centre of this barn when three separate rifle shots were splattered up against the wall behind us. We then did championship dives into the bales of hay which were in one end of the building and after this episode I always said that one of those bullets had my name on it but it had been spelt wrong!

This I said for forty-eight years until one day my wife was searching through a drawer at home and found a tag which we used to wear round our necks giving name, number and religion. My wife looked at this and said, 'But they've spelt your name wrong.' Sure enough, my name had been spelt Worswilk instead of Worswick and so I had to say, 'Well even our lot couldn't spell it right.'

So ever after that I have come to the conclusion that if I had been killed I would have had to be buried in neutral ground and my epitaph would have been fitting.

'Neither side knew my name!'

Arthur Worswick, Rochdale, Lancashire

My story about Dunkirk is perhaps a different one. My husband came from Folkestone and I from a small hamlet in the Elham valley, five miles from the sea as the crow flies. My late husband was in the Merchant Navy and had just come from an awful trip being attacked in convoy but also being mined in and around different parts of the war zone.

When Dunkirk started he went to Dover to volunteer to take a boat out to help, but was turned away when they saw from his books that he had just come off ship. So what does he do but buys all the cigarettes, chocolates, milk etc that he could find and we went down to Tram Road, Folkestone, where the trains pull up from the harbour at walking pace and alongside the road.

The people of Folkestone gave anything they could to those poor bedraggled soldiers on the trains. I was not married then but we went together, and my old school-mistress was there and she was very pleased to know my 'husband to be' especially as he was tanned with his travels despite his awful time.

When one of the trains stopped near us some of the Scottish soldiers said to him (my husband), 'What are you doing here, making money on easy street?'

He was also called a coward and I stepped forward and pointed to his uniform with a small silver badge in his lapel. Whether they knew what it was I don't know but they still spat at him saying, 'Get over there and pull your weight you scab. What use are you.'

My husband turned away and my schoolmistress said, 'Don't worry, they don't know what they are saying.'

But everyone was staring, saying, 'Look at him, dressed and washed against those poor devils.'

He wouldn't go again but sent his sister and me to give out what he could. He would have given his life for them. People said, 'Oh they get more pay than the forces.' Yes they did, but they had to buy clothes not given to them and when they were killed there was no pension for their wives.

That's part of my memory of Dunkirk. Of course I did see a lot of boats etc but I could never forget the unthinking hurt those words gave to me and to my late husband. He died aged fifty-five and is buried at sea. This may not be the usual sort of story, but it's true and it shows the other side of the coin.

Arthur wrote this poem when he was eighteen years old for his father, who was also a Merchant Navy man:

> The Red Duster
> On all the seas of all the world
> There passes to and fro
> Where ghostly icebergs travel
> and spicy trade winds blow
> a gaudy piece of bunting,
> a Royal ruddy rag,
> The blossom of the ocean lanes
> – Great Britain's merchant flag!

Peggy Pepin, Rushton, Kettering, Northants

I remember Dunkirk because I was one of those who spent two days and nights on the beaches before escaping. I was a private in a company which went under the name of 2 Base Petrol Filling Centre and as you can see from the name we dealt with petrol and most of our officers were employed by the big petrol companies in peacetime. We were stationed at a little town named Lomme le Marais where we worked a large petrol installation.

When we were told to evacuate we moved into Belgium and spent two nights on a farm but as the gunfire got louder and louder we were moved back towards Dunkirk. As we passed through Armentières the Germans were bombing the town. We continued in our trucks until we were about twenty miles from Dunkirk and then we parked our vehicles in a huge field where the engineers were going to blow them up. Our truck was parked next to a NAAFI vehicle which I remember had thousands of cigarettes on it and our lads took little time in relieving the truck of its contents! Then we were walking towards Dunkirk and all the time we were getting dive-bombed by the German air force and had to keep jumping into ditches some of which, even in May, were full of water. But eventually we made it to the beaches and it was an amazing sight of thousands of soldiers on the sands with hundreds of small boats coming in to pick them up a few at a time to ferry them out to the ships which were standing offshore.

My pal and I joined on the end of one of those queues but we had to keep taking cover as the Germans were dive-bombing and strafing and it all started again. Then darkness fell and the huge petrol tanks kept exploding and the flames lit the sky and we went and laid down in the sand dunes to wait for daylight and then we joined on to a great rope that was going out to a ship which seemed to be a long way from shore. When the rope rose from the sea towards the deck of the ship I could not hold on any longer and we had to turn back towards the beach and the sand dunes where we stayed until nightfall.

During the night we moved to what was left of the pier. There were great gaps in the structure that had been repaired by fastening stretchers and any other timber that was available but it was hazardous getting along the pier, I can tell you. But a ship had tied up at the end and it seemed to be our last chance and eventually we made it and we were helped aboard and led into the hold where we fell asleep on a huge pile of coal.

When we awoke the white cliffs of Dover were in sight. We were back in England! The ladies meeting us as we disembarked gave each man five Woodbines and a bar of chocolate and an apple but I remember that we had hundreds of cigarettes still in our kitbags which we had carried since dumping our trucks and rifling the NAAFI!

We were taken to Aldershot where we handed in our rifles and ammunition and spent two nights under canvas before climbing aboard trucks and then we moved to Marlborough in Wiltshire and joined up with other members of our unit but alas, some of them had not come back. We were given forty-eight hours' leave, which was just time to get home to see my girlfriend and my family and that was my experience of Dunkirk. When I came back I was only twenty years six months old.

Kenneth Hogg, Elsdon Grove, Bradford

On approximately 26 May we were called out on parade and the commanding officer, Major Adams, informed us that the Germans had smashed through Holland, with a sweep into Belgium, and that the whole of the British Expeditionary Force and French armies were retreating. We were to proceed in three platoons, to Bailleul and Dunkirk for evacuation.

We drew rations and my platoon, under the command of Sapper Sergeant Marley, was instructed to make for Bailleul, keeping to the side roads as much as possible to avoid enemy bombing and machine-gunning from diving Stukas. We were considered to be 'lucky' because we had a three-ton truck, but by this time all the roads and paths and tracks were so completely clogged that very little movement by vehicles was possible.

As we travelled along the Stuka and Heinkel raids seemed interminable and we were constantly forced to take cover in hedgerows, ditches and fields. Any nearby copse was a haven since the enemy planes seemed intent on obliterating the masses of frightened fugitives on the roads. I will never believe that they were mistaken in their target, because of the obvious miscellany of carts, bicycles, prams and wheelbarrows, even the odd mule or donkey, all piled high with bedding and furniture, seemingly 'all but the kitchen sink', and in many cases children too.

After each raid we would assist in clearing the wreckage and bodies off the road. On one grisly occasion the sergeant, with seeming callousness, kicked the severed limb of a child into a ditch, all the accompanying family having been wiped out. The stench of explosives and animals was appalling.

We reached Bailleul purely by guesswork, since all road signs had been removed. We encountered a Service Corps officer of whom we asked which direction to take to Dunkirk, only to be told 'look for the pillar of smoke'. Sure enough, away to our west we could see it. And also squadrons of German planes high overhead, weaving to avoid what we assumed to be the gunfire of anti-aircraft guns. At intervals along the route Military Police and other personnel instructed us on to our destination, telling us to make for La Panne village, where we would be directed to our embarkation points.

On route we slept in the fields and under hedges, living off poultry or anything else we could forage for ourselves. In some of the villages there were, even at this stage, shops still selling bread and cakes, and we traded anything we owned to be able to buy some. We stole eggs. On odd occasions we even enjoyed a stew of animal feed, cattle cakes, mostly mixed with potatoes. There seemed to be an age-old animosity between the French and the British, but in retrospect I think they had good reason not to like us after some of our activities!

On 29 May we arrived at the 'column of smoke' and La Panne village. It was a very small hamlet, and we were appalled by the sight. The dunes, beaches and approaches were all littered with guns and vehicles of every description. Other piles of equipment were scattered around almost like a huge breaker's yard. All of it was useless, having been sledge-hammered. Engine blocks, wheels, axles, radiators of vehicles, had been smashed, 'so as not to allow the enemy to use them', we were told. Other transports continued to arrive all the time, each new arrival leading to fresh orgies of destruction.

For mile upon mile between La Panne and a long stretch of sand at Bray-Dunes we could see what appeared to be lines and lines of ant-like figures, and the lines stretched from the dunes into the sea. There were boats and craft of every description scurrying from the lines and the beach. Further out to sea there were destroyers, sweepers, barges, even paddle steamers. It was all like a huge regatta.

The 'ants' were being loaded into the boats taking them willy-nilly out of the water. What appeared to be a breakwater, or a long sea wall, stretched further into deeper water and there motor boats were picking up 'ants' from this. We then realised that they were MEN not ants, and that they were OUR men and that this was the so-called embarkation point. Along the beaches there was a never-ending wheeling and diving of enemy planes, and a cacophony of sound from explosions. There was the banshee screams of Stukas, with the continuous answering fire of guns from naval vessels.

On 29 May we were met by a Military Policeman and instructed to proceed to a point on the beach where we could join up with the other engineers. Here I met up with old friends Dennis and Alan Sanders, who were brothers, and Keith (Kev) Hartley, who had arrived with one of the other platoons. I never saw our third platoon again.

Arriving at the beach we were told to make ourselves as comfortable as possible and to await our turn to join one of the long queues of army personnel. We were given a serial number and only when that number was called out would we move. The raids were becoming ferocious and the lines forced to break for cover, any cover, to get out of the way. We lay behind dunes, we burrowed into holes, scared stiff, more by the 'banshee' wails than anything else.

Out at sea some of the naval vessels and small craft were taking a pounding from exploding bombs and huge water spouts and I saw an old Thames paddle steamer called the *Crested Eagle* blown to the beach in a mass of flames.

At night it rained heavily which, although uncomfortable, gave at least some respite from the noise. After a sleepless, sand-coated night the lines of troops reformed, broke and reformed repeatedly. Those of us who had not had orders to move carried out searches for anyone with food. Soup stoves had been set up and we were able to join the long queues waiting to be given soup, accompanied by stale bread and tinned beef, which had been brought in, at no little danger, by craft returning from the UK.

A rumour circulated that a U-boat had got into the fleet of boats out at sea, and this then seemed to be confirmed by a huge explosion on a naval vessel there. We were told that it was the HMS *Wakeful*. There were possibly five hundred or six hundred men aboard and the loss of life must have been terrific although we saw accompanying boats picking some men up. One of those I remember was a whaler called *Gobberon* I think. The sinking was later supposed to have not been carried out by a U-boat, but a German motor torpedo boat.

The Stuka raids continued. Sometimes the planes,

after unloading their bombs, wheeled around to make machine-gun raids on anything moving below. Leaflets were dropped advising the men on the beaches 'give up because you have no RAF left, and all the generals have gone home'. The lads swore and they used the leaflets for earthier purposes! But a rumour was circulating that General Gort and his entourage had been called back to England, and these rumours led to a lot of pessimism and such comments as 'we will never get back' and 'they have deserted us'. These were doubts that were quite widespread.

Fear of the truth of such rumours there certainly was, particularly when we began to notice that the numbers of small boats were getting fewer each day and also the fear caused by a small number of acts of what could be called cowardice, brought on by terror. Terror is insidious, taking over the senses. On one occasion a young officer 'cracked' and broke away from an evacuation column, jumping into a small boat that was loading. He refused to get out and was shot to stop the panic that could well have followed. The nerves of many men gave way, leading to queue jumping, hustling others in front of them to scramble into boats that were already overloaded, or claiming it was their turn before someone else. Another rumour arose that we were going to surrender and that we had already asked for terms. This was not true, of course, but at the time it seemed to have credence. Such rumours create panic.

The evacuation proceeded however and, having decided that the end of the mole had sufficient water for shallow-draught vessels, a number of smaller craft came alongside and formed a chain which speeded things up somewhat.

By this time the air raids were fast and furious because the Panzers thought we were finished and heavy fighting was already going on around the perimeter with shells dropping on to the village of La Panne. Amazingly, I remember that during this time in the lulls between the raids there were scratch football games being played or we visited other sections on the beach!

Then, on 31 May, we were ordered to join the lines. We were told to destroy anything that would be an incumbrance to us, and to take mainly what we stood in, weight and space being the order of priority. Some of the chaps had smuggled pet dogs along with them but many of these were being thrown back on to the beach or into the sea. Two more boats, one an Isle of Man packet steamer named *Tynwald*, and another named *Ben-my-Chree* filled up and pulled away. We waited and went on waiting. Movement was so slow that once again fear of not reaching a boat began to take over. Fear that the boat would fill before we got into it. Fear of impending air raids.

Another vessel, the *Lady of Mann* slipped away, and then I was hauled aboard the *Manxman*. I have never appreciated anything so much as I did that mug of thick, sweet cocoa that was shoved into my hand! This was IT. We were finally aboard. All we had to do now was pray. I remember thinking, 'Please God let the bombers miss us.' It was 31 May, and suddenly I remembered it was my twenty-second birthday!

Packed like sardines in a can with shouts of 'hang on' we sidled away, skirting the protecting naval ships that were firing ceaselessly. We were on our way to Dover.

I tried to find Dennis and Alan, but was told by one of the other chaps that they had 'had it'. This was confirmed by my other mates. We looked back at something resembling a picture of Dante's *Inferno*. What we had witnessed there was a carnage. But soon, far ahead, we could see the cliffs of Dover, and I can tell you it was a glorious sight.

Arriving at Dover, boatload after boatload of tired, filthy, dispirited men were met off the gang planks by WVS ladies offering tea and sandwiches. I shall never forget one incident. Leaving the dockside we were confronted by a smart 'spit and polish' redcap who stepped up to us and ordered, 'Smarten yourselves up! Do you call yourselves soldiers? I could call you something else.' The mate I was with, a little ginger-haired corporal from Liverpool, seemed to resent this slur very strongly and drawing himself up from his five foot six inches by at least another two inches, he leapt forward and head-butted the MP with a terrible thud. The MP fell backwards in no condition to retaliate!

Then, in no uncertain manner and language I remember, the little corporal told him, although I doubt he could hear, that if he had undergone such experiences as ours for the past twenty-five days, he would have justification for criticism. However, we were not prepared to take it from a 'lickspittle' who had probably never even left Waterloo station!

I never saw or heard anything of suspected fifth-column activities. Yet from all reports the whole French area was crawling with them. There were stories of Germans being parachuted in dressed as nuns, who were only spotted because someone observant noted their sprouting beards and were apparently seen shaving! Also that fifth columnists, dressed as French military motorcyclists, were reported to be misdirecting and causing general mayhem amongst civilians and retreating forces.

To me, Dunkirk was a sad defeat, the defeat of what Mr Churchill had once spoken of as 'the best army ever to protect England and our allies, and well prepared'. There was, however, a kind of victory and a great pride in the truth that it was an incredible withdrawal of huge numbers of troops who would be able to fight again. As proof of that claim, after a spell in hospital and an eventful return to active duty I later served overseas in Africa, Egypt and Palestine.

E. G. R. (Reg) Bazeley, Bewdley, Worcestershire

Author's note: the above article was sent in by Wynne Bazeley as a tribute to her husband who died in April 1989. It is his recollection of events, written shortly before he died. In her words, 'He was, to the end, a man of quiet courage and dignity.'

I remember Dunkirk well. At the time I was a despatch rider with the 523 Petrol Company of the 50th Division. Prior to the retreat to Dunkirk I was with an advance party on our way to Brussels, and we arrived at a village just outside of the city. It was a lovely warm day, and late in the afternoon, and our cook had managed to make a snack of egg and chips. We sat on the floor in an empty school and I was about to tuck in when our commanding officer rushed in and ordered all of us to pack up as fast as we could as the Germans were already in Brussels.

This was the start of our long retreat to Dunkirk.

Dunkirk was rough, but to be among the refugees also retreating and seeing them strafed from the air time and time again was appalling. The poor women and children who could not get out of the way suffered most.

I remember some of our lads with a machine gun and a fifteen-hundredweight truck opening fire at the planes. One was hit and eventually two crew baled out. We were going to try and pick them up, but the refugees got there first. That was  the end of their war! We were told by one army officer that they had just about pulled them to pieces.

This went on for a few days before we eventually arrived outside Dunkirk, only to be told we could not go in as there were already far too many troops in the town waiting and it was being bombed time and time again. However, we were ordered to move again and finished up at a little place at the coast just outside Dunkirk called La Panne. Just before we went down towards the beach we were ordered by the Military Police to leave all transport in a field a few miles away. We went to the ration truck to see if we could get some bully beef and biscuits as we hadn't eaten for days, only what we could get now and then. To our dismay we were told to leave them alone as they had to be left for the retreating infantry, poor devils. As we returned to the beach on the front I noticed the bandstand at the end of the promenade. One smart alec in our unit said, 'Well I'll go to hell. They haven't even put a band on to greet us.' The full length of the beach was packed with troops. We couldn't see a patch of sand anywhere.

Being late evening we were ordered to stick together as a company. That was all right until the enemy aircraft came down the coast strafing, and it was every man for himself. Then the shells were screaming over the top of the sand dunes, some landing in the sea, some in the dunes, ships on fire, others with their bows stuck up out of the water. It's something I'll never forget. Some of the small boats, such as yachts and fishing boats, had sunk because too many troops had climbed on board.

Darkness arrived, much to our relief, so we laid down on the sand dunes so as to get as much shelter as possible, but the possibility of sleep was a long way off. Gun flashes, searchlights raking the sky, screaming shells, it all went on throughout the night.

Dawn arrived and it was a bit hazy, but at least it was dry. The lieutenant in charge of our party gathered us together and we worked our way to the sea edge. Then he said that anyone who could row a boat was to take one step forward. We all moved forward en bloc! Twelve were picked out, and the rest of us were told to keep together until he came back. That was the last we saw of any of them! So I thought, 'Yes Nobby, every man for himself.' I spotted a nice yacht which some chaps were wading out to. Being a despatch rider I didn't have a rifle, nor had I been issued with a revolver, so I was able to wade out a bit easier than some. Then I saw where a lot were dumping their rifles into the sea as they were getting into difficulties, having reached a boat. Then we were told, 'It's no good climbing aboard here. The engine's broken down!'

What a disappointment. On my way back to the shore I came across four officers pushing a rowing boat out over the rolling waves, so I gave them a hand and when they got in I did the same! I fully expected to be told to get off, but nothing was said, much to my relief. Eventually we clambered aboard a Hull trawler and arrived in Dover next morning without any further mishaps.

Alfred 'Nobby' Clarke, Ripon, North Yorkshire

At the time of Dunkirk I was on board HMS *Fitzroy*. She was a flat-bottomed, coal-burning little mine-sweeper. Before the war she had been used as a survey vessel somewhere on the rivers of China. There the rivers are shallow and *Fitz*, being built as she was, was an advantage. She also proved that at Dunkirk, where we were one of the few to be able to go right up close to the beach for rescue work.

The first couple of trips were extremely nerve-racking, not knowing what to expect when we got there and shocked when we arrived. But with all the activity we soon overcame that. I am not quite certain of times but I think we left Dover around midnight and left Dunkirk at about four in the morning, each time loaded with wounded and men in all types of mood. You could not describe them as soldiers, for a great majority had discarded their uniforms and equipment in the effort to wade and swim to the boats. A weird sight, seeing dozens of men clambering up the side of the ship (rope ladders provided) in nothing but their underpants, some even without those. There was no shouting or screaming except now and again from a poor wounded wretch who was soon quietened and comforted by his comrades.

Our work was carried out as quietly as possible. We would be close up to the beach and our whalers would be going back and forth, filling then unloading as fast as possible. A most formidable task for the many brave sailors who rowed long and hard for hours in their endeavour to get as many of the lads aboard and get them back safe.

It was an eerie sight, in the dawn of the morning, looking along that beach covered with thousands of men. But there was no time for thought or despair. We were all too busy and in too much of a hurry to ever consider the danger around us, even though many times the ships and beach were bombed and machine-gunned, all adding to the hazard.

The jetty to the right of us was constantly attacked and, further away from it, thick black smoke and glaring fires continued for days. On one of those German bombing raids I remember coming up on deck, off duty watch from down in the stoke hold. I believe it was the second day. Orders had been given that whilst sailors were busy in the whalers or doing other tasks, anyone else free could man the machine guns.

My moment came! Once my eyes got accustomed to the light I rushed to the nearest gun station. I saw two aircraft in the distance and with all the eagerness and excitement that only a twenty-three-year-old can have, I let rip. No thoughts of what I was actually doing – the reality of it was that I was playing with a machine gun and actually enjoying myself!

Rat-tat-tat-tat the gun went. Suddenly a stern voice called down from the bridge. It was the captain. 'Who's the bloody idiot down there on that gun? Get him off!'

The order was carried out. I was hustled away by a couple of hefty sailors who were grinning from ear to ear and pointing to the bow of the ship where the 'stays' were swaying lazily in the breeze. Apparently I had blasted it away from the mast! And the aircraft had long since gone out of sight.

Another time coming off watch I looked towards the jetty. Between us and the jetty was HMS *Skipjack*. I said to my colleague, Tony Ward, who worked with me, 'Looks like the Jack's ready to move off.' She was loaded and about to return to Dover. 'Where?' he asked. 'There,'

I answered, pointing in her direction, but she was gone – blown up in a matter of seconds. It was devastating.

The emotion shown by many survivors was slightly embarrassing at times. Men hugging and kissing you in their relief but it was overlooked by the knowledge that we had rescued them, that they were alive, well and happy again and we were helping to get the boys back. The sad moments, looking down on the deck at the rows of wounded. Some with eyes filled with tears and gratitude, others with no 'eyes' at all, while many without arms, legs and other parts of their faces and bodies, lay motionless, staring from behind their bandages, in wonder, expectation and terror.

I cannot vouch for what I am writing next but I did hear it from several soldiers. They related that some officers were held back at gunpoint from leaving the beach to board a ship BEFORE the wounded had been moved on board. There is no accounting for some. After all we are only human, though some are less than others!

My most vivid recollection was of a Tuesday morning just a quarter of an hour before midday. The petty officer, Tony Ward and myself were preparing to be relieved of watch. We were about to stoke up the furnace. One of us would open and close the furnace door and the other would shovel in the coal. Tony was on door, I was shovelling, or would have been, but at that particular moment there was an almighty thud and rumble. No doubt a mine or bomb going off and before it happened, as Tony was about to open up, I shouted out 'Not now! Not now!' Somehow (I can't explain it) I had some sort of premonition. Had the furnace door been open it would have caused a blast-back and further possible danger.

As I stated earlier, and it seems ages ago and my hand is now aching, HMS *Fitzroy* did five trips to Dunkirk. The Saturday, which would have been our sixth, left us in dock. The order went out for volunteers to go on other boats and make the final journey. I was doing my washing and no, I wasn't scared, but I had learned never to volunteer for anything! But Tony wanted to go, he did so, borrowing my No.1 'going out' uniform at the same time. He had a busy but quiet trip there and back, but my uniform when it came back was in a hell of a state. Dirt, oil, blood and no doubt sweat. The outcome was strange, although exciting for Tony.

Some time later, several medals were allocated to some officers and men of several ships. A number for ours. Tony was awarded a Distinguished Service Medal. Sadly though, much time later, when we returned to Chatham as survivors, Tony again volunteered for another ship. He was lost off Crete on HMS *Kelly*, which was commanded by Lord Mountbatten.

I was on HMS *Malcolm*, a flotilla destroyer, doing Atlantic convoys. Going through some of my old papers and diaries – yes I kept diaries, though much of them boring and repetitious – I found I still had a soldier's pay book I had picked up from the deck at some time or other during the Dunkirk trips. His name was Henry Connell, age twenty, from Birmingham. His army number was 2659011.

Anyhow, I have been writing since five o'clock this morning and it is now 10.20am. Arthritis in my hand is playing me up, and I am dying for a cup of tea! But there's one thing extra. Our small ships sometimes had the mickey taken out of them. But our reply was ready – 'Small ships – big men!'

Reginald Cannon, Brentford, Middlesex

I was in the 51st Highland Division which fought a rear-guard action at Dunkirk and I was taken prisoner of war. We were forced-marched through Holland where we were put on barges which were both lousy and dirty and then on to cattle trucks to take us to our camps where I was a prisoner of war for five years.

After four and a half years I made a 'break' but broke my ankle in the process and eventually my foot swelled up and I had to remove my shoe and tie it to my leg and I crawled away from the camp unnoticed. Unfortunately in doing so I fell in a hole which must have been about twenty feet deep and I woke up with water around my mouth and I think I must have been there about two hours. My greatcoat was about six times its weight with the rain and the water in the hole and I was so exhausted I was prepared to die there and then. However, on looking round I saw a light not too far away and as I couldn't walk I crawled up a field of sugar beet towards the light. During that time I needed the toilet but quite honestly I didn't have the energy to undo my trousers, so I just let it go and the only comfort I got was that at least it was hot. Eventually I got to a small croft and found an open door and crawled into it and fell asleep.

When I woke standing over me was a savage dog which was barking close to my face and every time it barked I felt its spit and at that moment I was afraid even to blink. Suddenly the door opened and the farmer came in and cleared the dog away by stabbing it with a pitchfork and then he took me into the farmhouse and gave me a bowl of broth and cleaned me up. I was there for an hour but he warned me that he would have to report the matter which he did and two Gestapo officers came on a motorcycle with a sidecar to collect me.

I was ordered to sit in the sidecar and they set off back towards the prisoner-of-war camp, but halfway there they stopped. They humiliated me by taking out my penis and threatening to cut it off but by that time I didn't care what they did. I was done for. They held me against a tree and threatened me but by this time I didn't really know or care what was happening.

I thought I was being sent back to the prisoner-of-war camp but in fact I was sent to Massbach where I was detained for two months and then I was taken to a salt mine to work. When General Patton's army came through and released us we were as happy as pigs.

I found out that the hole I fell down was in fact an empty turning-table for the trains, hence its size and when I was released I was awarded a forty per cent war disablement pension but I was scarred for life, which was helped by the butt ends of the Gestapo and their revolvers. It took nine weeks of careful handling by my own fellow prisoners to see me through.

Douglas 'Titch' Robertson, Tyrie, Fraserburgh

I was called up to the Durham Light Infantry on 17 January 1940, and then given a week's embarkation leave before being shipped to France to complete our training. That was towards the end of April.

In France we travelled from Rouen northwards to a place called St Pol in cattle trucks on the railway. Each truck had chalked on the side '8 *Chevaux Ou 40 Hommes*' (eight horses or forty men) with a bale of straw in each wagon. Comfort was non-existent, as you can well imagine, and everyone was pleased when we reached our destination where we were accommodated in bell tents. Each man had one seam of the bell tent, and all our feet pointed to the centre pole! Luxury indeed! Fortunately the weather was dry and fine, and being young lads and fit as fiddles, it really wasn't any hardship as we all thrived in the open-air life and settled down quite happily to army life.

We hadn't been there many days when we saw an RAF fighter crash about a mile from our camp, and I had the not-very-happy job of painting the pilot's name on a wooden cross. I have never forgotten his name. It was Pilot Officer Radford. He was the first war casualty for us, and then we realised that war wasn't just a load of fun.

A few days later the Germans broke through, and things started to hum, and we packed up and marched towards the Belgian frontier. Whether we ever reached it or not I couldn't tell you because for the next three weeks we were marching, digging in, battling, marching, digging in until we reached the coast and quite frankly I don't think by then anyone knew where we were. We ordinary squaddies certainly didn't know. We crossed several of the old battle-fields of the 1914–18 war and sheltered from dive-bombing and shelling in the old shell holes which, of course, were nicely lined with grass by now. I remember on Vimy Ridge I was lying at the top of a cliff with a few hundred feet drop before me, and being under shellfire for the first time I was terrified in case a shell hit the cliff face a few feet below me and sent me to the bottom. Dumb-bell that I was,

I did not realise that all the whistling sounds I could hear above the exploding shells were red hot pieces of metal flying about, and any one of them could have finished me off as they had already done to some of our company.

When the shelling ceased I could see some enemy tanks in the distance. I was told to stand down from my look-out post, and shortly afterwards we retreated a few miles and I was glad to get off the high ground.

Our transport when we came to France consisted of about ten lorries and a water wagon. We never saw any of that transport and we heard later that it had all been lost to dive-bombers. The only thing we did see was the water wagon every day when we started moving. The dive-bombers were a menace. They would attack us umpteen times a day, and we would have to dive off the road and spread ourselves in the fields until they cleared off. Noisy, whistling things they were, and we passed several crowds of refugees on the roads with their pitiful belongings who had been machine-gunned by these planes. I was surprised at the number of farm carts that were stacked with family possessions. A double mattress tied on top with an aged granny fixed to that. How terrifying for these old bodies when they were being dive-bombed or machine-gunned. I often wonder how many survived it all.

The weather was very hot and sunny all the time we were marching to the coast, and as we were all wearing army-issue woollen "long johns" our crotches were all sore with constant rubbing of the garments and perspiration. Consequently we were, after a few days, all marching with our legs as far apart as we could, officers included, and really looking at the blokes in front it must have looked quite comical. I remember that as we reached the top of a particular hill which was well wooded, we were once again attacked by dive-bombers and so we got off the road quickly and took shelter amongst the trees. When things quietened down a bit and we had looked around we found to our horror that we were sheltering in an ammunition dump! There were thousands and thousands of artillery shells stacked amongst the trees. I think it may well have been safer to stay on the road.

After about ten days of this caper, it began to dawn on us raw lads that something was sadly amiss. Armies didn't fight or win battles by retreating. An RAF lorry and driver had joined us, completely lost, with no idea where his unit was, so he just tagged along with us. A day or two later we were told that we were heading for Dunkirk, where the navy was waiting to take us home. A few more days, sore and weary, hungry, and a bit discouraged, we came across fields full of smashed-up British vehicles. There were guns, Bren gun carriers etc, all deliberately smashed and some on fire to prevent them being of use to the enemy, and some distance away I could see a great pall of black smoke which we soon realised was lying over Dunkirk.

Next morning we were paraded and marched four abreast down to the beaches which were a right shambles. I remember my horror at the sight because we had got this far still disciplined and with all our weapons. We could see several sunken ships with their masts and funnels above water. A couple of lines of trucks placed end to end running from the beach out into the water, making make-shift piers. We were being bombed and machine-gunned from the air, and shelled by German artillery, and then quite suddenly we were told 'every man for himself'!

That was the moment when we realised that we really were in a mess. The first thing we did was scatter off that dangerous beach, and took shelter in the sand dunes. My mate and I had been in our particular dune, feeling pretty safe for an hour or so, when suddenly we were joined by a few very noisy Frenchmen. They were so garrulous and argumentative amongst themselves that I must admit that we two climbed over the ridge into the next dune for a bit of peace! I remember that shortly afterwards a shell landed amongst the Frenchmen and wiped out every one of them.

By this time my mate and I thought we had better see what we could do for ourselves, so we went down to the beach again and could see a couple of lines of men standing from the beach out into the sea, with the most seaward men up to their necks in water. Enquiring, we were told they were waiting their turn for a boat to pick them up and take them out to a ship, and we had better get to the end of the queue. Can you imagine standing in single file, in water, being periodically shelled and machine-gunned, and waiting for a boat!?

We couldn't see any sign of a boat coming in, and couldn't see much future in that, so we continued along the beach in the direction of a proper pier where we could see troops moving all the time, presumably boarding a ship whose mast we could see above the pier. When we got to within about a couple of hundred yards we saw a couple of shells burst on the pier and blow a gap in it, and effectively stop the flow of men. We didn't like the look of that either, so we returned the way we had come, somewhat dispirited to say the least.

Along the water's edge there was a continuous line of flotsam and rubbish washed ashore from the sunken ships. Bits of boat, lifebelts, broken tables, chairs, tins, cans etc etc. We came across two halves of a canoe, and would you imagine it still had two perfectly good paddles floating alongside it. Nearby was also floating a ship's raft. So we took off all our heavy gear, rifles, packs, ammunition, tin hats, boots and piled them all on the centre of the raft, which was about five feet long by three feet wide, and took a paddle each and pulled off to sea in the direction of the nearest ship. The sea was comparatively calm but with a bit of a swell and we were slowly making headway, when alas, for some inexplicable reason, our craft quite suddenly overturned and there we were struggling in the water and all our gear in Davy Jones's locker. So we partly swam, partly waded back to the shore, two thoroughly wet and sorry spectacles with a goodly coat of thick black diesel oil to boot. What a mess!

Low in spirit and thoroughly and uncomfortably wet, we made our way back towards the dunes but, almost there, I turned to look out to sea and saw a naval boat rowing towards the beach in our direction. So we ran back to the water and waded out towards it, with me leading. I thought good, I'll be the first in this queue, no worry about getting aboard. Ha! Ha! The story of my life!

Two paces forward and three back! As soon as I put my hand on the gunwale, a sailor told me to wade round to the bow and hold the boat steady against the swell to make it easier for the crew to help the following troops aboard. Can you imagine it? Up to my neck in water, holding the boat against the swell, which every two or three minutes lifted my feet off the bottom, followed by washing completely over my head.

It seemed to take ages to fill that small boat, and when they had, they forgot about me and started to row over me until, between gulps of oily sea water, I started shouting, 'Hey! what about me!' Eventually one of the sailors grabbed me and pulled me aboard. ▬

We reached the parent ship, thank goodness, which turned out to be the HMS *Albury*, a minesweeper. I was put down in the fo'c'sle, where I received the best mug of tea I have ever had in my life. Real navy stuff. Hot, strong, sweet and with a generous ration of rum to boot. Shortly afterwards we heard the sweeper get underway, for it was loaded, and we must have been amongst the last boatloads out. I have often wondered if the *Albury* survived the war. I have never seen, heard or read any more about her since.

After a while I got permission to go to the upper part of the engine room, and hang what was left of my clothes over the rails to dry off a bit. Then back to the fo'c'sle in my birthday suit. As we got near to England I went back to the engine room to get my clothes, and they were nice and dry, but have you ever tried walking over engine room grids in your bare feet? I was hopping about like a kangaroo on those hot grids, trying not to put down more than one foot at a time. I wished at the time that I had a dozen feet!

However considering all that had gone before, this was the least of my worries, and I was in uniform when we landed at Margate to a hero's welcome.

I have deliberately left out the more horrific things that happened to all troops in action. Sufficient to say that my initial training had been completed the hard way. After just four and a half months in the army I considered myself an old soldier. Out of our battalion strength of approximately eight hundred men who went to France in April, only about two hundred and fifty finally made it back to England.

Fred Clapham, South Shields, Tyne and Wear

We had been marching around France for ten days in the rain. We were just about at the end. I was alongside a mate of mine called Coley, well we called him Coley but his name was Coles. Suddenly he said, 'Cliff, I'm gonna dump this bloody shovel,' and I said 'Don't do that Coley, we might need it.'

A few more paces on Coley called out to all and sundry 'Who wants a bloody shovel?' Needless to say I landed up with that 'bloody shovel'.

Dawn was approaching as we halted and the next thing I know our section was detailed to take up a defence position on the outskirts of Dunkirk. This was no job of joy I can tell you. Our position was on the south side of a fair-sized farmhouse, and the poor farmer played merry hell. He gave in after being threatened. The 'bloody shovel' sure came in handy!

We just about finished our trenches and were getting settled in, and those not on watch duty were using the house to rest in, when we heard a lot of bangs! We in the house rushed out to see what was happening. What we saw at the second lot of bangs was the start of a creeping barrage, and believe me that is not funny. We watched them as they came nearer and nearer. We got down in our trenches and TREMBLED as we did so.

Well, you may call it luck. I call it providence. When it was all finished we saw that the nearest line of shells stopped just about fifty yards in front of us. Then it began about twenty yards to our left, and carried on for another hundred yards and then stopped altogether. I know we are all human, but how can you relate another's feelings under circumstances such as that? I know how I felt. You shake and pray. Not aloud, but you pray that you don't get hit. Well we didn't.

When it finished it was about eleven o'clock. We were not on duty and so we went back into the house. Imagine our surprise when we got in the house. We saw two smartly dressed women sitting there, so composed! I don't know whether you know the smell of fried liver and fat, but the house reeked of it. Obviously while the shelling had been going on they had fried the liver and fat for us. Now I have never been a lover of liver and fat, but I can say without shame that I have never enjoyed liver and fat again in my life as I did that morning on the outskirts of Dunkirk. And I know I never will.

The battalion was reassembled and marched down to the beach forty-eight hours later. I have never seen anything like it. Men in ranks of columns of three every-where. We did the same. After some time came the cry 'every man for himself'. What do you do? Everyone broke up.

There were men going everywhere. Coley and I started up the beach. I said to Coley I was going to look for a vehicle that would run. Coley said, 'You do that, I'm going to have a lie down.' So I said, 'Here, you have your bloody shovel back.'

I wandered off and never found anything. Then came the Stukas with their bombs and machine guns and wing-wailers. Unfortunately no RAF! All hell and no salvation. This passed and I then went to find Coley. I found him after about half an hour after searching. He was sitting upright in a small trench. I got in beside him and said to him, 'You were glad you'd got that bloody shovel.' Coley didn't answer. I went to shove him and as

I touched him he fell at one side. He was dead. No marks or bullet holes and no blood. But he was dead. Panic. What do you do in this carnage? Dead and injured lying around. I spotted an officer with RAMC chevrons, and went to tell him and told him my mate was dead with no marks. His reply? 'It happens soldier.' He came and had a look at him and said, 'I'll take his dog-tags. You bury him if you wish.'

I buried him on the beach with only a 'bloody shovel' with a tin hat on top. What a tragedy. Poor Coley had only been married for six months. What a terrible shock. Not twenty-one years old, but dead. Where is the justice. So this is war – we must be mad, British and German alike, but I had more to come. I wandered on and around the beach, how long I know not. Eventually I found some of my platoon and asked if I might join them. They didn't mind. They were not going anywhere, and neither was anyone else unless they found a vehicle or a boat!

We wandered around for some time, about thirteen of us, which is about half a platoon, plus a lieutenant and sergeant. If we found a vehicle we were going to head west from Dunkirk and hope for the best. Eureka. We found a Bren carrier. We got aboard, then someone spotted a sailing boat or barge a fair way out to sea, so instead of setting off west we decided to try to reach it in the carrier! It just goes to show how panic or joy spoils your reasoning. We drove straight into the sea!

Yes, you will say, so-and-so idiots, didn't you know that the motor will drown when you get so far out? But we didn't think about that. We did get a long way before the motor drowned, and there we were then, stranded. The others started jumping off, but not yours truly. Why? Because I'm only five feet four inches high, and the water came over the shoulders of the others! There I sat on top of the carrier, alone. What was I to do. I couldn't even swim! I slid gently down the side of the carrier, then hung on with my head above the water.

Then I took a deep breath and let go of the carrier and went like hell with head under water for the beach. My chest gave me hell, but I kept going. Don't ask me how, I just kept going. I don't know, except possibly the answer was self preservation! Suddenly my head came out above water. Then I remember I stopped and saw the rest of the lads waving. How long it took me to join the others I don't know, nor did I care. I had survived a watery grave. We sat down there on the sand for a time, how long I don't know and I didn't really care just as long as I was alive and well.

Anyhow, we decided to get up to carry on searching and some time later we found a rowing boat in good nick. So we looked for something to serve as oars so we could row out to a boat. But thirteen men could not get in the boat at one time so we sat in the boat for rehearsal and found it would only take five men and two rowers which of course meant six were left behind on the beach. It took a long time to get to the boat with their improvised oars, but they made it there and back.

Just after they had started they decided that they wouldn't be able to do it there and back again, so the only way would be to take the remaining six on the first trip. No one volunteered to drop out so we squeezed in and all went very well until about half way there we began to take in water. I think we behaved quite well! We were ditching the water with tin hats until we came alongside the boat and then panic arrived. Everyone in the rowboat grabbed for the lines hanging over the side, and the row boat capsized taking about four men into the water. Ropes were being thrown out everywhere!

I was lucky. I was aboard. Three of the four men in the water could swim; but one couldn't, and a great effort was made to keep him afloat and to get a rope around him and eventually this they managed to do. He was hauled aboard and then the three swimmers were pulled in afterwards. It was decided we would sail at dusk, and this we did and fourteen hours later we were towed into Ramsgate.

That is what happened to me at Dunkirk. No doubt there are hundreds of stories of valour and self-sacrifice which went unsung and honoured at Dunkirk. I am seventy-one years old now but I still think there are a lot of men of all the services who went unrewarded for their efforts.

Clifford Homan, Rushden, Northamptonshire

Strange as it may seem, a number of writers about Dunkirk stories appear to be able to remember the dates of their experience, but in my case the only date I remember was my twenty-first birthday on 27 May which was spent in a barn a short distance from the blazing town of Estaires. I was sheltering from torrential rain and enjoying a meal of Maconochie stew, which was to be our last meal of any description until arriving back in England. But the main story which I wish to relate is the subsequent events after my 'birthday party' and a lack of information which our infantry unit in the West Yorkshire Regiment enjoyed.

At the end of the day, that is 27 May, we were advised we would be going to a rest camp, and we were marched through the night and the following morning to what we were told was Hill No. 60 of the 1914–18 war. That day was spent snoozing and sheltering from the rain in the woods, again moving out as darkness fell. Anyway, as we progressed we realised we were returning to the UK. Amidst the confusion of abandoned vehicles, flooded fields and disappearing officers, we made our way to the coast. Another night was spent a short distance outside

Dunkirk, this time in a bed in an empty house. Finally arriving in a square in Dunkirk our small group, by this time reduced to about ten, were advised by our commanding officer to wait while he went to arrange transport home.

We never saw him again, but learned that he had arrived back home four or five days before us! We waited patiently in the square which fortunately had air-raid shelters, because shells started falling in the area so we dived off into those shelters.

A soldier jumping into the shelter struck the butt of his rifle on the ground firing a bullet which hit one of our party (Cyril Rigby), taking off his knee cap.

We bandaged him as best we could, got him to an unmanned first aid station then luckily found an American nurse doing her rounds. She re-dressed the wound and went on her way so the next thing was to find someway of getting poor Cyril back to a ship! Two hours later a passing ambulance convoy picked him up and we went to the quayside with him to be confronted by row upon row of ambulances! After handing our comrade over we were told to make our way to the beach. 'Chuck' Skillbeck

and myself were so ignorant of the situation that when we saw a group of soldiers marching along a jetty we remarked 'Let's hurry, that could be our regiment'.

We made our way around the blazing oil installations to the beach to then be met by thousands of soldiers queuing on the sands. During the three nights and two days on the beach I came across an abandoned RASC stores vehicle and having a battledress blouse and shirt with two bullet holes, received whilst in action on the Le Bassée canal region and feeling in a really grubby state I changed clothes from top to toe!

Now having lost all sense of day or date, we moved up to the mole in batches of fifty and eventually boarded the Royal Naval ship which I think was HMS *Exeter*, disembarking at Folkestone. At the railway station we were directed to either of two trains. I chose the one which went to Blandford, Dorset and the other, I learned later, went to Manchester which was my home town!

On our journey, wherever the train pulled up at stations we were overwhelmed by the local ladies with tea, sandwiches and buns, also blank telegram forms to advise our relatives of our safe return. To these ladies the Dunkirk veterans must forever be grateful.

Our injured comrade Cyril Rigby never returned to his home in Knaresbrough. Regretfully, I was never able to find out what happened to him.

Finally, as far as I could check I eventually received all

my twenty-first birthday presents and cards and, indeed, even a birthday cake baked by a friend's mother. Regretfully it was beyond the eating stage!

Ernest Jones, Bolton, Lancashire

Author's note: the 1940 photograph is marked from a bullet passing through Mr Jones's wallet!

On 30 September 1939, I got married on a special licence at Bridport and the following day we went to Southampton and my regiment sailed for France. Later we relieved a French division on the Maginot Line and that division, I learned later, got back to England. When Field Marshal Rommel invaded France, we retreated back to the Somme where we had put up our last gun barrage. In the meantime, I now understand, that our troops were being evacuated back from Dunkirk, where I believe about three hundred thousand men escaped but about thirty thousand men were captured.

Our guns were situated on the edge of a wood, mostly sheltered by trees. We were firing over the crest of a hill as the Jerrys were on the other side, about six miles away. They also had to elevate their guns to clear the hill between us which made their shells go over our heads. Early one morning before it got light we had orders to move out. Within ten minutes the Jerry bombers struck and blew our gun position out of the ground.

Two of my brothers were also involved at Dunkirk. My oldest brother was in the Royal Navy and he was presented with the DSM by the Queen Mother after the evacuation. My younger brother was also in the BEF, with the Royal Tank regiment and he managed to get home from Dunkirk. Unfortunately I didn't!

I was taken prisoner of war and everything of value was taken from us. We were forced-marched through France, Belgium and Holland and when we got to Germany we were put in cattle trucks till we got to Poland. Everybody by then was covered with lice and had dysentery. Later we transported to Marienburg labour camp. While we were on the march from France, we received one drink a day and one piece of bread. I am sure it was eating dandelion leaves that kept me going!

Towards the end of the war the Russians were pushing the Germans back on the Eastern Front and I was working on a farm near Danzig at the time. We had to march back in the snow through Poland until we got to Germany and we finished up in Lübeck. Soon afterwards we were liberated by the Yanks. During the five years I spent as a prisoner of war many of my friends died, some were shot and some committed suicide.

At one time I was in the sick bay with chronic sciatica caused by unloading sugarbeet. Each railway wagon held twenty tons of sugarbeet and we started work at 6am and didn't finish until the wagon was empty. It took the biggest part of the day to empty it. In doing that unloading I must have pulled a nerve in my spine which affected my sciatic nerve and I was in terrible pain before I was allowed to be transferred to the sick bay. In the bed next to me was a chap with his leg off. One day he received a letter from home stating his wife had run off with a Yank, and soon afterwards he committed suicide.

That was my Dunkirk! Five years as a prisoner of war. I believe that all the prisoners of war captured never received compensation for all their pain and suffering that they went through. I got to the point where I used to envy the criminals that were serving time in Dartmoor. At least they got three meals a day, a bed to lie on and a wireless in their cell, and were allowed to go to church on Sunday. When I was demobbed in 1945 and came back to civvy street I just felt like a fish out of water.

Richard Legg, Bath, Avon

I got called up in 1939, did my training at Dover Barracks and had my twenty-first birthday there. When we went to France I was posted to Roubaix where I was a batman and driver. I was in the 30th Field Regiment of

Royal Artillery, 4th British Division. The regiment was first sent to Belgium, but later on we knew something was wrong because there was so much activity going on suddenly. The officer I was batman to came in late one evening and said, 'Martin, get all your gear packed up. Be ready to leave at short notice.' I asked if anything was wrong and he said, 'I'm afraid so.' We were going to try to get back to England.

When we did set off the drive was frightening, wondering what would happen. My thoughts all the time were of my family at home. At daylight it was a question of all lorries heading one way, about three abreast for Dunkirk. I remember dive-bombers coming over and all the traffic stopped and we went into ditches, buildings, in fact anywhere to get away. Myself and another soldier went into a house, and there were two women there and we put them under the table and got under the table with them and down came the ceiling and the walls were shattered but the table saved us and the women.

We had to get into the lorries quick, so that we wouldn't hold anyone up, and so we didn't wait about. At that time, because of that, we lost our interpreter but we found him later, walking, as the traffic was so slow.

Twenty-five miles from Dunkirk we had to drive our lorries into a field and park them radiator-to-tailboard. Officers were telling troops to take anything they wanted from the stored lorries, but only what they could carry

in their small pack. Everything else was to be left behind. I can remember that we took a load of Mars bars to keep us going! Now we started the walk towards Dunkirk. There were now nothing but troops, and as we looked back later we could see the sky bright. All the trucks had been set alight so that the enemy couldn't use them.

We saw two motorbikes in a gateway and I said, 'Let's see if they will go.' Yes they did, so we did a shuttle service to the footbridge over the canal near Dunkirk. After that we had to walk to Dunkirk on the sand dunes and beach. The German planes came over and all we had was .303 rifles, one anti-tank gun which was fired from the top of a car that was left there. Then we were on the beach, with troops everywhere and men walking into the sea. Some were drowned because they couldn't swim and they died as they tried to get out to the boats. In some areas panic began to set in. One order we had was to throw away our rifles as we didn't want them on the boat. The next thing is we had an order that no one would be allowed on the boat unless they had a rifle. Panic again to get one!

It got worse so in the finish they had rows of troops set

apart from the sea to the sand dunes with rifles loaded and orders were given that if anyone tried to pass those points 'just shoot them'. It worked OK! In the finish, regiments had serial numbers and when yours was called out you made for the jetty for loading on to the boats.

I remember my officer ordered me to swim out and get a small rowing boat. He reckoned that he had a compass and that we would be able to get home all right! For the first time in my life I refused and said no, the only way to get home was to stay with the regiment. Of course he could have shot me I suppose, disobeying an order, but I think he was in more panic then me! I won't mention his name. He'll remember if he's still alive. He got transferred, back in England, to another regiment.

I well remember how the German dive-bombers came over to bomb the ships. It seemed if they sank the ships then they would get the troops.

One night I dug a hole in the sand and got in it and went to sleep. I was in a panic when I woke up. My regiment had been called and were on the jetty.

Imagine troops the full length of the jetty width with German fighters firing shells which made holes so that we had to get round somehow or jump over. The moving was so slow. Sit down. Then up. Move a few yards. I was lucky. I came over on the destroyer HMS *Wolsey*. They brought up buckets of water and dry bread to start with and then tea and soup and, eventually, a stew.

The ack-ack gunner was good. He brought down one plane that tried to dive-bomb us. Then we landed at home. It was a lovely sight, land with trains waiting and cigarettes etc. Our regiment was sent to Tidworth to start, and then to Yeovilton, where all the people treated us so well.

When I arrived home on leave to a little village called Semer [in Suffolk], where my dad was the village black-smith, all the village turned out including the vicar and his wife. I was presented with a leather wallet with £25 inside. Later I had a plaque given to me. I remember my dad putting his arms round me and saying, 'My goodness son, you've certainly been through something.' I said, 'I don't know, what about all your men in the First World War in those trenches.'

After the regiment was regrouped we were stationed near Newbury, where I met a wonderful Berkshire girl who has now been my wife for the last forty-eight years and we have three wonderful sons.

Ken Martin, Hungerford, Berkshire

In 1940 I was nineteen and working as an executive Officer in the Post Office's London Telephone Service, at Waterloo Bridge House, which stands at the south end of Waterloo Bridge. This incident happened during the early days of the evacuation – probably about 27 or 28 May. It

was a brilliant summer day – the
weather was good all that week.
I came out about twelve noon to
go for an early lunch. We had,
of course, been told on the radio
that evacuation from Dunkirk
had started but up to then had
seen no signs of it.

I had just started walking
south – towards Waterloo Station. From time to time we
had seen soldiers, sailors and airmen on leave in London,
who were staying at the servicemen's Union Jack Club, in
Waterloo Road, SE1 – a hostel mainly for those on leave.
But this time I saw three young men who were not as
smartly dressed as most men on leave tried to be at that
time. They were in stained and crumbled denim 'fatigues',
two of them had only trousers and singlets and light
khaki shirts open at the neck, and these two were *bare-
foot*. They were moderately sunburnt, and one of them
was casually swinging a *German helmet* (the first I had
ever seen) by its chinstrap.

They were smiling, carefree, looked tired, but relieved
– just glad to be alive. They strolled on towards the
bridge. We had yet to experience the German air intru-
sions near London and the beginning of the Blitz. It was
seeing these young men which for the first time brought
home to me the reality of the war in France.

In the succeeding days we had daily accounts from the papers of the numbers lifted from the beaches, but I cannot recall seeing again any comparable soldiers. I presume that later escapers were taken to regimental and other depots and kitted out properly before going on leave.

This sense of shock would be consistent with them being from the first of those rescued – possibly on 27 May the news that Dunkirk was the evacuation point had not yet broken. It would also be consistent with there not being yet any full-formed and operating organisation which was dealing properly with the needs of the returning men.

Rex Parry, Stafford, Staffordshire

I joined the 15th Field Park Company in France in late 1939, the company being stationed near Lille at a small town called Seclin, and we were billeted in an old factory which made porcelain and ceramics for electrical and telephone overhead wiring. It was a small company of about 150 strong. We sat on the Belgian frontier until 10 May 1940 when we moved into Belgium, near to Waterloo. Within an hour of arriving we were being bombed, but the destruction was mainly in the village, leaving many dead who, I remember, were mostly women.

In the retreat I remember we were sent out in small groups to scuttle canal boats and block the waterways, and deprive the Germans of this method of transport. Our unit was part of the 3rd British Infantry Division under Montgomery, and no one was informed of what was happening, or the German successes. Eventually a few of us were taken into a British Guards division, and we retreated steadily to Dunkirk, stopping some enemy units with our delaying tactics, and over a period of three weeks we arrived at La Panne, tired and weary after continuous shelling and bombing. We had not had our boots and socks off for weeks! We were hungry, tired and totally bewildered.

A senior officer put us on parade on the sands. I think it was at night time, and many artillery shells landed amongst us, and many were wounded, including myself. For three days and nights we lay there wounded, hungry and thirsty. During this time Messerschmitts patrolled the beaches firing at any target, but one day men of the Lincoln Regiment came along and carried the wounded on any kind of stretcher, even doors, anything at all.

We were taken near the jetty at Dunkirk, and slowly into small boats that were rowed out to a destroyer. As we got near one destroyer I remember seeing it bombed, and it was on fire. Some of us finally got on a destroyer, and were taken below deck. The Messerschmitts were still at it, and all the destroyer guns were firing and to us below the noise was like a shipyard with hundreds of blacksmiths and rivets banging away.

As far as I can remember it was 6 June when we arrived at Folkestone where we had food and drink and lots of nice people helping us, and I finally arrived in hospital on a 'Kent and Sussex' bus. Some ambulance!

I was moved to different hospitals and was an in-patient for nearly nine months and then on sick leave, and eventually I rejoined my company.

Funnily enough, I remember the sunny days of wheat and barley growing in the fields of Belgium. But I also remember the constant machine-gunning from the air and being under attack from German mortars and getting exhausted and dirty. And we still had faith and strength to carry on and discipline was good. And the information was NIL. Just do as you are told and carry on.

Raymond Earnshaw, Welwyn Garden City, Hertfordshire

I was called up in September 1939 and went to France at the beginning of 1940. I was a gunner and signaller for the Devon Heavy Regiment, sent to extend the Maginot Line, but I did not expect to get into any action!

My first involvement with Dunkirk was when we had to blow the guns up and then we were told to make our way to Dunkirk. The only signpost we had was the black smoke billowing over Dunkirk. It was a few days to get there. We had to sleep rough on the way. One incident I remember was that I slept with pigs one night and early the next morning the farmer came to feed them. What a din. It's a laugh now, but not then!

Eventually we arrived at the sand dunes to find hundreds more there. We had to line up day in and day out. You would be shot if you rushed the boats. We were often strafed by the German fighters, and as we dived for cover one of my pals got a bullet through the lapel of his coat. You couldn't get much nearer than that. We were in a position where, as I faced the sea, Dunkirk was on my left and I would imagine that we were roughly two miles from Dunkirk itself. As I turned round on the dunes, I was overlooking a school. Some said that it was a school for the blind, but as the shells screamed over from destroyers I saw six little children walking up the steps hand in hand. I often wonder since if that school survived all that shelling.

A large ship was offshore just to my right and six dive-bombers attacked it. Sailors were diving overboard and it was then burning and I can remember a plane doing a victory roll over it. We were glad when it became foggy to give us a rest from the German fighters. It became clear that our time was running out as not only did we have the fighters and the bombers to put up with, but you could hear the rearguard getting nearer and nearer every day as the perimeter that they were holding shrank.

As I waded out to get on to a boat when my turn came, I had to climb a rope ladder. I remember it was a Dutch cargo boat. I had my trouser leg bottoms tied up, and when I went to lift my legs out of the water I couldn't. The water was hanging in my trousers and I couldn't lift my legs. So my mate had to undo the string on my trousers, and let the water out before I could get aboard.

We eventually got away, but we had a bomb drop each side of us whilst we were leaving but we got through all right and landed at Margate. I can remember just being glad to be home.

Stanley C. Dilley, St Albans, Hertfordshire

I volunteered in September 1939 and joined the RASC, going to France in November. As a driver of a troop carrier I had taken the Guards to the front line in Belgium during mid-May. It was from here that I was ordered to make my way to Dunkirk where I was on the beach for three days. Eventually I was taken off by a British destroyer, the HMS *Winchelsea* and brought back to Dover on 30 May.

My orders when the retreat started were to make my way from the Poperinge area to Dunkirk and on the way to destroy my vehicle. It must not fall into enemy hands.

Near the Belgian/French border I came upon a canal and decided to put the engine into gear and let it go into the depths. I had a few extra pieces of clothing so I had to decide quickly what to keep and what to destroy. There was a brand-new pair of army-issue boots. Sensible, I thought, to put them on and sink my old pair. With hindsight that was not very clever! I then had to walk twelve or more miles to Dunkirk and those new boots rubbed my feet raw.

When eventually I was told to embark on the *Winchelsea* it was moored by the bow, stern out, to enable a quick getaway. Quite an awkward moment from jetty to ship via orange box when your feet are killing you!

I was on the beach at Dunkirk for three days, being shelled from land and dive-bombed from the air by the Germans. Our days and nights were spent in holes scooped out in the sand, hoping we would therefore avoid all but a direct hit. Not all survived and a very sad, vivid memory, is passing a pile of bodies with tin hats on chests as I made my way at last to the jetty.

The first night on the beach we were all excited to see lots of green lights at sea and thought it was boats coming to our rescue. Imagine our disappointment at daybreak when the lights proved to be millions of fish giving off fluorescent light.

My worst injury was caused by a very young, nervous Scottish soldier on the ship returning to England. We saw some bombers approaching. Thinking it was the enemy coming to bomb us he grabbed my leg in a vice-like grip, and the resulting bruising lasted for some weeks. Thankfully, though, the planes were British going to bomb the Germans!

At last we reached Dover and then the tea was handed out to us by the WVS. It was the first hot drink for days and it is still the best I have ever tasted!

Peter W. Butcher, Great Doddington, Northamptonshire

I am a Belgian and I was actually there in Dunkirk on the beaches and witnessed it all without realising its importance. My father and mother and brother and me tried to flee to England. After many adventures on our bikes we got caught between a battle after leaving Gravelines and just outside the town. We nearly lost our lives there. There was a canal. We were first in a farm-house looking for shelter as we were shelled from the Germans and then the British army. We were in between!

The refugees still on the roads nearby were all killed, but the shelling got worse and we were so cramped inside we decided to get outside in the grass. I well remember May was a lovely month: it was warm, above me was an elderberry bush in flower, bees were humming, but the battle hotted up so my father decided to make a run for it.

I got up and I realised that I had been lying on a dead soldier's boot. A bullet from somewhere had struck him. It could have been me! I had to ride my bike again and my legs were as lead, I have never experienced anything like it since. Bullets were whistling in front of us. Then we came to a canal and we had to pay a hundred francs to cross it. That was a lot of money. Meanwhile somebody had stolen my mother's luggage from the bike at the farm.

Anyway there we were, in front of us a long beach. Four hours' walk in beach sand pushing a bike (for safety's sake) on a scorching hot day. We left the noise of battle after us and plodded on. Our mouths were sore from thirst and our lips swollen but at long last we came to Dunkirk. We found a little chapel where a priest gave us a drink from a fountain.

Never has the best champagne tasted so good! And there on the beach were all these soldiers lying on the dunes smoking and resting. I could see some little ships but I did not know what it was all about.

I know now! We didn't stay long. We went on our bikes back home and after a few days we reached Antwerp

again and we saw the cathedral and we just wept with joy.

Not so many years ago my brothers took us back to the farmhouse and to the canal and to Dunkirk. But strangely we couldn't find that little chapel. We also spoke to a former mayor of Gravelines and he told us that three thousand people had died that day, both soldiers and civilians. We saw the little bridge which they battled over. We went over the road where the refugees were killed but it was now just a busy road. Then people were hanging in the trees, blown up by the shells.

Yes I had my war! I was twenty years old and my youth was ruined in those war years. But never mind, I have got a lovely daughter and son and my husband, who was in the invasion of Normandy, is still alive aged seventy-eight.

Cecilia McNicholas, Mansfield Woodhouse,
Nottinghamshire

In the spring of 1940 I found myself an NCO nursing orderly in a casualty clearing station at Béthune in Northern France. We were running a tented hospital for the men of the BEF during the 'Phoney War'. Without any previous medical experience, I had had eight months' training and was now in charge of a surgical ward. My orderlies, young ex-coalminers from Birmingham, had had four months' training! But all was well; soon experienced nursing sisters arrived from England to watch over the activities of us amateurs.

But a few weeks later the fighting broke out in earnest. It was considered that the situation would be too dangerous for the women and the sisters were ordered back to England. I am told that some of them actually wept in their anger and frustration when they knew that they would be sent home. But we who were left quickly found ourselves in a situation of complete chaos. Isolated from surrounding units, cut off from our higher command, and without orders, our colonel found himself thrown back upon his own initiative. We had only one course – to make for the one haven which remained open to us – Dunkirk. Arriving there, and having re-made contact with command, we were ordered to set up a hospital for the wounded in Dunkirk.

For this purpose we were given a large château on the outskirts of the city. Already, when we moved in, it was little more than a shell. There were holes in the roof, no glass in the windows, no water in the taps and no power in the electric wires. The city itself seemed like the abode of the damned. The oil tanks had been set alight by bombing and shelling. A cloud of black smoke hung over it, making it almost as dark by day as by night. The underneath of this cloud was reddened by the light of numerous fires, which cast a flickering red glow over everything It was like Judgement Day [had] come.

In the lowest cellar of our mansion we found an ancient iron pump, which when energetically cranked would yield a thin stream of brackish, greenish water, and most of the time this was all we had for our medical and culinary use. The colonel allocated one of the best downstairs rooms for the operating theatre. Since there was no glass in the windows the only way to keep out the dust of the outside world was to close the shutters, mercifully still intact. We drove one of our trucks up to the window, took off one headlamp and brought this into the theatre on the end of a long lead. All the nursing orderlies were fully employed elsewhere, so the driver was detailed to hold the lamp over the surgeon's busy fingers. Alas, he had never seen sights like this; in the middle of the first operation he fainted and the lamp clattered down on to the patient.

I was busy in another part of the building supervising the intake of what seemed like an endless stream of wounded. Never had I seen such a concentration of bruised and broken bodies. Most had been lying in the field for many hours, some for days, without medical attention. Never did I see such obstinate determination to stay cheerful. Never did I hear a word of complaint

or self-pity. I said to myself, 'Whatever happens to me after this, I will never complain about my life again' – a resolution which, alas, I have not kept during these fifty years as well as I ought!

I saw our officers (the doctors) worked up to, and sometimes almost beyond, the point of breakdown. I saw our orderlies trudging in and out, in and out, with the endless train of stretchers, while almost asleep on their feet. Soon every square foot of floor space was taken up by the rows of stretchers. One then had to decide which cases were most fit to be left in the open.

I saw two young nursing orderlies, only lately from the mines. They had armed themselves with the largest syringes they could find and charged them with enough morphia to poison half a regiment. Nothing was under lock and key; we had no locks or keys! They were going up and down the serried ranks of stretchers, giving a jab here and a jab there, wherever they thought they found human suffering coming to the point of culmination. Ought I to have reprimanded them and taken the syringes away? I found that I had not it in my heart to do so. Medical advice and orders were, in the circumstances, far out of reach. Our doctors had been worked to the point of breakdown. Many poor souls were not getting the alleviation which they needed. In circumstances of such stress and suffering the human frame can take far more opiates than in the normal way. I don't think they killed or seriously harmed anyone; and they certainly saved a lot of suffering. Sometimes it is better to look the other way.

I don't know how long this continued; with loss of sleep one loses track of time; a week, ten days maybe. Then one day we were all summoned to the basement of our château. The sergeant major was there, with his tin hat under his arm. He looked grim. He explained that the last hospital ship had left for home. The evacuation was finishing that night. One more ship, with good fortune, was due to leave. Our unit had been promised places on it. But high command had ordained that for every hundred wounded which we would leave behind, ten orderlies and one officer must stay and be taken prisoner with them. Out of a hundred of us, thirty must stay. 'Now look 'ere; I've got a 'undred pieces of screwed up paper in my 'elmet 'ere; thirty of them has got crosses on them; you comes up 'ere, you takes your piece of paper; and if it's got a cross on it, then Gawd 'elp yer – ye're for it!'

Loss of sleep undermines one's powers of judgement. The rumour had spread that the Germans were taking so many prisoners that they were standing them against a wall and shooting them rather than having the burden of feeding them. In our rundown state perhaps we half believed it. It was a tense moment, fumbling in that tin hat for one's piece of paper ... I was lucky.

Hours later we were down on the beach, four long lines of us, two British and two French; even in a time of disaster, one must be fair! There followed six hours of sporadic shellfire. And here an interesting psychological point was to be observed. As one heard the whine of an approaching shell, a babble of apprehensive conversation and comment broke out in the French ranks; the British crouched down and froze into silence. It was marked. We were different. But who were the better? Who can tell?

In the small hours, to our infinite relief, we saw the form of a destroyer slip silently and diffidently into the cluttered harbour, littered with sunken ships. As it came slowly alongside our wharf, we, poor landlubbers that we were, waited for the gangplank to be put out. It became clear that the occupants of this ship wished to be away as soon as might be. We heard a sailor's strangled voice call, 'Come on Tommy, JUMP for it.' Suddenly we realised there was not going to be a gangplank!

As one body the four ranks surged forwards, leapt the gap, and swarmed on board. A few minutes later I found myself in what I supposed was the wardroom, deep in the bowels of the ship, jammed into a solid mass of khakied humanity more tightly than any sardine in a tin. The thought occurred to me that should we be torpedoed or bombed, no single one of us would have a moment's chance of survival. I do not normally suffer from claustrophobia but I had an attack then! I am quite small and by keeping a low profile and squirming and pushing and squeezing, a quarter of an hour later I emerged at the top of the companionway on to the open deck.

I judged that we were headed south-west, parallel with the French coast. When suddenly we turned due west, heading for Dover. The engines revved, the ship sprang into life like a living thing and started to cut through the water at a speed which I found breath-taking. The wind in that night air was distinctly chilly. I joined a group of soldiers who were sheltering in the kindly lee of a gun shield. Soon a burly sailor appeared from the gun turret to explain to us that the decks were cleared for action, that should anything untoward occur, all merry hell would break out round that turret and we would BE IN HIS WAY!

Obediently we left him and went aft to the stern of the ship. But the night air remained cold, very cold. Slowly, one by one, almost insensibly, we found ourselves creeping back into the friendly lee of that gun shield. Soon it was densely populated as before. Our burly friend returned. He was wringing his hands. He seemed distraught. 'Boys, boys, *please!!* I may have to FIRE this bloody thing!' A few minutes later a lone plane flew overhead. Was it a German raider who failed to see the silent form slipping by in the darkness? Or a guardian angel from the RAF sent to protect us on our way? I shall never know.

Hours later, in a semi-comatose condition in the train that was trundling us along the line from Dover to Aldershot, I thought of the high hopes which had held the hearts of the valiant little British Expeditionary Force as it had gone forth only a few months previously to do battle with the dragon. And now we were returning like a pack of beaten dogs, scurrying for home with our tails between our legs ... That is how I felt.

Then I looked out of the window. The trackside houses were decked with flags to welcome us. There was a large notice, 'We are PROUD of you.' Indeed we had come home!

Lawrence Edwards, Strontian, Acharacle

I am a Dunkirk veteran with a medal and certificate but, strangely enough, I have never even seen Dunkirk! I was a member of 3rd Royal Tank Regiment and together with the Rifle Brigade we were put into Calais to hold back the Germans on the roads leading to Calais and Dunkirk and to defend Calais, as Churchill told us, 'to the last man'.

Movement on the roads was nigh impossible. They were choked with people (women and children and French soldiers) attempting to get into what they thought was safety in Calais. What a hope. Every so often the German Stukas would come spraying bullets and small bombs down the road. It was utter chaos and pandemonium each time when the Stukas had come. The sight was terrible. Wounded and dead people and animals, particularly horses, lying everywhere. Having eventually managed about four and a half miles out of Calais my tank broke down and had to be abandoned after being disabled. My crew and I joined up with the refugees until we came to some of our lorries with ammunition and petrol for the tanks. The lorries had found it impossible to go forward and had to pull back into Calais with the throng.

In the meantime Calais and the citadel were taking a lot of bombing and artillery fire and flames were everywhere. It was the 'flames of colour'. A book by the late Airey Neave described it accurately. Things were very bad at the docks. We were ordered to dump everything we could in the docks, lorries, guns, even broken-down tanks. The spoils of war were everywhere. People were fighting to be allowed on transport ships taking off all surplus service personnel but it was not possible to take any. For a while it began to look as though I, with some others who had been out to do a job outside the docks, were going to be left but fortunately another small boat made the attempt and took us off along with some French troops.

Sixty of us out of a force of five thousand were all that were taken off. Some of our tanks did go some distance outside Calais and drew some of the German armour from Dunkirk and the Rifle Brigade continued to defend Calais and the citadel until the bitter end, even though both were blazing infernos.

Some historians think that Calais and its defence did a lot to distract the Germans from Dunkirk. Others that it was troops sacrificed for nothing. I don't know. I lived to fight on the rest of the war but, on reflection, it seemed we achieved very little.

Fred Kite, MM and two Bars, Stoke-on-Trent,
Staffordshire

I was serving with the East Surrey Regiment at Dunkirk and we were situated in and around a brickyard at Furnes [Veurne] in Belgium, as part of the last organised defences of the evacuation of Dunkirk. The evacuation had been going on for over a week, and for five days of this we had held our present position.

Most of us were young, all of us were tired, weary, and I am sure somewhat bewildered. We had been without food for days, and we had little knowledge of what the true situation was. Our company strength had been 128 men but that number had changed dramatically during the previous two or three weeks, as each action had taken its toll of our officers and men. My platoon commander, Bob Emett, had been the first of our officers to die. He had been shot, along with his batman, in our first action. Mr Montague, another of our platoon commanders, had died a week later when we were ambushed while on patrol. He had escaped the first concentrated burst of close-range fire, which had cut down several of our number, but was hit by a burst of machine-gun fire as he lay within a few feet of me. He was giving instructions as to how to try to extricate ourselves from the situation when he was killed.

We had been in our present position for five days and it was now 1 June. Most of our problems here had been from shelling and mortar fire, interspersed with machine-gun fire from several hundred yards away. Fortunately it was not too accurate but the 80mm mortars had our range spot on, and never left us alone for very long.

Yesterday had seen us under attack from German infantry. They must have come up during the previous hours of darkness because we didn't see them coming until, following a short burst of shelling, they launched an attack on our left flank, from the cover of stacks of bricks in the area. It was at first thought that the casualties were much higher than they later proved to be, as several men we thought had died had, in fact, been taken prisoner. Many were wounded during the action.

It was this action which lost us our last platoon commander, though not as a casualty. He, along with two NCOs, could not be accounted for after the action and they subsequently faced charges some months later in England. After the attack the remainder of the platoon were withdrawn and used to strengthen two other platoons which were themselves under strength.

There were examples of courage and unselfishness during the action. One instance, of a corporal who picked up a stick grenade and threw it back at the Germans, but was shot and wounded and subsequently taken prisoner. Another of a soldier who had tried to help his mate who had been wounded, only to be taken prisoner along with his friend, who was a lad from Sunderland who had married a girl from Lyme Regis, where he had been stationed before sailing for France.

Earlier, in the morning our company commander, Major Nash, made his rounds and gave us the sad news that one of our local territorials, Private Sales from Chertsey, had just been killed by a sniper. He took two other men and myself to a brick shed which had three small holes in its wall. He placed one of us at each hole, told us roughly where the sniper was thought to be and told us to try and find him. After a very short time Private Jackie Buck, at the centre hole, said he had seen the sniper and tried to indicate his position to Private Green and myself, but without success.

Foolishly we both moved to either side of Jackie and were all looking out of the same hole with our heads together. Suddenly the sniper fired, and the bullet hit the brick on the inside of the hole immediately in front of my face and ricocheted on to Jackie's chin and down into his chest. Bill Green ran for a stretcher and was soon back with a first aid man and our company commander, but nothing could be done. Our mate Jackie was already dead. It was obvious that the shot had been fired from a high position and slightly to our left and Major Nash said that the sniper must be either on top of one of the stacks of bricks or in the nearby buildings. So he decided to send me out to try to outflank him.

My orders were to make my way out on the left flank, and then work my way forward using whatever cover I could find, and take up a position in one of the three cottages that were about two hundred yards in front of our position. The idea being that the sniper would not expect us to have anyone behind him, and would be more likely to show himself and give me a chance to get a clear shot from close range. I was also ordered to keep a close watch on our own open left flank, and report back if I saw any signs of an attack from that side. Otherwise I was ordered to stay out until I was relieved. I must admit that I was more than a bit scared out there by myself, and the hours seemed endless although things were very quiet and only a few shells landed anywhere near and not close enough to put me in any danger. A few tiles fell from the roof, but I never saw any signs of the sniper. I think he must have moved out before I took up my position.

After several hours I began to see quite a bit of movement on my right front. It was a hundred yards or more away, so I wasn't too worried. I knew they would also be seen from our company lines, though our troops could not engage them as we had no high explosives for our mortars, and the only artillery had spiked their guns and had left for Dunkirk three days ago. At about this time I decided that I had better take a look out on the left flank. There was a road on the left side of the cottages, and on the far side a strip of woodland about fifty yards wide, beyond which lay open country.

I dashed across the road and made my way carefully through the trees to the far side but there were no signs of activity, so I returned to the cottages where I again took up my position of observation through the holes in the roof. I immediately saw three German soldiers less than fifty yards away. It was almost certain that they must have passed by the side of my cottage during the few minutes I had been away. It was a long time ago but nevertheless I remember well how I wished that I had my Bren gun, which was my usual weapon, and not the Lee-Enfield rifle that I was holding. It was difficult to line up my sights because of the roof timbers. It cost a few more precious seconds, and I intended to take the man furthest away and hope to get a second shot at one of the others. But before I could fire he began to move to the right, making a moving target rather than a more or less stationary one. Whilst he was moving away from me I dropped my sights to the second man and squeezed the trigger. I didn't get a second shot. The two remaining men had taken cover and my immediate concern was that they would work their way back to me but they probably didn't know where the shot had come from as I saw no further signs of them.

It was now getting on towards evening and I was more than a little worried about my situation and kept thinking about making my way back to our lines. It was very quiet at the time and then suddenly I heard the familiar 'plop' of German mortars. Then the bombs came in.

I often wondered afterwards if the two men who had been on reconnaissance patrol, on whom I had fired at earlier in the day, had anything to do with it but at the time I just cowered under a table and shook with fright as the roof fell all around me. How many rounds were fired I can't even guess. It seemed a lot at the time but I don't suppose it lasted for more than a few minutes. Not long afterwards I heard movement nearby and suddenly I heard my name called from below.

It was Private Bill Green who had come to get me out. I was down to him in seconds and never more pleased to see anyone in my life! He told me that twice during that afternoon a Corporal Crowter had been sent to find me but each time he had returned and said that he couldn't get through because of heavy machine-gun fire. Bill had come out off his own bat because the company were pulling out. No one had sent him. No one had ordered him to. He had taken a great risk to save me being left behind. God knows what would have happened to me if he had not come. Maybe I would have been taken prisoner, but maybe my two fleeting acquaintances of the afternoon may have had other ideas! Bill told me that we would have to be careful on the way back because things were a bit dodgy in places, to say the least. After about a hundred yards we were faced with an open space about thirty yards wide, with no cover of any kind. Bill told me that there was at least one machine gun, and possibly two, covering the area and the only way was to run for it.

We were able to get a flying start into the clear area by going back ten or fifteen yards and then going like bats out of hell, and we were a good halfway over before the Germans opened fire. It was unbelievable. The ground around us became alive like the surface of a pond in a heavy storm of rain but our talisman was working overtime, and in the face of all the odds we got safely across.

The company were already on the move, and as we tacked on the back, one of the lads stuck a half-eaten tin of cold stew in my hand. It was the first food I had had for more than two days. So on into the evening dusk we marched, sometimes on roads, sometimes on grass, and I remember little about it, apart from once being stopped and warned to be absolutely quiet.

I understand that at one point we actually passed through German lines. The credit for this must be given to our battalion commander, Colonel 'Nipper' Armstrong. He was a fine officer and awarded the Distinguished Service Order.

It had been daylight for quite some time when we reached the coast somewhere south of La Panne, towards which we made our way over the sand. The sight was devastating. There was equipment everywhere, including arms and ammunition, just dropped by those who had passed that way before us. I still feel pride when I remember that every man in my battalion still had his equipment and carried his weapons and we were not the first or second or third to pass that way. We were the last!

We eventually arrived at a place where there was a large building right on the beach and my company was sent into the building to rest, out of sight of enemy aircraft. Almost as soon as I sat on the floor one of our NCOs, Corporal 'Dixie' Dean, came up to me and asked if I had any shaving kit. I told him that mine had gone

up on one of our trucks days ago, probably along with his! But I suggested that we go out on the beach and look amongst the many packs that littered the area.

I remember how long it took us to find a razor each. Every pack seemed to contain Odol toothpaste and Palmolive shaving cream, but no razors! Unfortunately when we set out we walked back along the beach the way we had come and when we got back to the building it was empty. Our company had gone. There was no sign of them, even along the beach. Dixie and I set out towards Dunkirk and after a while we passed near some houses. He suggested that we look for a couple of bikes! As luck would have it we soon had a bike each, and I was in favour of riding along the road but Dixie wouldn't have it.

'We will be safer on the beach,' he said.

So we wheeled the bikes down to the water's edge, where the sand was firm and began to ride. It wasn't a pleasant ride. There were bodies everywhere, many covered in thick oil from the ships that had been sunk. But there was nothing we could do for them. There were a great many dead, but no wounded had been left behind. Thank God, as there would have been nothing we could do for them either. Very soon we were forced up on to the soft sand and could no longer ride the bikes, so we dumped them and continued to walk until I felt just about shattered and said so to Dixie. 'What about going off the beach and walking on the roads. It would be much easier,' I said. But he didn't want to know. He said that if we took the roads we would either 'buy it' or 'go in the bag'.

So we split up and I went off on my own. Some hours later I was still walking, taking the odd rest now and then, but I saw no enemy troops and was never fired upon, although the road had long since left the coast. The only people I saw were a small group of sappers and I marched with them for a short distance until the officer in charge told me that they had a job to do and my best bet would be to make for the coast and keep on it until I got to Dunkirk.

So I set off on my own again and after a while I made the beaches at La Panne. Things were very different here. There were hundreds of soldiers, many up to their chests in the sea, waiting for small boats to pick them up and take them to ships out in the deeper water. I made my way to join them, but on reaching the water's edge and seeing the length of the queue I decided to turn it in and went back to the dunes to rest.

I can never understand why, but as I sat there I turned to look at the sky and as I looked I counted thirteen enemy fighter planes gliding out of the clouds with what appeared to be their engines cut. It was terrible to see because, as I remember it, their engines suddenly roared into life and the machine guns opened up, pouring their fiery tracers into our men who were packed tight like at a football match. God knows how many were slaughtered. And so I again set out along the beach towards where a pier of sorts had been made by lorries which had no doubt been run out on to the sand at low tide and there on the beach I saw my commanding officer. I was back with my battalion!

Shortly after rejoining my unit we were strafed by two German fighter planes, but amazingly we suffered no casualties. On their second run they passed a little upland of us so we did not come under their fire, but everyone in our battalion still carried his arms and we poured lead at them as fast as we could reload our weapons. I don't suppose the planes were in much danger from us, but it was an act of defiance just the same, and probably made us feel a lot better and not quite so helpless. Somewhere between La Panne and Dunkirk we left the beaches and I can well remember the scenes of devastation as we made our way through the streets to the dock area.

Not a building was undamaged and several times we had to climb over heaps of rubble or skirt round bomb craters which hampered our progress, and as daylight began to fade we arrived at the embarkation area and took our places in the queue leading to the mole from where we hoped to be taken off. I don't know how long we had been there when the shells began to fall on us. I certainly can't remember them coming in. Maybe I had gone to sleep on my feet for a few moments, something not impossible when one hasn't slept for more than an odd hour or two for days and days on end, or maybe they were using high-angle howitzers, which would account for the absence of sound until the shells were almost on you. Some of the shells were very close and those of us involved had to take cover for a while. When we rejoined the queue I had become separated from my company again!

After the queue had moved a couple of times I found myself near a little hut near the beginning of the mole. There was a naval officer inside and he informed us that the evacuation would end at three o'clock in the morning, at which time the last of the destroyers would leave. I remember sitting down at the side of the hut and though there was little talking I could hear that there were French troops lining up with the British waiting their turn to be taken off.

That was my last recollection of that night because I suddenly woke up with warm sun on my face and realised that the evacuation was over and that I had been left behind. There was no one left at all. Not one single person. Just the dead, many of them covered with greatcoats.

First I moved away from the pier but I didn't go far. One of the first things I did was to change my rifle for a Bren gun which I found, complete with a full magazine, though what I proposed to do with it all on my own I will never quite know! I suppose it just seemed the right thing to do at the time. There was still no sign of another living soul, so I turned back to the mole and walked right out to the end and sat for a while until I realised that I just had to get a drink from somewhere.

So I went back off the mole and into the town, and wandered about for a little while and then caught sight of a soldier and, although he was not wearing either a hat or a tunic, I was sure that he was French. I watched him go into a house and I went up and knocked at the door. It was opened by the same man. I saw that the room was full of French soldiers. They just stared at me without any kind of greeting whatsoever. I asked for water and the soldier who had come to the door gave me some raw red wine from a mess tin. I thanked him and walked away, leaving him and his friends to continue their wait to be taken prisoner by the Germans.

Back at the beach I began to search for food but without any luck so I again walked right out to the end of the mole and laid down on the floor. It was late in the afternoon when I observed movement but it was much too far away to make out any details. But there was no doubt about it there was someone there, so I just watched and waited and after what seemed like ages I could see a small group of people coming towards me. Many times during the ensuing years I have wondered what I would have done had they been German troops. Would I have opened up on them with my Bren gun? Or would I have thrown it in the sea and surrendered? Even today I honestly don't know. I know what I would do now, but then I am not the same person I was fifty years ago!

But as the people got closer I realised that they were British. There were six or seven officers, some of whom were wearing service dress with the red tabs and hatband of staff officers. One was a lieutenant in the East Yorkshire Regiment and, strange as it may seem, I had met him before in a factory where we had been billeted in Roubaix in northern France. The only other rank was a sapper who had just met the officers, and he turned out to be one of the group I had met on my lonely march to Dunkirk. The senior officer, I think, was a brigadier, though I am not certain at this late stage fifty years later. He gave orders to look for a boat in which to get away but the order only seemed to apply to the sapper and myself as no one else made any move!

We eventually found a small motor launch bobbing about a hundred yards or so from the shore and, mostly through the efforts of the sapper, we got it to the mole and made fast to one of the ladders, up which we climbed. We reported back to the senior officer who said at first that we would not all be able to go and because of my Bren gun I seemed to be the only one sure of a place in the boat! But in the end we all got in, only to find that the engine wouldn't start! I think the decision to drift out and rig a sail was made in the hope that we would be seen and picked up, so we worked the boat along the mole towards the sea.

I don't know how long we had been messing about on the boat when someone called out that a ship was coming. It must have been cut off from our line of sight by one of the breakwaters, because in no time at all it was alongside and we climbed aboard as quickly as we could. I was the last to leave the motor launch and climbed the ladder to board the ship. Suddenly I noticed the brigadier's leather cane lying on the floor of the launch so I went back and picked it up. I never saw the officers again or the sapper. I don't know where they were taken when they got on board but I was taken to a little mess deck, no doubt where the crew got their meals. I was given a lump of bread and a piece of meatloaf. I was also given some tea in the tin that the meatloaf had come out of! It was swimming in grease and made me feel sick as a pig. I still have the officer's leather cane somewhere in my loft. There were no other troops on the small ship and although it steamed for several miles along the coast before turning for England we didn't pick anyone else up.

I was later put off the ship at Dover where they put me on a train to Bovington Camp and where I rejoined my regiment a few days later. I never gave it any thought at the time, or until years later, but I wonder could it be that I was the last man to leave Dunkirk?

Ron Davison, New Haw, Weybridge, Surrey

One of my earliest memories is of the evacuation of Dunkirk. I was a member of the ambulance team run by the WVS in Cannock, and one afternoon at about four o'clock we were told to report at Lichfield to take wounded from Dunkirk to Burntwood which had been turned into a military hospital. We arrived at Lichfield with about six or seven ambulances only to be told that the train would arrive at Trent Valley much later than expected. However, we decided not to return to Cannock and so we went on to Trent Valley and lined up at the station, ours being the first ambulance.

It was some hours later, after the sirens had gone and all the lights had been put out, that the train slowly

Mrs Lane, centre in white blouse

pulled in. It was a wonderful sight coming in so slowly, with the white-topped carriages showing their red crosses, even in the dark. Soon we were called forward and our ambulance loaded with one officer on the bottom bunk and two other men on the top bunk.

I always remember that we lost our way to the military hospital, and on the way the two boys at the top bunk talked away and I remember one of them saying that the officer on the bottom bunk looked or sounded sorry for himself and so we stopped the vehicle and I flashed my torch on to him to have a look at him. Of course he was dead. I asked the remaining two if their parents knew that they were safe and took their phone numbers to let them know as soon as I could. We eventually delivered them safely to Burntwood where we discovered as they got out of the ambulance that they were still covered only in blankets and their wounds were becoming gangrenous.

After that we went back to Trent Valley and collected two more loads of men, one of whom on the journey died in my arms. It was four o'clock in the morning before we were told to go home. In Cannock Square there are two telephone boxes and so we decided to ring up the parents of those whose phone numbers we had and taking half of the numbers each (there were two drivers to each ambulance) we made the calls. My first call was to a London hotel. The night porter, when asked for a Mr Benn said, did I want Mr Wedgwood Benn. I said I didn't know but I wanted to tell him about his son Anthony. I have never discovered whether it was the present Anthony Wedgwood Benn, but then I have never tried to find out!

Dora Lane, Rugeley, Staffordshire

At the time of Dunkirk I was a nurse at the emergency military hospital near Lichfield. We had five hundred members of the forces, mostly soldiers, injured and shell-shocked, arriving by convoy and arriving throughout the night.

I remember that twelve of those soldiers were put to bed in a ward upstairs as they could help themselves a little and

then the rest of the night was spent settling in all the others.

Next morning I went back upstairs to the twelve to prepare them for the doctor's visit and, lo and behold, every bed was empty.

I searched high and low as they were only clad in pyjamas and eventually I came across them, still all in their pyjamas, returning from the village.

The village was three miles away but they were carrying a gramophone with a big horn and loaded with records that one of the villagers had given to them.

They all looked so funny that I had to laugh. We must have looked a real odd sight wending our way back to the hospital.

Later, I married one of those soldiers and we had forty very happy years together, with four children, two boys and two girls. Sad to say he died just before celebrating our ruby wedding.

Bearing in mind that I was working at a military hospital and that my husband was a wounded soldier, you can imagine the delight he took in telling everyone, 'The first time I met my wife, she took my trousers off!'

Joyce Etherington, Colne, Lancashire

During the first months of the 'Phoney War' my Field Park Company of the Royal Engineers was employed on supplying the 'furniture' for the defences on the boundary of France and Belgium. Our area was the Lille–Roubaix sector. There the company supplied hundreds of wooden duckboards, A-frames etc, which made up the firing areas for the infantry, incorporated with underground HQs, as per World War One. The 'new' thing was the tank traps, huge sloping areas dug out and then a vertical wall that the enemy tank would not climb over. After this had been completed it was normal 'works' until we received orders to pack up and the company was fully mobile, 'ready to move'.

Our objective was Belgium and we moved as part of the 3rd Division under a Lieutenant General Montgomery. We crossed the border and made our way to the outskirts of Louvain. At this time I was the bridging section sergeant and we carried the folding boat equipment which could make a bridge of nine tons across water, also a complete small girder bridge for small gaps, again nine tons.

After a brief period, a few days, I was told to have my section and its vehicles ready to move in twenty-four hours. Having just crossed the border we all wondered why we were headed back in that direction. Being a very small 'cog' in the wheel of war we did as we were told and finally, two days later, we halted in the area north of Lille, about ten miles from where we started. I took quite a while to find out that the 3rd Division had moved to the east flank of the BEF and was covering the area the Belgian army had been occupying.

Then further orders moved us in the opposite direction of the fighting area and finally, after using some of the bridging equipment – putting them at selected sites as per map references – I was told to carry enough explosives to blow them up if ordered. Otherwise, the explosives would be left at the site so other sappers could blow them up later on. This was very confusing as there were all sorts of rumours about enemy agents, parachutists etc etc. What was happening? Finally I was told that the company was going to return to the UK. 'How?' I asked. 'More details later'. So by the time we reached the town of Poperinge I had used up the bridging equipment and just had the vehicles and men.

However, things changed dramatically at a town called Furnes where I detailed men for various sapper's jobs, mainly with explosives, and with the remainder headed for the coast. I found that overnight I was 'in charge' of the remaining men; all officers – the company sergeant major and the quartermaster – had literally 'vanished'!

So with the remaining men and vehicles I took a road towards the coast, and here we met with the unfortunate refugees, on foot, by car, horse, bicycle – anything with wheels – and so we crawled along at about five miles per hour. I decided to turn off this road at the first available turning but before we could do so the German air force took us by surprise and machine-gunned the road. Everyone took to the ditches and we were very lucky as the bullets and cannon shells hit the centre of the road and *outside* the ditches; the casualties were the vehicles but luckily I was able to load the men and equipment into two 'runners'.

So we did finally find a road to the right and off we went. The question was, where to? Luckily we met an NCO motorcyclist and he said, 'Head towards the black smoke – they are waiting along the beach to take you aboard ships to England.' The road towards the smoke led us to the Military Police barrier where the instructions were to smash up the vehicles, engines etc and then go onto the beach at La Panne and join the queue for embarkation on the ships. Having smashed up the two vehicles we made our way to the beach and there we saw hundreds of men on the beach and in the sea, standing up in the water. Everyone seemed to say, 'We are NOT going to stand in the sea and wait,' so we made our way along the beach and scooped out the sand and slept. We were awakened by shouting and found that once again the German air force were having a go at the unprotected troops. This time they used the Stukas as well. Luckily the bombs and bullets missed our little party and we dug a little deeper in the sand.

As there were no cafes or restaurants available we had to go thirsty and hungry. Still, we were alive and decided to make ourselves as comfortable as possible until the morrow and then we would have a look at the beach as far down as Dunkirk town as we had seen ships coming in and out.

The morning came after a restless night, mainly cold. As breakfast was not available we had a conference and I said to the remaining men that if they wanted to split up and find their own way home, that would be in order. So about ten of us set off down the beach towards Dunkirk. Men were still standing in the water and we saw that several folding boats, the sort that made the class nine bridge, were being used by the navy to carry troops out to the ships at anchor. After watching two of them capsize by overloading and the big waves, we passed along the beach. Once more we were treated to a raid by the Luftwaffe and once again were very lucky; they seemed to be aiming at the troops standing in the water.

We carried on down the beach, disregarding the orders of several officers who wanted us to join the 'queue in the sea'. Our remarks were unprintable after seeing what happened to some of the men standing in the water! Ten

Ken Naylor,
front right

or more minutes later we were rewarded with a marvellous sight, a ship's lifeboat, upside down at the water's edge. At this juncture I must point out that all Royal Engineer recruits were taught to row 'cutters', which were large enough to have two men to each oar and carry about twenty-five to thirty men. I inspected the upturned boat, found that there were no holes or cracks and that the bung, a large brass one which screwed into the bottom, was intact. So with the help of some other soldiers we turned the boat right way up, all intact, plus enough oars to have eight rowers, plus one for me to steer with as the rudders had been lost. Turning the boat bow-on to the ships at anchor I decided to head for a destroyer three-quarters of a mile out. By this time I had accumulated a number of helpers etc so I told them they could come with us – some would double-bank on the oars and the others would sit in and do as they were told.

The boat was pushed out into about three or four feet of water and everyone put in place. The oars were placed in the water and I gave the command 'give way all' to the rowing rhythm of 'IN-OUT, IN-OUT' and we were under way, straight for the destroyer.

Looking back at this particular moment I was very proud of being a 'sapper' and the men who were rowing. As we neared the destroyer there was a motorboat pulling several of our old FBE boats back to the line of waiting soldiers and I heard the sailor in the bows say to the naval petty officer in charge, 'What about this lot, chief, shall we give them a tow?' and the reply was, 'No, they know how to row. They'll manage.' And so we pulled alongside HMS *Codrington* doing the proper drill of 'Toss Oars' and 'Lay in Oars' and then everyone filed out and aboard the ship.

Down below we had a mug of tea and a couple of man-sized sandwiches. 'Make yourselves comfortable' we were told, and with the food and the warmth of the ship we must have slept for quite a while as we were told we were in the Channel on the way home.

We came in at the docks at Dover and were directed to the station and told to board a train which we did, and after cups of tea and sandwiches and a cigarette we got off the train at Blandford. Here there was a large reception camp with orders to 'Give your name, number, rank etc and go over to Tent B and draw ten shillings' which we did and found other tents where you could also draw ten shillings. The thing was to find a way out of the camp and a bus to Bournemouth and a tram to Christchurch where my mother lived. A good bath, shave etc etc and next day back to Blandford, to find out where my unit was. 'Here's your warrant, take these men to Codford St Mary in Wiltshire and join your unit.'

Now for the big surprise. Arriving at Codford St Mary we found our long-lost officers, CSM, CQMS etc, all waiting to re-equip us with new battledress, rifles, equipment etc and the cheerful remark, 'The 3rd Division is being re-equipped and will be the first division to go back to France.' After having all that trouble to get OUT of France we all wondered how we were going to get back in!

However, the army is always full of surprises, and we were paraded as a company a few days later and His Majesty King George VI and our illustrious (later) divisional commander Monty gave us a few words of support for the forthcoming return to France, presented a few medals and a soldier's farewell. However, within forty-eight hours France had signed up with Hitler and did not need our help any more!

Ken Naylor, Woodchurch, Kent

I was with the BEF from early September, in the RASC, billeted at a small village in Écourt-St-Quentin until the Germans broke through and then – nothing but chaos. We were feeding the 98th Field Regiment with petrol and ammunition. Our officer commanding, Captain Webster, had us on parade and told us we were going to Dunkirk and may get a boat to England, but we may not! He said that lorries had to be left in a field indicated by a redcap (military policeman) but on reaching this man my officer commanding went ahead, so I followed him in my lorry of course.

Then we drove through the night until we pulled into a small village (Westende) a few miles from Ostend, where as much damage was done to the engine as possible. Then we clambered on to another lorry and arrived at Dunkirk beach early next morning. We took shelter in the dunes and there in the morning some time later on we went to the beach where we started digging trenches in

case of any aircraft. During the day we were machine-gunned. I was there about three days, on the beach by day, back to the dunes by night. It poured with rain one night.

Eventually our officer commanding took us to the jetty at the end of which was a destroyer, the HMS *Winchelsea*. We climbed on board. I sat where I could on the open deck, not aware of the fact that I was near to one of the ship's guns. Suddenly I heard 'bang'. The gun was fired at a German plane and I have never heard such a bang in my life.

We then set sail for Dover (thank God) where we were treated like heroes with cups of tea etc along all the stations along route to Exeter. We camped under tents in St James's Park football ground. My wife had already received the postcard given to us by the people at the stations as we passed through and then sent on to relations. They were issued by the army and she came to Exeter for a weekend.

I might add that we were ordered to dump all our belongings except rifle, gas mask, gas cape and groundsheet. But I still bought presents for my wife, mother and father and sister and I kept them and got them home. My wife has still got hers!

Wilfred A. Gingell, Bath, Avon

Going into Belgium with the 7th Battalion, Worcestershire Regiment was a wonderful experience. The Belgians loved us and we were going in to save them from the Boche. It was flowers all the way – IN!

It was on 21 May 1940 at Velvain [Wez-Velvain] that we in the headquarters company came under really heavy shellfire. We just lay in an orchard and felt the ground trembling and erupting all around us. That seemed to go on for hours, but eventually it stopped and my friend Adrian Stephenson, who had been lying beside me, said he was wounded. Sure enough a piece of shrapnel had gone through his haversack, his mess tin and personal belongings, ripped his tunic and shirt, and just made a bruise on the middle of his back. So fortunately there was going to be no purple heart for him that day!

It was at the Bassée Canal that I was sent to follow a telephone line, because we had lost touch with our forward companies. I finally came to the end of the line, in the middle of a great expanse of open country, dominated by a village which I presume was Bassée. I was questing around for the other end of the line when two of our infantry men approached me. They were going back towards battalion headquarters and asked me where I was going. On my pointing to the village ahead they just laughed and said, 'You'll be lucky, because the Germans are already there.' So that solved my problem of the line fault!

On 27 May we all became front-line troops. Our signal section made for a farm on a ridge which dominated our positions. We reached a barn and then we came under fire from the farmhouse, or so we thought. Our officer asked for someone to bring a Bren-gun section to our position. I went and was lucky enough to find two men and a Bren gun who were willing to accompany me. On returning to the barn Second Lieutenant Cheshire came to meet me, and said they were being fired on from the farmhouse. Without thinking I said, 'I'll get them', crawled under the wire and with fixed

bayonet went after my Germans. Looking back on it I probably deserved a medal for that, but also looking back I realised that if Germans had been in the farmhouse my medal would have certainly been posthumous, so I am not complaining! If Germans had been there they must have run away. Anyhow the farm was cleared and by that time Adrian Stephenson had joined me and we made our way to the other side of the farm, where we had a clear vision of two long lines of tanks, stretching back over the horizon.

French tanks we thought, and big ones at that. We were really enjoying the views when suddenly we were raked by machine-gun fire and chips of bricks and mortar from the wall behind us showered down. We went down on our knees wondering where the hell the fire was, then came more flying brick dust and mortar. By this time we were as flat as the gas mask on our chests would let us get, our only protection a wire fence, and some grass growing against it to the height of about twelve inches!

We didn't even raise our eyes for about five minutes, then I began to wonder if I could get a bullet in through the eyeslits of the leading tank. How foolish can you get! Fortunately for us a haystack to our right had been set on fire and the smoke was billowing between us and the tanks. We nipped around the back of that farmhouse double quick, and there we solemnly shook hands. Even now I don't know whether to laugh or sweat when I think of it. Anyhow that was the start of our retreat to Dunkirk, although we didn't know it then. After two or more abortive last stands we started our trek to the coast.

And it was refugees all the way. Roads packed with them. We lived on raw eggs most of the time, and we milked cows who were bellowing in their stalls with overful udders, then we freed them to roam and often get killed. We saw scores of bloated bodies, animals and humans on our weary march back. And weary we were. I have never been so tired before or since. We stopped at one place and made a lovely bed in a pigsty, but we weren't there long enough to snatch even five minutes' sleep. One of life's major disappointments!

We passed through Tournai just after an air raid. There were telephone wires, debris and bodies everywhere. One body was perched flat on top of a wall with its two legs sticking out of its back. We didn't stop and we didn't get any cheers from the people. In fact it was thumbs down for us, and what could we do or even say, to cheer them up except, 'We'll be back.' Even then they didn't believe us.

We trudged through mile after mile of open country, us (the BEF), some French, some Belgians, and scores of refugees with their carts, handtrucks and bicycles piled high with bedding. There were old folk and children. Then some biplanes came over and everyone said the Germans had no biplanes but they strafed us just the same although they didn't come very low because everyone in that column was firing at them with all they'd got, including anti-tank rifles. I do remember seeing a French soldier cowering under a lorry. I gave him the thumbs-up sign, but he refused to be cheered!

As we were nearing Dunkirk we began to find vehicles and even tanks, in the ditches. Then we came upon the now famous NAAFI wagon abandoned in the ditch and I think just about everyone who got out of Dunkirk plundered that vehicle! It was a godsend. No one took too much, because it had to be carried, and we were already loaded with personal belongings and weapons.

By this time we were thoroughly mixed on the road with refugees all marching at a steady slow pace but from our rear we heard a commotion. It turned out to be a French horse-drawn artillery troop, coming at full gallop scattering people in all directions. I think it was then that we taught the natives a few swear words! By this time we were getting very thirsty, as well as hungry and tired, because the local farms were boarding up and locking their wells. I can see their point now but at the time it seemed most inconsiderate.

We stayed on the outskirts of Dunkirk on 29 May because of the lack of boats at the beach. Our section were in some dark cellars. All were thirsty. A Frenchman took some of us to where there was water. I prepared to drink it but it stank like sewer water, and I opted to stay thirsty! But many drank the stuff. I have often wondered if that Frenchman was a fifth columnist, because by that time they were rumoured to be everywhere.

On 30 May we went onto the beach amongst the sand dunes. Many times I have been asked what it was like, but my impressions are hazy. Just blue skies, sand and sunken ships scattered all around so far as the eye could see. I went to sleep for how long I have no idea, but I was awakened to share, with six others, a tin of bully beef. It was grand and we did appreciate it. Then we were told we were embarking from the jetty. I shall always remember a sailor standing at the end of the jetty marshalling us forward. He was so calm and so young, practically everyone gave him something from our NAAFI loot! He was so reassuring. He said, 'the RAF were keeping the skies fairly clear over Dunkirk' which was nice to know because we had hardly seen a British RAF plane since 10 May!

The jetty had a hole blown in it but that was planked over so what was left of our battalion, about eighty of us at that time, boarded a paddle steamer without haste or confusion. They packed us in all right, but we didn't care because at last we could go to sleep. I think some sailors brought tea round, God bless them. We didn't know what was going on, but we felt that we were on our way.

Eventually we were roused to see the white cliffs of Dover looming ahead, and there another big surprise awaited us. We were feted as heroes by those marvellous people of Dover. They showered us with sandwiches, boiled eggs, and stamped postcards for us to fill in to tell our folks we had 'arrived home'. We thought we had been defeated, and had let them down, but they wouldn't have it. We were the heroes. We were their 'boys', that was all that mattered to them.

Eventually I was granted leave and I returned to my parents' house. I will never forget the words that I saw on a plaque on the wall, 'We are not interested in the possibility of defeat in this house.'

John W. Carter, Kidderminster, Worcestershire

I remember Dunkirk. I was driving a YMCA van at the time. We were asked to visit a country house in

Cheshire where men from Dunkirk had been taken. It was a warm sunny day and the men were sitting about in the garden in all sorts of uniforms and parts of uniforms. So far as I can remember no charge was made for the tea and 'wads' we handed out.

Usually when we arrived at a gun or searchlight site there was plenty of chat and banter but this time everyone was quiet. No one spoke. I got out of the van and spoke to a sergeant who was sitting on the grass. He was drained of life. I sat beside him and took his hand. I asked him why there was such stillness among hundreds of men.

'Well,' he said, 'we expected to be rejected when we came home because people might have thought we had run away, but it wasn't like that, we were overwhelmed. All the way up from the south coast whenever the train stopped, we were greeted with open arms and with every sort of affection. Our boys had come home.

'But we shall go back,' the sergeant went on, 'one day we shall drive into Berlin.' I saw him several times after that. When the time came for him to move on with his re-formed unit he asked if I would write to him. He said he needed a pen friend. I agreed and wrote to him for several months and had notes back and then they ceased. I often wonder what happened to him. And did he ever get to Berlin?

Mary Hamer, Harlech, Gwynedd

My brother was called Sidney Barley and was aged twenty when he lost his job with the firm he was working for because it was closing down, and after trying for three months to find work he walked in one day and told us that he had joined the King's Own Scottish Borderers. My mum was heartbroken. He went for six months' training and a week after he had finished his training he came home on a week's leave and then war was declared and he was sent straight to France. As he was coming up to twenty-one I bought him a gold watch. Dad wanted him to leave it at home, but he went off with it on. We never saw him again, because he was at Dunkirk and only seven soldiers came home from the whole of his battalion.

Mum got a telegram, 'missing presumed killed', and later on she got his medals, but she never believed he was dead right up to the day that she died. But Dad and I knew he could not be alive because if he had to go out into the sea he wouldn't be able to do it. When he was young a boy at school pushed him in the deep end at the swimming baths and after that he was terrified of water.

One of the lads that came back later came to see Mum said my brother was the life and soul of the battalion and the last he saw of him was on the beach at Dunkirk. He had heard him say to another chap, 'I'm going back to Lille. I'm not going in the water. So long, chum.'

Alice Jacklin, Leeds, West Yorkshire

On 10 May, 1940, we were stationed on the French/ Belgian border when we were informed by our company commander that Germany had invaded the Low Countries and that we would proceed into Belgium immediately. During that day we experienced for the first time bombing and machine-gunning from the air and also witnessed the bombing of towns and civilians. After three days we finally got to our advanced defence positions which were little more than slit trenches in the ground and about 5pm the following day, 14 May, we were ordered to stand by our battle positions.

Just prior to the stand-to, I had found six eggs which I had put over a fire to boil for tea for myself and my mates. We never did taste those eggs which, if the fire kept going, would still be boiling! Suddenly we were in the midst of heavy shelling and fighting continued all night and at dawn we were driven from our position with heavy losses.

From here onwards we were in retreat, sometimes in small isolated groups, sometimes in large numbers, as we met up with other retreating soldiers. On 28 May a composite force of many regiments, of which I was a member, started an attack to try and link up with the French forces. During this engagement I was at first slightly wounded in the side of the face, followed shortly afterwards by some more severe wounds to my left arm and hand. I had the wounds dressed at a first aid post then I was placed in an ambulance which was going in a convoy to Dunkirk. I remember the driver being told to drive like the wind and we eventually arrived in Dunkirk after being attacked by aircraft and tanks on the way. During that trip we lost two ambulances and only the skills and bravery of our driver got us through. We arrived in Dunkirk on 30 May.

The sight was both appalling and frightening. The town was virtually destroyed and under continuous attack. We stayed on the beaches until 1 June when we were told that all wounded were to go along the mole, which was a jetty leading out from the beach, and board a paddle steamer which was tied up at the end. Whilst proceeding along this pier we were dive-bombed and although several boats had near misses, I didn't see any direct damage done. I remember remarking to another soldier, 'If this is the best they can do, we have nothing to fear.'

On boarding the vessel all the wounded were sent below deck but the bombing continued and apparently the captain decided to pull away from the pier and stand off from the beaches. We had hardly started to move when several bombs struck the ship causing severe damage and setting her on fire. The decking that was above us collapsed inwards trapping us in total darkness with no way out.

We kept up our morale by singing the songs of the time, and after what seemed many hours, but was probably only a few minutes, a seaman on deck cut a hole through to us with an axe. I reached this opening at the same time as another soldier but he stood back and said, 'After you.' My reply was 'No, after you.' This was repeated three times when a voice behind us said, 'If you two buggers can't make up your bloody minds move over and let me through.' We moved quickly!

Out on the deck many people lay around dead and the ship was on fire and it became obvious that without pumps she wouldn't be saved. Consequently the order came to abandon ship. It was at this time that I realised that most of my clothes had been blown to rags. I was in the bow, having put on a lifebelt, and was preparing to jump overboard when an RAF bloke asked if I could swim. I explained that I could and the belt would help. To which he replied, 'I can't swim but this is where I learn.' I never saw him again but I hope that he made it.

After some considerable time in the water I was rescued by a small boat that took me and several others across to another ship and we arrived in Dover at daylight on the morning of 2 June.

As we arrived, the shout went up of 'let go' and the anchor slid down and a soldier lying next to me said, 'Oh no, not here as well.' He had mistaken the anchor noise for aircraft machine-gunning.

I was placed on an ambulance train which took me to Yorkshire and after an operation I was detained in hospital for six weeks before being granted six weeks' home leave for recovery.

Dunkirk is an experience I would not like to repeat but it taught me the value of comradeship and its effect on different people. I have returned twice since, not only to look again at the places and remember the people, but in particular to pay homage to my friends who never returned.

Thomas 'Darkie' Hammond, Thorrington, Essex

M y husband's battery was on the mole at Dunkirk during the evacuation of the army. Whilst he was there some very tall soldiers went by, uniforms rather worse for wear, but marching very smartly with shovels over their shoulders. My husband asked, 'What mob do you belong to, mate?'

He got a very quick reply. 'Don't you know. We belong to the Bullshit Brigade.'

They were in fact Grenadier Guardsmen. My husband said later that you would have thought they were changing the guard at Buckingham Palace.

He returned home on 7 June and I remember him telling me he came home in the hold of a large ship and that had they been bombed they would have all drowned like rats.

Shortly afterwards my husband received the Military Medal and a citation commending him for attending wounded men under very heavy shellfire and keeping his guns in action on the mole.

It was with great pride that I accompanied him to Buckingham Palace when he was decorated by King George VI in February 1941.

My husband's name was Sergeant S. C. Collins of 17 Battery, the First Regiment of the Royal Artillery. Sadly he died four and a half years ago.

Mrs P. M. Collins, Lichfield, Staffordshire

I was living with my parents at Nottingham in 1940 and I was eleven years old. I remember that my father had a large map of Europe on the wall on which, having listened intently to the news on the wireless, he would move little flags, mounted on pins, backwards and forwards on the map according to the news that had

been received. At the time of what ultimately became known as 'Dunkirk', I clearly remember him saying, 'I don't like the sound of this.'

My special, but rather sad, memory of that time is this. One day a huge open lorry came down a rather long road, laden with our soldiers covered in all the grime of battle on the beaches, most of them with bandages on various visible parts of their bodies. Others we found later were badly wounded elsewhere.

They had come straight from the beaches, received emergency treatment on landing here, and the army was now looking for people who would take them into their homes whilst they sorted things out. There were two or more to a house.

I shall never forget the sight of those lads, piled in a lorry looking for homes. The real sadness of it didn't hit me, being only a schoolgirl, but it is something I shall never forget.

Thelma Montague, Oakham, Leicestershire

The first time I realised the horror of war was just after Dunkirk. I lived on Barrack Hill and every day soldiers struggled up to the barracks. They were holding each other up and some had rags wrapped round their feet, and their clothes were in tatters.

There was not enough transport to run them from the station, so those who could stand were sent walking. People who were awaiting news of their loved ones were asking them which regiments they were from and giving them tea and cigarettes and trying to help as best they could, but all the soldiers wanted was to take off their filthy clothes and get some sleep. There were few cars around and even less petrol then, and the sight of seeing those men staggering up the hill will always be with me.

I also remember the trains rushing on the middle line through Newport station, and scraps of paper and parts of cigarette packets and anything which could be written on being thrown from the windows to let their relatives know that they were alive and back in this country.

As soon as the station was clear, railway personnel got down on the line and collected every scrap. They were taken to the stationmaster's office and carefully read and if the names and addresses could be understood every person was notified and told that their loves ones were safe and had passed through Newport.

Joan Morgan, Caerleon, Gwent

We had been on the move for some hours when I first became aware of Dunkirk. That happened when a German plane flew over and dropped a lot of leaflets. The leaflets told us that we were in a hopeless position, but that if we surrendered we would be well treated. I remembered that there was a note in it telling us to look towards the coast where we would see the port of Dunkirk burning. I showed the leaflet to an officer but after he had read it I remember he remarked 'I should hardly think that is true'!

A few minutes later a German shell came over and burst about four or five hundred yards past our position, soon followed by some more ranging shots till they had our range almost to the yard. We opened fire with our four guns, but No.2 gun recoiled and failed to 'run out', so we were down to three guns. The Germans started firing again and got a direct hit almost immediately on our No.3 gun, killing the detachment. They also hit the dump of ammunition that we had placed there not long before.

Now we were down to two guns and our ammunition dump had been hit. However, whilst all this was going on I was taking down firing orders till all at once the line went dead. We didn't know what damage we'd done to the Germans but they had certainly done plenty to us. Two guns were out of action with several men killed and others wounded. The ammunition had been destroyed and there were shells all over the place. When the firing stopped we buried our dead in the cottage garden on the other side of the road and the padre was there and some of us stood still while he read a short service.

My mate and I then set out to try to trace the fault on the firing line. We followed the line till we came to the top of a hill where we could see right over an open stretch of lovely countryside. Looking around it was obvious some action had taken place there. There were lots of shell holes and sitting in a shallow ditch still holding the handset to his ear was our signaller. He was dead.

Just near to him was a farmhouse so we decided to have a look into it. We thought it might have been used as an observation post. As we opened the door we shouted 'anybody there?' but there was no reply so we went in. In one big room we found about a dozen people seated on chairs around the walls. I spoke to them in my poor French, but they just stared at me with frightened eyes, none of them even moving their heads or answering me. They all just seemed to be in a total state of shock. What could I do? Nothing. Just return to the troop or what was left of it.

As we were returning we passed a cottage that had been used as a first aid post. Parked close to it was a three-ton lorry. The driver was still at the wheel but slumped over it and a sergeant sat at his side also slumped in his seat. Both were dead. My mate took a look into the back of the truck and then said to me, 'Here have a look in there.' A shell had landed in the back of the truck smashing the floor and killing about a dozen men who had been passengers in the back of the truck. The bodies of these poor men were in a heap, some hanging through the blown-in floor. They were just a heap of smashed-up flesh and bone, arms and legs blown off. There didn't seem to be much blood so I thought they, including the sergeant and the driver, had probably been killed instantly.

Soon we got the order 'prepare to move'. Moving and halting all night we found ourselves at a crossroads by the time it was light. We put the guns into action, one on each side of a narrow lane that ran towards a farmhouse and other buildings set amongst some trees. Along this lane were about a dozen or more abandoned three-ton lorries and some Bren-gun carriers. During this time we saw a lot of the German air force, most of them fighters flying very low and we wondered why.

They seemed to fly about uninterrupted by any ack-ack fire or any British fighters. Eventually we were told to take the transport and make for Dunkirk.

We didn't get very far because the roads became blocked by all sorts of abandoned transport. Several of the fields were flooded so our motors were driven into the flooded fields as far as it was possible. We all set out to walk the rest of the way and what a sight met our eyes.

I couldn't get over it. There were transports of all kinds, light tanks and lots of Bren-gun carriers. There were guns of all sizes including six-inch howitzers and some real heavy guns still covered in grease from the first war; hundreds of tons of ammunition of all sorts and small arms, mortar bombs and thousands of rounds of artillery shells and cartridges.

At one crossroads as we travelled on was the remains of a French horse-drawn transport unit that had been caught by the German bombers. There were dead men and horses and smashed-up vehicles all over the area. The horses had their teeth showing and their eyes had the look of terror in them even in death. Soldiers were making their way along the road and I saw two German airmen that had been taken prisoner being escorted to Dunkirk. They were smiling away with their faces. No wonder when they saw all the abandoned war material lying all about them. What became of them I have no idea.

Even then we could not grasp the seriousness of the situation. A soldier only sees his own unit's part in a battle, and he hasn't much time or knowledge to think about what's going on elsewhere. As we got nearer to Dunkirk the roads were more clogged than ever but as we walked over the sand dunes what a sight met our eyes. It was then that it struck home to us our plight.

There was an awful feeling that we had been let down somewhere, that it should never have happened. That we had not stood a chance right from the start. The beach at Dunkirk was crowded with men, and several queues had formed right up into the sea.

Just offshore were a couple of warships and two more destroyers lay on their sides in shallow waters. What do we do now we asked, but who knew the answer to that question? We hadn't been there very long when a squadron of German planes came in, machine-gunning and bombing and there was nothing to stop them anyway.

We were sitting waiting for the next air raid when there was the sound of shells passing overhead. The shells landed on the beach just at the water's edge right among a group of soldiers, killing some and wounding others. The wounded were taken to the first aid post that had been set up in a building near the shore. Now that the Germans had got some artillery within range life became very much more uncomfortable. Although the shelling wasn't heavy, one couldn't tell just where they would land. The beach offered a big target so that the German gunners couldn't miss.

During the late afternoon we were told to fall in and we formed three ranks and the regimental sergeant majors called us to attention. A major addressed us saying, 'We are going to march along the beach in a smart and soldierly manner so keep in step.' The RSM then gave the order right turn, quick march, but it wasn't easy to keep in step because footsteps can't be heard in soft sand and the RSM had to keep shouting 'left, right, left, right'. It was almost dark when we got towards the harbour at Dunkirk and there we had to await further orders. Some planes were flying overhead and there was a bit of an uproar when one man struck a match to light a fag. 'Put that bloody light out,' was the cry. Eventually we formed a long queue on the harbour wall but we had to keep to one side and so leave a gangway for the stretchers to pass along to the front of the queue ready to be loaded on board a ship when it came.

We didn't know all this at the time. We just waited patiently. The Germans kept shelling the harbour area. They must have known about a ship and the long queue of men along the harbour wall. Most of the shells dropped in the water, but some hit the harbour wall, killing and wounding more soldiers. It was a terrible time, waiting there not knowing what was happening and expecting to be blown to bits or wounded at any moment.

There was no panic, everybody was calm outwardly but we must all have been keyed-up within. All at once the long queue started moving but not before all the stretcher cases had been taken on board. There was a big gap in the harbour wall where a bomb had hit it and a gangway had been put over the gap to form a bridge. It was slow progress till we got to the gangway as we could only pass over it one at a time. Once over it was a clear run to the ship. At the foot of the other gangway on a ship stood an officer of the Merchant Navy. I remember he was shouting, 'Any more for a trip on the Saucy Sue?' like they do at the seaside in peacetime. Once on board I went down below with hundreds more. I just lay down and can't remember anything else till I woke at Dover.

I was told afterwards that the ship was the *The Maid of Orleans*. It was attacked several times during the short voyage home but I was fast asleep, quite oblivious to anything. How great to see the white cliffs of Dover and the port again.

We were a strange collection of men that landed and then entrained at the port. Some of them had hardly any clothing but that didn't matter. We were home. Many hours later we found ourselves in Northampton. I can tell you that it was great in the pubs that night!

Ted Mortimer, Gedling, Nottinghamshire

It was dark when me, Jock and Tom reached the beach and everything was so quiet. There was none of the activity we had seen on the outskirts of Dunkirk. 'For Christ's sake settle down,' was the greeting we got! We plonked down there in the sand and slept. We were woken as dawn was breaking and the site was then unbelievable. Just a mass of bodies coming alive, then all hell let loose as the Stukas started their dive-bombing.

We saw bodies flying in the air, and men lying flat in the dunes, their bodies jumping as machine-gun bullets hit them. After a while things became quieter and lines of men formed out to sea to catch the boats. I can still remember being amazed at the orderly manner in which the men lined up and waited. There was no panic.

For three days the three of us waited, all lined up together, and we saw men being taken to the rear of the lines, some dead and some badly wounded. I marvelled at the dedication of the stretcher-bearers, some of whom were conscientious objectors but who had volunteered for services in the Medical Corps. On the fourth day we got on a boat and on the way home we were strafed again by a German plane. Tom received a belly wound which was bad, and all we could do was put our field dressing on him. We had no other medications, not even any water and it wouldn't have done any good. As we neared Dover Tom asked us to lift him up. I can still remember that as we lifted him he looked towards England and saw the cliffs and then he just sighed and died in my arms. I can remember looking back towards Belgium and I remember the fear and anger that I felt on the beaches, but for the first time I felt hatred and I screamed terrible obscenities at the top of my voice at those who had been responsible.

If I wrote a preface for your book I would write, 'If there is a place called HELL in the hereafter then those that survived the beaches at Dunkirk need not fear it for they have already been there.'

Henry Pusey, Hounslow, Middlesex

I joined the navy just prior to the war after completing my training at Chatham. I was posted to HMS *Gossamer* which was a Halcyon class minesweeper. We spent some time at Harwich, Dover and Grimsby before arriving at North Shields. I remember we were in the cinema when a message was flashed on the screen telling us to return to our ships at once. We sailed about midnight and after two hours or so the captain, Commander Ross, informed us that the army's position had become desperate.

Our orders were to cruise off the beaches and survey the situation. Not being aware of any troops, only heavy shellfire, we headed back to Dover only to be told to alter course and return to the beaches. By this time it was daylight and I couldn't believe my eyes. The beaches were teeming with troops and from that morning the worst ten days of my navy life were to unfold.

At this time we had been joined by a handful of British and French destroyers, plus some of the smaller ships. Troops had already begun to wade out to sea up to their necks, either to be rescued or sadly, in some cases, to drown. We eventually managed to load about four to five hundred troops and returned to Dover. As can be imagined, disembarkation was done with speed. A quick clean of the ship and we were off again. The oil tanks in Dunkirk harbour had already been bombed and shelled and the heavy pall of smoke could be clearly seen at Dover.

By the time we returned to Dunkirk it was quite dark and a hospital ship had been ordered to enter the harbour to pick up the wounded but hadn't a chart for the harbour. We lowered one of our whalers and a crew took the chart across. Whether it was fate or not I'll never know, but whilst waiting for our boat to return one of our destroyers, HMS *Wakeful* passed us. Minutes later she was gone, be it by mine or torpedo I don't really know. The screams for help took me a long time to forget. We saved about sixty or seventy but had to leave in case the E-boat or sub was still around. By the way, we never saw our boat's crew again. I still think about them and wonder if they were ever picked up.

We made our way towards the beaches and with the aid of small boats we loaded again and were soon on our way

to Dover. Just a couple of hours and we were off again. We laid off the beaches that night waiting for daybreak although we still loaded some troops. Our captain had warned us that the German air force would probably attack at dawn. How right he was.

Many of the troops had found shelter behind sand dunes and abandoned equipment. Still there were many who were isolated. Suddenly, without warning, German fighters came in low over the beaches, machine-gunning the troops. It was all over in five minutes and the scenes were terrible. The only way I can describe it is like a farmer cutting corn. We carried on loading that day and returned to Dover, cleaned the ship and returned to the beaches. As days passed it became obvious the troops were getting more and more desperate. We gathered together some small boats (these were left to drift as the destroyers became loaded). We rowed inshore and loaded and then rowed back to the ship, always desperately overloaded. As the situation got worse some troops actually threatened to shoot us if we didn't make room for them on the boats. After that we were armed with pistols and had no further trouble. Nevertheless some chaps couldn't take any more and I saw a few end it all by jumping overboard, even one in Dover harbour.

Days seemed to drag, and on our next trip we were told to enter Dunkirk harbour at night, a frightening prospect. Anyway we inched our way in very slowly. As we approached the mole we shouted to the troops to jump aboard. No lines were put ashore. We dwelt a few moments and backed out. Believe me, we were fully loaded. It seemed it would never end and don't believe people who say you can't go without sleep. Admitted, we stood up and 'cat napped'.

Eventually, although we didn't know, we set out on our last trip. Fewer and fewer troops were now coming home. Although only half loaded we set out to Dover. Remarkable as it may seem, we were alone. Suddenly about twenty dive-bombers attacked. The captain ordered us to batten all the troops below decks. My nerves were stretched to their limits and I actually hoped a bomb would hit us. Amazing as it was, we suffered no damage at all and arrived safely at Dover.

We were granted three days' 'Dunkirk' leave. I went home, met my father who didn't say a word. Then I shed a few tears and went to bed.

William Cassell, Redcar, North Yorkshire

I was in the 16th Field Regiment Royal Artillery and did service in France from 5 September 1939 to early June 1940. I remember when we were on the retreat, we were told to forget the retreat and head for the Albert canal as we had to stop the German advance, so the troops who were already at Dunkirk would have a better chance to get away. For two days we shelled the Germans and we did halt their advance. I remember we had nothing to eat, and no sleep.

I remember when we had fired nearly all our shells, we had orders to save two shells so we could spike our guns when the time came, and to get all the smoke shells we had as we would be firing them at first dawn. The idea of this was to get the Germans in a panic thinking they were under attack, or even gas. It must have worked, as they stopped firing at us.

I remember when we got orders to spike our guns and vehicles, I remember how downhearted I was when we went back to the gun to see what damage was done. It was like losing a friend. I remember the trek to Dunkirk, although at times I must have been sleepwalking. When we got to the beach at Dunkirk we were told to go into the sea until it was too deep to go any further, as there was a ship coming to pick us up. After standing in the water for three hours, we were told 'no ship, so go back into Dunkirk and find some place to billet'.

I remember our troop found a large house with no tenants, so we claimed that and managed to get a little sleep, but nothing to eat. It was Sunday, and the Germans were bombing and shelling Dunkirk. I remember thinking we will never get away from Dunkirk, so I was surprised, when we got orders to parade in the street at five as we had to be on the pier at 5.30 as there would be a ship for us.

When we got to the pier there was a trawler waiting with a wooden plank fifteen foot long from the pier to the trawler. The Germans were shelling the pier and there was a short time between shots, which meant that one person had to get across before the next shell. I remember that dash along that plank! Several of my mates fell off, never to be seen again. I don't remember much about the crossing as I slept on the deck. But I do remember the lovely cup of tea and food the WVS had waiting for us at Dover.

Wyndham G. Marshall, Rotherham, South Yorkshire

During the 1939–1945 war, at the time of the Dunkirk evacuation, I was the sister of a male surgical ward in a large base hospital in Surrey. We had received a convoy of six hundred patients from France and in my ward of sixty-two beds there were sixty French soldiers and two Scots. All were in a terrible condition. Uniforms had to be burned of lice, and once all were made comfortable, clean and in bed, the doctors did a ward round. I went round and shaved all those with beards!

The following day, whilst in the operating theatre with a patient, I received a message to return to my ward as an important visitor was expected. The visitor was Her Majesty, Queen Elizabeth, now the Queen Mother, who spent the day touring the hospital. For over

an hour she talked to the patients in my ward, speaking fluent French and asking questions about those who were screened and just back from the theatre. She requested to see and handled the items which had been removed from the patients, such as shrapnel, bullets etc. I remember her saying, 'Do please tell them that I have seen their souvenirs when they wake up.'

Our ward, an army-hut type of building, on that very hot May day, had received from local nurseries tall blue delphinium flowers. With green beech leaves we stood them in buckets on the floor right down the centre of the ward.

This visit was not reported in the press and no photographs were allowed. The Queen looked so beautiful and with her smile and charm she put the staff at ease and chatted informally to us about our work in wartime conditions.

The French soldiers were given the opportunity to stay in England and to join the Free French Forces or to return to France. Only three stayed. They were from the 3rd French Infantry Regiment. One had his regimental badge which was a circle of laurel leaves and a wolf's head in the centre. This he gave to me when they left and each soldier put on a lucky charm, a silver madonna, a black cat and a horseshoe.

Myrtle Paton, Chilham, Kent

Strange isn't it, how memories start to flow back when one sits down to think. Yes, I remember Dunkirk. A very warm and sunny May in 1940. The war had erupted into something real and decidedly menacing. As a young soldier of nineteen, I had enlisted in the Royal Corps of Signals, TA, was eventually attached to a Bolton Artillery Regiment, the 53rd Field RA. We moved to France in the spring of 1940. When the German push started into Belgium, the regiment, then stationed around the Lille area, was moved into action stations, over the border into Belgium. As the fighting intensified, withdrawal became inevitable.

Our signals detachment pulled through Lille. I recall how this once-peaceful city lit up the sky, red with the flames of burning buildings. Things looked really black when the order came to render all usable equipment useless. All the instruments we had carefully maintained! Wireless sets, exchanges, telephones etc, smashed beyond repair. From then on it was orderly withdrawal to the coast. The area of Dunkirk. The BEF was to be hemmed in to a shrinking perimeter with the port and stretch of coastline, known as Bray-Dunes, the best chance of evacuation. We lost one of our signals detachment at the village of Poperinge, when a shell burst shattered his leg. I found out later, much later, that this chap came from the area where I now live. However, the group of us who struggled towards the coast had to abandon our vehicle. The lowlands had been flooded and we struggled through hordes of pathetic refugees.

Eventually we came within sight of the port of Dunkirk. By now, we knew the evacuation of the army was no rumour. The burning town was under intense attack from the Luftwaffe. A decision had to be made about the best point for being picked up. A senior officer directed us to Bray-Dunes. I was only aware of soldiers at this stage. The civilians seemed to have disappeared. On the dunes, slit trenches were prepared hurriedly. No one knew how long we would have to wait, but meanwhile eyes scanned the blue skies above. Down the coast, columns of thick black smoke arose, as droning planes shed HE [high explosives] upon the blazing port.

For me it was like taking part in some great epic. Barely a year ago I was doing a fairly routine clerical job, going to night school and generally enjoying life. And now, as I look out to sea, there lies a hospital ship, heavily listing, having been struck by bombs. On the shore, washed up by the tide, oil-covered bodies, still with lifebelts on, waves gently lapping over them.

Ships of various kinds lie off the shore, as small boats come in close to take off the troops. And then, the noise, as rifles, Bren guns and assorted weapons open up, and soldiers rise up from their slit trenches, firing furiously, as the Luftwaffe roar overhead. At the time we prayed for the appearance of the RAF but we were not to know how desperate a position our own air force was in. As it turned out, every plane was going to be needed for the coming Battle of Britain.

Meanwhile there was no panic as troops lined up at the water's edge, to clamber aboard the boats. This meant wading out to about chest level. It is now 30 May, and our small detachment reaches the water line. Shelling of the beaches is a hazard but the rearguard holds off the leading Wehrmacht units. I still had my rifle, water bottle, pack and ammunition as we scrambled and lumbered towards the large dinghy which lay offshore.

Willing hands helped to pull us into the boat, which

held about twenty-five men. We made towards a paddle steamer, called the *Glen Avon*. She was listing to one side but was apparently still seaworthy. In a fairly modest swell, each man clambered aboard. I remember going down to a warm area near the engine room, to dry off. There was a tremendous explosion. The whole ship seemed to shudder and then steady. It turned out to be a near miss but I realised (much later) how many men, having boarded ships, never made it out of the Dunkirk mayhem. We were lucky.

The paddles of the old tub began to thrash away as we slowly pulled away from the beaches. I couldn't help thinking of those oil-covered bodies left there on the shore, as I gazed at the receding figures of those still waiting to be picked up. The noise and the long columns of smoke became less obvious, as we drew further away from the continent. Sailors came round with chunky corned beef sandwiches and steaming mugs of sweet tea. What bliss ... I couldn't remember what we had lived on for the last few days. Well, we were now in the hands of naval personnel. Brave men indeed!

The old steamer eventually made it to Harwich – 1 June 1940.

Alex Martin, Manchester, Greater Manchester

I was a lance corporal in the Sherwood Foresters in 1940, and I was attached to the headquarters of the 3rd Infantry Brigade. During the withdrawal to Dunkirk we made our headquarters in the cellars of a tobacco factory at Roubaix. Around 10am a despatch rider came down from the front with a report that the Germans had released gas. Due warning was passed to all personnel.

Some time later and being off duty I was in a cellar which had a grate on to the street level. The atmosphere of the cellar was musty and I was writing a letter home. The town was being shelled when suddenly the smell in the cellar changed. Being unable to define the smell I shouted 'gas'. Masks were donned and then the answer was revealed. A petrol tank had been hit and the fumes, together with the cellar smell, had produced my 'gas'!

Later at Bray-Dunes, some three or four miles from Dunkirk, we were in a small copse and when the German planes came over, strafing with machine-gun fire. We took shelter in slit trenches and dugouts made by troops who had preceded us. I was with a sergeant of the Intelligence Corps and we found a well constructed dugout, just large enough for the two of us. I had two tins of mushrooms and a bottle of wine and my intent was to get the latter home! Anyway my companion persuaded me to

open it. We had consumed approximately one-third when the German planes came over again. Unable to find the cork quickly I stood the bottle up in the sand and went under cover. Some ten or fifteen minutes later the German planes had gone and we emerged – to find the bottle gone!

About an hour later we heard a Frenchman singing, obviously through drink. We looked around and there he was sitting on the ground with his back to a tree and my now-empty wine bottle by his side. Someone said, 'Shoot the bugger.' I replied, 'Not likely, he's better off than us. He doesn't even know there's a war on!'

Shortly after that we met a private soldier from the Devonshire regiment who had become detached from his unit and he tacked on to us. Overhead there were clear blue skies and an aerial dogfight was now taking place at a great height. 'Devon' stood up, minus his tin helmet, although we were still being strafed, and looking up at the planes he exclaimed, 'Ee, ain't they up a depth!' Six hours after I was taken off the beaches at Dunkirk all sailings from France ended.

Claude 'Mush' Noble, Selby, North Yorkshire

Do you remember May 1940? Hitler's troops had bypassed the so-called impenetrable Maginot Line, and they were relentlessly pushing our BEF towards the French coast. The outlook was grim as we geared ourselves for a possible invasion. A Sunday of prayer was announced and every church, chapel and synagogue in the British Isles was packed to capacity. Strange, isn't it, how in adversity we usually acknowledge our weakness and turn to a higher power! Help did come, although many a life perished. From every port and harbour along the south and east coast of England all types of craft – any boat that could face the sea – rushed to the rescue of our troops, hurrying back and forth across the Channel, snatching weary and bedraggled souls from the beaches and sea around Dunkirk

My fiance had embarked for 'somewhere in France' on 13 January 1940, and his parents and I watched anxiously day by day, hoping against hope that he would be amongst those rescued. Then came that dreaded yellow envelope, 'Regret … died from wounds …' The long hot summer dragged on until September, when suddenly a card arrived from Belgium. He was alive! He had been picked up unconscious and operated on by a surgeon who was miraculously on the spot at the crucial time and who specialised in that type of wound. He regained conscious-ness four days later in Ghent hospital, only to find it was now in German hands and that he was a prisoner of war.

Year followed year with the fluctuating fortunes of war – our flagging spirit spurred on by the gruff voice of our 'bulldog' Prime Minister, Winston Churchill. I remember

Wilson Sadler, front right

coming home from Sussex through London and seeing the long queues of people with their pathetic bundles of blankets, waiting to descend to the comparative safety of the Tube stations, not knowing whether their homes would still be standing when they next emerged.

London, Coventry, Plymouth and countless other cities, towns and hamlets were taking an unmerciful battering from the Luftwaffe.

Then into my own little world came a ray of light. In October 1943 there was suddenly talk of an exchange of wounded prisoners of war, and in November 1943 it materialised, with joyful reunions. The result was that the following year, in February 1944, we exchanged our marriage vows and endeavoured to erase from our memories those weary years of separation.

Oh yes, despite everything, I have a lot for which to say 'thank you'.

Eileen F. Sadler, St. Ives, Cornwall

I remember the night. Clouds were receding before a greying sky in the east and then imperceptibly, the colours changed, and one could feel that a glorious summer sun was bursting to peep over the horizon. I rested my elbows on the wooden farmgate and gazed across the river. Apart from the dawn chorus of the birds in a nearby copse all was still. It was the epitome of peace, and all seemed right with the world.

Unfortunately this was not an English river, but the River Dyle in Belgium and I was on guard duty. Up till now we had been billeted in northern France, spending our days on manoeuvres, exercises and digging a network of trenches. We did a short stint in the Maginot Line, which was supposed to be the impregnable fortress for France. The odd shot was fired to show that we were still at war and we did patrols to see who and what was going on at their front.

It was 10 May, 1940 when the silence of the 'Phoney War' was suddenly shattered. Machine guns and mortars lashed through the trees and suddenly we were learning what real war was all about. The incessant noise of firing, Stuka dive-bombers pounding our positions, whilst the artillery on both sides constantly whizzed overhead. I was a stretcher-bearer with three other bandsmen and we seemed to be always on call. We were kept busy taking ammunition, food and cigarettes up to the troops and returning with the maimed and wounded casualties. The days seemed to be scorching hot and we soon discarded the gas masks and other equipment that seemed to impede our treks to the front.

The following days and nights were full of incidents too numerous to relate. Some tragic, heroic, fearful and even humorous but after four or five days of this impasse, inevitably something had to give. The advancing German troops had by now captured bridges to the north and south of us, trapping the whole BEF in a pincer-like movement. We were told to pull back to straighten the line between the Belgian and the French armies. This brought us back to our second line of defence near to the River Lys. Our unit was holding the canal at Froyennes near Tournai. Here, in an abortive counter-attack, we were ambushed and twelve men died. The villagers respectfully buried them in the local cemetery, and each year on 20 May, the day that they died, a simple service is held and posies are laid on their graves.

The next few days were a repeat of our first encounter. Nothing could slow or stop the remorseless Panzer tanks with their volume and fire power. Another tactical

withdrawal took us back to
our third and final line of
defence, a twenty-five mile
perimeter arched around the
one and only port available,
which was Dunkirk. Three
army corps held this line whilst
the battle raged and the Royal
Navy joined in with shelling the enemy from well out to
sea. Evacuation had already begun days before, and
already many of the wounded and the non-combatant
troops had gone.

Finally orders went out for the corps to withdraw in
reverse order. We withdrew independently, in relays, so
as not to alert the enemy and we estimated that we had
eight or nine miles to go. We had no maps or directions
but they weren't needed, because the pall of smoke
over Dunkirk and the endless roads filled with human
panic and misery were sufficient. Refugees and troops
of all the Allies trudged in dejection and defeat along
those roads, with prams and bicycles and carts, along
with the carnage of military equipment. From a lorry I
took a Bren gun with ammunition and a supply of
tinned herrings and stewed steak. Both were essentials
for survival!

We left the road and had a snack at a farmhouse, and
there a frightened horse joined us, and enjoyed the

French bread which we gave to him. My pal was a real country lad from Devon and so he suggested we ride it into Dunkirk. Like an idiot I agreed and so we rode the horse towards Dunkirk until a couple of miles out of town soreness to my backside called a halt.

Soon I found myself on the dunes near the beach with my young pal. Wounded were lying all round, mostly from the consistent dive-bombing and strafing of the Luftwaffe. We set to and dug hollows to protect the wounded that could not be moved and sent walking wounded off to the queues near to the mole. We replenished our dressings from ditched ambulances nearby, forgetting now about food and sleep. The long queues had decreased and scattered parties were everywhere. It was a bizarre scene, blazing oil tanks and docks, constant noise and day turned into night by the pall of the thick black smoke.

After a couple of days of this I was approached by a young officer. I told him what I was doing and my unit and he told me that he had been watching and had seen what I was doing. He then told me that he was transferring me to his own regiment and so, as of that moment, I became a Royal Engineer! At 10pm that night I reported to him, as instructed, on the mole.

Soon we were treading carefully over the gaps in the planking and climbing down the supports of the mole on to the deck of a fishing smack from Lowestoft.

Daytime loading had been suspended due to heavy losses, hence the night-time loading. I remember being handed a half loaf of bread and some water which I promptly wasted by falling asleep! The noise and bustle of docking disturbed my sleep and we stepped ashore at Margate in Kent. Here we were given tea and sandwiches and sent off to a train nearby which headed north.

It would be four years to the day before this journey could be reversed and the long hard slog back the way we had come would start again.

Alex Turner, Crook, Co. Durham

At the time of Dunkirk I was aged eighteen and serving an apprenticeship as an electrician at Ramsgate. One morning on going to work on a ship in the harbour I found that the approach road was closed and a police barrier was across it. However, I was allowed to pass as I was working on a ship for the navy. Everything appeared to be normal and I went aboard the ship and joined my mate in the engine room. At about ten o'clock it was my practice to go up to the sailors' home to get a can of tea but when I got up on the deck I saw a destroyer at the pier head and it was packed with troops and that was the first time we knew that something was going on and had gone badly wrong.

The troops were in a terrible state. There were French and Belgian as well as our own and soon people from town were coming down to give assistance, handing out food and cigarettes and anything they could lay their hands on. My mate and I got hold of an elec-

tric wash boiler and filled it with water from a fire hose and brewed tea and handed it to the troops and they certainly needed it.

The next day there seemed to be a vast armada of little ships arriving. I have never seen so many small ships together and the whole harbour was full and Pegwell Bay was crowded with larger vessels. They were all types and it seemed that anything that could float was there. I even remember seeing the *Massey Shaw* which was a well-known fire-fighting boat from London. For the next few days the sea was as calm as a millpond and so calm that even rowing boats could be towed across but I remember that for days a great pall of smoke drifted along the horizon. It was Dunkirk burning.

In the evenings I spent my time giving out and collecting postcards from the troops at the railway station, to be sent to their families telling them that they were home and safe. A remarkable thing was that we never got bombed, although I remember one or two German planes coming over to have a look at us.

Eric Martin, Rugby, Warwickshire

I, like thousands of others in their late teens, joined the Territorial Army early in 1939. Thus I found myself as a driver in 226 Field Company of the Royal Engineers in my home town of Reading, and I was mobilised just before declaration of war. Eventually we joined the BEF in France in January, 1940. We spent the next three to four months working on defences in the Douai/Lille area which, of course, when it all happened, was rapidly bypassed! We were moved up to the Belgian border early in May, but it was on 10th May 1940 when Germany made its move and, so far as I was concerned, I am still somewhat amazed at the happenings and experiences of the following three to four weeks.

I think that around that time luck took a hand in things that happened to me. Firstly a change of NCO led to my being moved to headquarters section driving a stores lorry. Had I remained with my Field Section undoubtedly I would have been captured, along with all my other friends. After considerable confused movement we were told to abandon our vehicles some two days' walk from the coast and so joined the stream of troops of various countries together with so many refugees, all en route and away from the advancing Germans.

As night approached it was decided that we should try to get some rest in a barn near the road. A fellow driver – Les Howard – and myself decided that we would try the hayloft and sleep we did, such that when we eventually woke up everybody else had gone and it was just getting light. We quickly got our bits and pieces together and I started down the loft ladder. Suddenly I froze as I heard the barn door creak as it was opened and I quite expected the worst. In fact, a voice said, 'Oh! There you are!' Our quartermaster, orderly room sergeant, and a French liaison officer had come back to find us. Luck again! We pressed on as fast as we could but didn't catch up with the rest of the section, and entered the outskirts of Dunkirk about 10am on the second day. The French officer disappeared into an empty building, I think a school, and came out with a large pot of cold coffee and a bowl of sugar. I tell you, it was nectar! We wended our way through damaged and burning buildings and eventually came to the seafront when an amazing scene of men, vehicles and equipment all over the beach and foreshore met our eyes. I remember taking shelter in a basement bookshop during one of the Stuka raids. Looking back I think how stupid it was because we wouldn't have stood a

chance if the building had been hit!

Our French officer decided he would leave us to report to any French unit he could find and suggested that we continue to walk towards the harbour. We came to an RASC lorry where the crew were issuing corn beef and biscuits and that was the first food we had for three days. All I can remember is enjoying that food whilst sitting on the steps which surrounded a statue. Was it Blériot's? All I remember is that it was a statue. Shortly after resuming our 'stroll along the prom' a naval officer perched on top of a beach hut shouted for us to join a line of troops sitting on the sand and almost as soon as we joined the queue we were up and moving towards the harbour mole. We could see the oil tanks across the harbour entrance burning and pushing out thick smoke that certainly hindered the Stukas, but suddenly a flight appeared and started to scream down to offload their bombs and machine-gun the beach. I recall we had dropped off the mole and on to the beach and I did my best to emulate the ostrich! One sight, however, left me astonished. I was lying on the sand below the mole wall and looking across the harbour entrance, I saw two figures run for cover into a building and then within seconds it disappeared in a sheet of flame and smoke from a direct hit. Even today I cannot really explain my thoughts at that time.

After the raid we clambered up on the mole again and walked on, balancing on single planks in places where it had been hit. We then embarked on what I gathered was a Scottish pleasure steamer. It might have been called the *Lochgarry*? We cast off and moved from the mole at about 3.30pm. Such was my short period in Dunkirk. Luck again!

But our troubles were not completely over. Once clear of the shore we found ourselves in the company of a destroyer and a small Dutch coaster. Two or three times the Stukas came in, despite the firing from the destroyer. We were fortunately on the top deck and there was a certain fascination even then in watching the damn things screaming down at us to release their bombs and open up with machine guns. I remember saying to Les that it was amazing that they did not hit us and he casually replied, 'No, but the funnel looks like a bloody pepperpot.'

One Stuka was hit and the pilot bailed out and the coaster picked him up. The suggestions from those on our deck as to what they should do with him I leave to your imagination! After a while things quietened down and the destroyer came alongside, wished us luck, and went off at full speed. We pulled along at half speed – apparently a near-miss at the stern had damaged one of the propellor shafts. I think it was about one o'clock in the morning when we arrived at Dover. I am sure many of us didn't realise we were coming back to England but thought we would just go down the French coast to reform and resume the fight. Little did we know what had happened!

I recall the fantastic work that was put in by the Salvation Army, the Church Army and the WVS, and practically every other organisation you could think of, in producing sandwiches and mugs of steaming tea for us as we boarded the train soon after disembarking. We were all soon asleep. I recall waking just as it was getting light and realising that we were slowly moving through Reading station and I was home! We ended up at Blandford camp for a week or so and then rejoined our unit or rather what was left of it, at Monmouth. As we had all got split up, even Les and myself were thought to be missing. However, we were quickly given some pay, a rail warrant and sent off straightaway on leave. I remember having a drink in the local with the family and my much older sister remarking that the 'boy' had gone away but the 'man' had come back. Some of the events had certainly left their mark on a twenty-year-old I think.

Perhaps as a postscript I must say that as my grand-daughter and grandson have grown up I have tried to explain to them, when they are watching *The A-Team* or the like, that they should realise that real bombs and bullets hurt! But looking back, compared to many, I had an extremely easy trip over. Luck again?

Peter P. Kingsley, Ipswich, Suffolk

I was stationed on a farm near Louvain in Belgium in early 1940. I was a corporal in the South Wales Borderers, and our unit was a standby unit, ready to deploy anywhere as the need arose. So we were all virtually on duty twenty-four hours a day, and we had very little sleep. I was in a slit trench on my own when the first attack came. It came first from aircraft, and then I heard the rumble of the tanks, and then everything went quiet and I must have dozed off because when I awoke there was not one of my unit around me. They had all gone.

I didn't know whether the Germans had passed or not. All I knew was that the sun rose in the east, and so I must go west, and so I started to walk rapidly westwards. On my way I saw a lot of people away in the distance and I kept out of sight until night fell. I snatched a few hours' sleep in an old barn and then carried on, still westwards. I had no idea where I was, but I guessed that I was heading the right way.

On the second day I met up with a Sergeant Parsons who was in the Royal Engineers. He was also on his own, having lost all his platoon, either missing or killed. But what he did have was a fifteen-hundredweight truck which was OK by me! He said if I helped him I could ride in the truck with him. His job was to destroy three bridges, one at Geraardsbergen over the River Dendre, then the bridge at Courtrai over the River Leie, and if there was any powder left he was then to destroy the bridge over the Ijzer at Bergues. At least I now knew where I was heading!

That night we placed eight charges on the bridge. Two were on the uprights and six on the girders. I was anxious to get away, I can tell you, but the sergeant said we must make sure the bridge was destroyed. However, all went well and the two butresses were blown to bits and the whole bridge fell into the river. There was no way then that the Germans were going to drive into Geraardsbergen. We drove all that night although we could not travel fast owing to the road being blocked all the time with carts and bikes etc. But we managed to get to Courtrai by daybreak.

I remember I was very very hungry and the sergeant said to look out for food. I went up to the front door of a large château and knocked and a lady came to the door in a nightgown. My French was not good, neither was her English, but I managed to convey my hunger and she went into the house and returned with two large French loaves and a pound of cheese, and a jar of pickles and

four bottles of wine! She asked how far away were the Germans and I said I wasn't sure but not more than fourteen miles. I shall never forget that feast. It was the best I had for months!

Courtrai was very busy, everybody rushing here and there, but me and the sergeant got on with our work and we had it all set up by three o'clock. Then a British Guards officer came up to us and told us to hold everything until all his men came over. And they came in 'dribs and drabs'. By the time they had passed over both the sergeant and me were getting 'itchy feet' and we finally blew the bridge about nine o'clock that night and we then had to scrounge some petrol off the Guards' captain!

Now we had only four limpets left for the bridge between Poperinge and Bergues and the sergeant said it would not be enough, but there was no more to be had. When we got to the Ijzer the bridge was massed with people, soldiers, trucks, carts, bikes and even prams, and again we had to wait until the traffic eased. We had placed our Burrowite limpets all together to make the greatest impact. This Burrowite was marvellous stuff. It takes the strongest form of resistance and it blasts into whatever it is up against. There was a clock mechanism on these, so we timed them for 9.30 that night, and we got the hell out of there quickly, not waiting to see the result of our work. Everyone was hurrying to Dunkirk, that's the only word you could hear.

Then we had our first bit of bad luck. The truck got stuck in a ditch, and we had to abandon it. I was sorry to see it going up in smoke and we had to walk every step into Dunkirk, which was pandemonium. So the sergeant and myself went down to the beach straight away. We kept on going until we were out of the crowd because they were all bunched together and sitting targets. When we were down beyond the dunes we spotted a boat about half a mile out, and so we shouted and waved until it saw us and came in just before dark. We waded out to it and clambered aboard. It was called *The Barnacle* and was skippered by a Mr Whitaker. All together we numbered twelve, and we set off for Ramsgate.

How we got there I shall always ponder. The boat was an old one and the engine was misfiring, and it creaked at every wave, but we made it to Ramsgate and as soon as I landed I kissed the ground and the sergeant said to give it another kiss for him as well. So I did! Myself and the sergeant parted company at Ramsgate, me to return to my unit which was being reformed at Ascot, and the sergeant to go up to Redcar to his unit. I have never seen or heard of him since.

When I met up with my unit in Ascot they were all

astonished to see me alive. Everyone thought I had bought it when they had last seen me in a slit trench at Louvain, but I was only sleeping so, as you can see, I was one of the lucky ones. Later in the war I got wounded but that's quite another story!

John Jones, Builth Wells, Powys

After we landed in France our convoy route eventually followed through Belgium and along the roads of Roubaix, Menen, Poperinge, Ypres, Oudenaarde and Kemmel and so along to Brussels. The Germans were invading Belgium and France at a fast rate and when we were going up through these areas the German airborne troops were baling out in the fields left and right of our convoy. This was our first sight of airborne troops and parachute landings. Where they went to nobody knew. It appeared that their object was to intercept and cut us off from the coastal ports.

We continued our convoy route and [were] eventually on the road to Louvain, which is east of Brussels. We progressed several kilometres in an easterly direction but had to turn back to Brussels where we virtually stayed put in our lorries as a base but spent two or three days 'rounding up' and seeking out on foot German fifth columnists. We handed some over to the 'safe custody' of the Belgian police.

From then on it was 'escape' to the coastal area of Dunkirk. The Germans were rapidly advancing in large numbers and there were no French or Belgian forces to be seen. Somehow we had instructions to concentrate on getting to the Dunkirk area. About half-way between Brussels and Dunkirk we received an order, by way of a motorcyclist despatch rider, to destroy all our vehicles, equipment and stores. Apart from the workshop vehicles, others contained defensive and assault stores, explosives and land mines. We pulled into a field, parked the vehicles close together, and after removing anything useful to ourselves, fixed explosive charges. There were more than was really necessary and it destroyed them all, including all the equipment and stores.

Then came the scramble to the coastal area. About thirty miles to go and all on foot. We mostly sheltered under hedgerows or where there was any cover by day, and walked along the roads and lanes at night. Except, that is, for when there was no obvious air attacks. The Germans kept passing by. Small cars and motorcycle combinations with machine guns always on the alert. On one occasion we had to take shelter in a farmyard, so we climbed up on top of a stack of baled straw in the middle of the yard area. The Germans went round our stack several times and then questioned the farmer at the farmhouse. He must have known we were there, as when we arrived a light went out in his house. But then the Germans departed. It was a narrow escape.

We continued after dark and made slow progress by helping each other along. I was a young man of twenty-five. We had others in our little group who had served in the 1914–18 war and some others were not so physically strong. After walking all night for two or three days we finally arrived at the centre of the promenade at Dunkirk. We had virtually carried two or three of our group between us because their legs had given in. Our unit as a whole was scattered everywhere and some had not even made it into the town.

We walked along the seaside front and beach to Bray-Dunes, supposed to be the expensive suburb of Dunkirk. And then a person, very tall and smart and with an arrogant manner and a German accent but in the uniform of a British major, came up and told us to get back into the land away from the beach as there would not be any ships for us. He turned out to be a German fifth column agent, but we never took any notice of him, because he did not appear to be helping our objective. He was too clean and tidy to be one of us. Cutting across the low-lying fields before getting to the beach we were heavily attacked by German fighter-bomber planes and we were very lucky to make it to the beach. Many never did. After two days on the beach, waiting and looking out to sea for any boat, we were instructed to clear inland again. Because of the air attacks and no shelter and no sign of any boats this time we did go back to the promenade and down to the basement of a hotel and sat quiet on boxes that had been left behind by the unfortunate proprietor.

All long the seafront the hotels were deserted. There was still no boat in sight, so being hungry we went for a walk along the beach from Bray-Dunes to Dunkirk harbour to see what we could find. We found abandoned army ambulances on the beach and had a good feed of tinned cherries and Carnation milk. Someone had used the flat-top ambulances when the tide was up to make a landing stage to a ship and then, naturally, just sailed away! The cherries and milk were very good. We returned to Bray-Dunes and lined up in proper order again on the beach to walk into the sea up to our necks to get a boat as some had appeared on the horizon and some smaller craft ventured to come in closer. We had two or three days of this procedure, taking shelter in the dunes when the ships had sailed off elsewhere and were not available to us, or had been sunk, or when there was an air attack. We must have entered in and out of the sea about ten times altogether.

We were an easily visible target. Before leaving the hotel basement for our final line-up in the sea I was talking in the basement to another young person (not of our unit) and he said to me, 'Is your name Stribley from

Portsmouth?' He turned out to be the young brother of a boy who was at school with me. He knew my younger brother better. After dodging through several more air attacks and five days on the beach we had the luck to get in a naval rowing boat. It was a scramble to get in the boat and we were soon pulled up and we were sitting all around the gunwales, about twenty-five to thirty men – grossly overloaded but somehow still afloat! The tide was going out fast. Because of the shallow water the sailor rowed us out to another motor launch and then by this launch to a minesweeper that had just appeared on the skyline. We both sailed towards each other and eventually we scrambled on board the deck of HMS *Halycon*. The other boat we were expecting to get on, I believe was HMS *Skipjack*, which I believe was later sunk. Another narrow escape! Several ships in the actual harbour were sunk. That included a hospital ship which had just taken on a large number of walking wounded. It was near the Dunkirk mole.

The sailors on the *Halycon* made us as comfortable as could be. They helped us move around the deck and supplied a limited amount of dry clothing and a welcome cup of hot tea. We had already just dumped our rifles which we had hung on to up to now, on the deck. Before getting on to the *Halycon* an army officer who had been attached to our unit was so 'exhausted' he refused to get into the rowing boat. Another sergeant had to threaten him with his revolver as he was holding up the evacuation of the beach. Eventually we bundled him into the boat. After dodging through several air attacks the *Halycon* steamed round the harbour area and picked up many more survivors.

We had a chaplain who was attached to our unit and we had carried him in turn for about the last ten miles on our shoulders. He was frail and weak and lost his 'sense of direction'. When we arrived in Dunkirk near the harbour approaches we had to leave him and we were very fortunate in being able to hand him over to some medical troops but we never saw him again. I wondered later on, whether he was on that hospital ship in the harbour, but I cannot remember who he was.

Before leaving the beach it happened that another army chaplain came along from the Dunkirk town area and into the dunes and men who were there collected together around him and the chaplain conducted a short non-denominational service.

It seemed an eternity before the *Halycon* turned her bow towards England. It was from then on a comparatively peaceful trip across the Channel – only two air raids and no damage. After about three hours we docked and tied up in Dover harbour. A hospital train was waiting at the docks and we were glad and thankful to sit in peace and quiet with hot tea and buns provided by the WVS ladies and the Red Cross.

Then we were off – up and around the London area and down to the Oxford area and so on to Tidworth camp in Wiltshire where a majority of our unit had somehow managed to reassemble like a lot of homing pigeons! We never all came back across the Channel on the same boat. It was a miraculous achievement that somehow or other we all finished up together.

Leon G. Stribley, Hitchin, Hertfordshire

I was sent to France with the British Expeditionary Force and was a driver in the 13th Troop Carrying Company of the Royal Army Service Corps. We had quite a job, I can tell you, in bringing back British troops when the German army broke through Belgium and northern France. I can remember that, without any warning, the whole company was suddenly assembled in a field and the commanding officer told us that it was now to be every man for himself and to abandon our vehicles and make our way to Dunkirk. Looking back, we owed our safe journey on foot to the company sergeant major because the officers had disappeared!

The oil tanks burning gave off smoke that could be seen from miles around. It was as we came into Dunkirk that our company got broken up and I was left on my own. It was afternoon when a Sherwood Forester infantryman said, 'Can I keep you company?' and I must say

I was pleased to have him along with me. We shared a foxhole and saw the German aircraft firing at the troops at the beach and also trying to bomb the ships. When they dropped bombs on the beach it appeared to be a more muffled sound on penetrating the sand.

Whilst on the beach we watched the troops at the water's edge in quite orderly manner waiting to get away. However, we decided to wait longer because mass queueing gave the German air force a better target and we felt our chances would be better if we waited.

The troops were by now thinning out in the area where we watched but of course this operation was taking place over many kilometres of beach. May I say that the beach where we were had sand dunes, then the beach, and then a shallow approach of sea and so, as people were being taken away, troops were wading out with rifles above their heads with a grim determination to reach their objective.

Suddenly on the horizon we saw a larger craft making its way towards us and we decided we would have a go. It anchored quite a distance from the beach and then a motorised craft made its way towards the beach and we knew by now that the procedure was to wade out to meet it. When we got to a big ship it turned out to be HMS *Wakeful* which was an old destroyer. When I was on board I was told to go to the bows of the ship and down a few wooden steps beneath the deck where we were given cocoa in our mess tins and a bacon sandwich which I can tell you was the Ritz after what we had been through recently.

HMS *Wakeful* stood by picking up troops for many more hours and finally we set sail with about six hundred and fifty on board. It was now late evening and I hung my greatcoat, respirator and steel helmet on a nail and we sat quietly by the light of a single light bulb. Then we heard the news that we were going for England, and we were surprised because we thought we were being taken further down the coast and by that time we were all in good spirits because we were returning home and we were in the hands of the navy.

Unfortunately that soon came to an end after we had been sailing for a short time because she was then hit by a torpedo in midships, and was very soon left with the bows and stern in the air almost like a letter V. The single light that we had went out and so we made our way up the wooden steps which were now at a crazy angle to find the deck a huge slide. Although it was dark the sea was strangely illuminated but it was silent, with the exception of other survivors, but we had no life jackets and only thirty of the people on that boat were saved.

Apparently most of them were trapped and didn't have any chance of survival.

Names were not being taken when we boarded the ship and so I wonder if the relatives of troops who died that night were told that their sons and brothers and fathers died in France or Belgium. Because there were no records taken we can only speculate as to their fate, and even after all this time that still worries me.

After being in the sea for some time I then saw some coloured lights near to me and two sailors in a rowing boat came and, with some effort, picked me out of the water. I was put on board a smaller naval vessel but I don't know its name. I was given some blankets and a tot of rum and I stripped off my wet clothes and I can still remember shivering and my teeth chattering. I was twenty years old but I would get over it!

At early dawn I was told to go to the deck to be transferred to another boat. I had only a blanket to wear but as I got on board the new ship it was a tremendous sight. It was a cruiser named HMS *Calcutta*. Her guns were blazing at the sky and I can remember the pride that I felt in the British navy and the way they were going about their job in bringing more troops back from the beach. Yes, I was back at Dunkirk again! No words can describe my feelings at that time, but neither can they describe the dedication that was shown by the navy and all the small-boat owners during the evacuation of Dunkirk.

Forty-nine years later, in 1989, I wrote to *Searchline* on television asking if they could find a sailor who owned some white shorts which he had given to me on HMS *Calcutta* to supplement all the clothing that I had abandoned. I had kept the shorts as a souvenir and they had his name printed inside and it was a Mr Young from Liverpool. I have been in contact with him since.

Another sailor who was on HMS *Wakeful* also got in touch with me and he tells me that at the time of the attack he was going to the toilet and so was in a different place than he would have been and he was able to escape! He told me he must be the luckiest person in the world. His name is Mr Stanley Crabb and he lives in London. I also heard from a Mr Spicer of Bracklesham Bay in Sussex whose brother served on HMS *Wakeful* and died, as did the brother of a Mrs Barnard from Newcastle.

It is all very sad and I often think [of] what happened and how I was one of the lucky ones.

Stanley Patrick, Kettering, Northamptonshire

I was in the regular army when war broke out, as an infantryman in the Royal Berkshire Regiment. I was stationed at a place called Arras which was near the Belgian border. When the German offensive started in May, 1940 I was just about to go home on a spot of leave to Blighty, and I didn't realise then that I would be going home shortly in any case but via Dunkirk! Chased home, to be exact.

As soon as the German attack started we were rushed right through Belgium where we got a hero's welcome from the Belgian people. They cheered us and showered us with cigarettes and chocolates and flowers and I can tell you there were plenty of kisses from the women! Anyway we were rushed right through Belgium but I think that we came back faster than we went.

When the Germans started to attack we had to retreat, and I remember going through a forest where it was all uphill and we had to run carrying all our equipment including ammunition boxes. It was agony. We came to a canal where it was quiet for about a day or two, and then the Germans caught up with us and gave us everything they had got and I remember that was my baptism of actual warfare. The shelling was frightening. A shell landed in one end of the trenches that I was in and killed four of my mates. We had to stay in that trench for many hours. Then we got orders to withdraw, but before we withdrew our sergeant told us to put our mates, who had been killed, in sandbags and get their identity discs from around their necks. That was the most sickening part of it because they were in pieces. That was my first experience of death but not my last.

I don't know where it was, but we were retreating for days and nights when a message was received to make our way back to Dunkirk as fast as we could. Quite honestly that was the first time I had heard even the name of Dunkirk. We didn't even know where it was and before we found it we had a few brushes with the Germans on the way. I remember one instance we were in a farmhouse under attack when our two-inch mortar finally ran out of ammunition. The lads wanted to fire at the machine guns across a field but all they had left were smoke bombs and so we ran away from the farmhouse and in frustration they just slung the gun in the general direction of the Germans!

I was on Dunkirk beaches for about three days and I must say that everybody that got away from those beaches must have had a charmed life. The only fighting we could do was a rearguard action to allow the rest of the British Expeditionary Force to withdraw. It's funny, looking back, but I remember that when the Stuka dive-bombers kept coming down and machine-gunning, all you could do was to put your head in the sand and somehow you never worried about your backside being hit.

I finally got on a boat but I remember that we had to wade out some way to it because the jetty had been bombed and I think that the name of the boat I got on was the *Isle of Man*. It wasn't a big boat and as soon as I got on it I looked around for some space but I couldn't see any so I just flopped down where I was standing and it wasn't long before I fell asleep regardless of what was happening around me. However, I was soon to regret it because afterwards I found out I was right underneath a Bofors gun and it opened up whilst I was asleep, and frightened the life out of me!

Finally we reached Folkestone and there were so many ships in the harbour that we had to anchor alongside two more so that when we got off the ship we had to get on the other two ships before finally we were landed. There we were met by nurses and the people of the town handing out cigarettes and tea, cakes and chocolates. There were a lot of stretcher cases on our boat and we were all put straight on a train to get away from the town.

I was hoping we were going to London but it went straight through and we finished up at Halifax where we were marched to a big empty factory and we stayed there enough time to have a good old army stew and then told to get back on to the train again, not knowing where we were going. It was only a short trip to Huddersfield where we were met by coaches and buses and private cars and taxis to take us all to the public baths where we enjoyed a good swim and clean-up.

After that we were taken to the local police station because we were being put in civil billets until our units were sorted out. I had a mate with me from Stepney who I had met on the beaches at Dunkirk and so we stayed together from then on. While we were all being sorted out at the police station, my mate suddenly spotted his brother whom he hadn't seen since leaving England and I can still remember the joy and excitement on his face at that time.

I was billeted with a Mr and Mrs Earnshaw of Gledholt Road, Huddersfield and this was my most trea-sured moment of the war. They looked after me as though I was their own son and I shall never forget them. They gave me everything they had and treated me like a lord and I shall never forget the time when, having a bath one night, Mr Earnshaw noticed I had a wound on my leg and he told his wife and she dressed it for me. She used to knock on my bedroom door to wake me in the morning and I would answer her, but after she noticed the wound, when the knock came a voice shouted, 'Stay where you are, I'm coming in,' and it was the maid with the breakfast tray, so I had my breakfast in bed and was told to stay there.

They made a right fuss of me but everyone had

forgotten that an army sergeant would sometimes come round and knock on the doors where the soldiers were billeted and tell them to parade on a grass verge at the top of the road. Apparently when the sergeant knocked on my door Mrs Earnshaw came out and told him to go away as I was sick and I couldn't parade that day. Can you imagine that happening in the army!

We had to go to this parade while the army sorted out who was missing, killed or taken prisoner and to get as much information as they could about them. I think we must have lost about three hundred men from our unit on the Dunkirk beaches. I still think a great deal about Mr and Mrs Earnshaw and I may sound silly, but for people like that I would have faced a hundred Dunkirks. They were wonderful people.

Ted Hatchman, Dagenham, Essex

After a two-day journey by train from Britanny, we arrived in northern France, somewhere near Lille. It was night-time and as we were unloading in some station yard we had our first session of bombing. From there we were given the job of keeping the roads clear for the military. I think it was up near the Belgian border. After that all I seemed to remember is marching everywhere and anywhere, getting bombed and machine-gunned in the process!

My first contact with the Germans was in the Carvin–Seclin area. We were put in a defensive position on a river or a canal, and near us were some railway sidings. The bridge across the canal had been blown. It was just sagging in the middle. It was here that I saw my first Germans. I was platoon runner at the time so when the sergeant went on a recce he took me with him. The Germans were on the other side of the canal amongst some factory buildings and we were on the top of a railway embankment when I saw them.

I remember I started jumping up and down like a bloody two-year-old, pointing them out to my sergeant and shouting, 'Germans!' The next thing I knew he had pushed me down the embankment saying, 'Get down you silly bugger!' We were there for about twenty-four hours, mortar-bombed and shelled etc and then we got ordered to get out. We needed no second telling. We did!

We rejoined the company and saw a lot more of the French countryside as we got our usual quota of bombing etc. Marching here and marching there, I can't remember much about places or dates, but it was about this time when I lost contact with my company.

Later on two NCOs and myself, with an officer, were told to take a load of barbed wire to a wood three or four miles away. Whilst unloading the wire a German spotter plane came over. We thought it was a Dutch plane and waved to him! The officer went back to the company, telling us to wait in the wood until the main body of men arrived. It didn't! But we hadn't been in the wood long when three dive-bombers plastered it. All of that effort for just three of us and a pile of bloody barbed wire!

By this time there was such chaos we were just wandering around, and after two or three days we came upon a Royal Engineers bridging company who were billeted in a large house. The area seemed to be alive with activity but one of the NCOs told me to see if I could scrounge some tea for them. They went up some steps into a large room and I went off and found what had been the cookhouse and made some tea. The cooks and everyone else were packing up, and the engineers were blocking the road with their bridging equipment.

Finally, after some time I got the tea and went back to the room where I had left them, only to find that they had vanished! I kept looking for them but no luck! The engineers then arrived outside and kept shouting for me to come on, as the Germans were here, so I got on the lorry and went with them. Later on, I found that the men I had gone to get the tea for had all been captured in that room whilst I was away getting it, and had spent four and a half years in German prison camps. It was certainly my luckiest cup of tea!

Anyway it seems these engineers had been ordered to make for Dunkirk. On the outskirts of Dunkirk we were stopped by some Military Police, who told the driver to dump the truck in a field. There were hundreds of them, or so it seemed. They then sent the engineers on their way into Dunkirk, and me being in the bloody infantry had to stay! When they had a good-sized crowd of infantry (all types and different regiments) we had to go with an officer to a canal or dyke where we were part of the rearguard action. The only problem was there wasn't much action.

We were there about a day and then told to get into the town and down to the docks. I went through the town and it was in ruins. It was still being bombed and shelled. One night-time we were told to get on to the mole, which was a long jetty going out into the sea. It was badly damaged by shells or bombs. As I was going along it I heard someone shout, 'Here mate.' Looking down I saw a small boat. I got down and in the boat was an RN rating and a civvy. I think there were about eight or nine in the boat when they took us out to sea, and put us on a larger boat. I was the first on, and told to go down to the hold which was empty.

I sat down and I was out like a light! When I woke up the hold was full of soldiers both British and French. I got up on deck which was full of Frenchmen, and it was by now daylight. Some Hurricanes flew by towards France and I remember one of them dipping its wings in salute and there in front of us was Blighty. We landed at Ramsgate to a right royal welcome. Why, I don't know. Cigs, tea, chocs, etc. They posted cards home for us, then on a train to Shrivenham in Wiltshire and what a rest we had there.

Jim Hall, Hinckley, Leicestershire

I was in the 5th Northants and for some reason I had been appointed 'sniper' and given the job of going out for a few hours at a time carrying a rifle and a few rounds of ammunition to stop German snipers coming through. The Germans preferred to work in twos. My job was to try and find them coming through and if possible see them off. I was the only sniper in our company, and British snipers (unlike the Germans) worked in ones. As far as I was concerned, it was easier to work in ones anyway. The reason was that you were not bothering about looking after the other man, and as long as you knew your own job it was up to you to look after yourself. As a sniper, you should be able to do this.

There were no particular rules to obey. You were there. Your job was to stop other enemy snipers from

coming through who were
getting ahead of our troops
and picking them off. My job
was to make sure that none of
them got there, and I tried
obviously to do that as effectively as possible. I did hit
German snipers. I can remember roaming around in a village

that had been evacuated and suddenly feeling a movement. It was a 'feeling' of movement somewhere ahead
and not a sighting. Knowing that the Germans worked
in twos, the first thing I had to do was to find out where
his mate was. I knew from experience that there would
be a 'mate' somewhere, and I wanted to know where the
second man was before I went for the first and gave away
my own position.

Assuming that there would be two, I used to look
round carefully to try and get an idea of what position
the other bloke would be assuming. If you saw them
moving from one house to another you would know that
his mate should be fifty yards behind or fifty yards in
front because they always kept in sight of each other.
You wouldn't have far to look before you could see the
second movement.

I reckon I found and hit nine or ten pairs of German
snipers, so that in total there were probably eighteen to

twenty men. I remember one specific incident. It was fairly typical.

A chappie had got himself up on a roof, knocked a few slates away and he was hidden up there, overlooking the village square. Anybody walking into the village square had had it – he'd got a good field of fire. He was roughly in the centre of one side of the square and his mate was in the corner, and they effectively covered the whole square that way. The way they positioned themselves they were also protecting each other.

I shot the first one from a bedroom window. He had had a shot at one of our officers in the square. I saw roughly where the flash came from, so I went up into a house opposite and shot him from the bedroom window. Then, of course, his mate had a go at me but he was too late. I shot him also.

I found the second man's position by the flash of his rifle as well. He hadn't waited until he saw me. That was the thing. I was firing out of the bedroom window and there was only the end of my rifle at the window. He saw the flash and must have assumed that I was a lot nearer to the window than I was. By firing he gave himself away so that was his lot because I was able to fire straight into the corner of the square, straight into where he was.

Their bodies weren't retrieved so far as I know. We didn't bother about that at the time. The first one I had shot was hanging out of the roof and then suddenly he dropped forward. I didn't bother even looking at the second one.

I have to say, though, that the accuracy of the German snipers was good. Their failing was that if they didn't get you with the first shot then their firing got very inaccurate and they seemed to lose their nerve entirely.

Edgar Rabbets, Boston, Lincolnshire

Author's note: Below is an extract from the diary of William Leslie (Digger) Kerley, maintained at Dunkirk contrary to King's Regulations. This has been reproduced from the original diary and some words are missing due to being illegible.

20th May: Tired, very hectic day. Shifted. Returned shells whistled overhead. Heavy guns rumbling all day. Set Dis [means wireless set unserviceable]. Got good coat.

21st May: Heavy shells last night. Guns on all day. Very hot. Fixed up loud speaker in set. Had letters from home and Margaret. Pleased indeed. Saw Roulon bombed to blazes. Pretty horrible.

22nd May: Rain for first time for weeks. Left battlements for good. 2 corps HQ. Pinched gallons of port and wine in Armentières, also lemonade. Slept in open, a bit drunk. All kinds of liquor. Armentières is hell.

23rd May: Arment. Bombed to blazes. Retreated once more. Set stocked with wine. Leaving here again. Gunned hill. Left 10. Nice town, Arment. Jack and I first in Brewery. Burst door.

24th May: Very hot. Slept in straw cart. Armentières bombed to billy-ho. Not much food. Can see town burning. Bags of smoke. Saw cuckoo. Refugees all on road ... mentally deficient let loose.

25th May: Scores of bombers raided Armentières. Left farm six o'clock evening. Arrived another farm eight. Had supper in farm. Took place of ditched lorry for 5th Div. Damn it. Hazzybrouke Woods.

26th May: Three o'clock in the morning. Passed thro' Arment. Burning. Scrounged more drink. Arrived 3.30. Good farm. Heard nightingales lovely. Bombed farm at nine o'clock. Worst yet for me. Hazzybrouke Woods. Thought we were finished when bombers came. *Memo.* Rotten here. Bull frogs croaking all day. Bombers bombing. Me working. What the hell.

27th May: Guns and bombs. No sleep yet. Tons of bombing near us. 11.30 night. Couldn't get control. We are nearly finished here. Enemy very near only small gap left. Rain. I have pretty low feeling.

28th May: Guns very near. Low ceiling keeps bombers away. Thank goodness. Retreated. Saw some dead friends. Awful wrecks. Almost surrounded by enemy. Enemy right round us. Path broken by …(?)

29th May: Shelled on road. Dunkirk. Joined retreating convoy. Dumped set. Saw horrible bodies around. Came to shore for destroyers to take us off. Bombed all day. Narrow escape. Saw old mate from Catt [Catterick].

30th May: Too much sand about for my liking. Never did like seaside. Expected to go last night. Boats didn't turn up. Am going from shore to a shared dugout with officer. Endy, Dubby and Jock missing. Left Dunkirk 01.30 morning. Lots of men killed on mole. Shelled to blazes.

31st May: Arrived Margate. Lovely to be back. Had some grub. Went to Doncaster. To sleep pretty fast. Good rest. What a change from three days ago. Only Corps Sig here. Palled up with RE and ASC blokes.

1st June: Paid ten bob. Went out good fun in Doncaster. Fairground, good dames. Good beer. Good everything. Good weather.

2nd June: Had a (?) lady's house tea and supper. Game of darts etc. Not bad dames around here. *Memo.* Worst week and yet best week I've ever spent in life as yet.

William L. (Digger) Kerley, Loughborough, Leicestershire

CROSSES

Each life has its crosses
And each soldier has his share
From a trip across the ocean
To an envied *Croix de Guerre.*

There are many crosses by the censor
Far too many so it seems
There are crosses in his letters
From the girlfriend of his dreams.

There's a cross that's worn by heroes
Who have faced a stream of lead
There's a cross when he is wounded
And a cross when he is dead.

But there's also a cross of mercy
That quite a few may own
To a soldier it's a second
To that of God's alone.

It's a cross that's worn by women
When we see it we believe
We recognise an angel
By the 'Red Cross' on her sleeve.

Corporal Mitchell seated centre, Haute Kreis,
Elbing, Germany, June 1944

This poem was written by Corporal William Mitchell of the 2nd Battalion, The King's Royal Rifle Corps. He was captured at Dunkirk and wrote this poem whilst a prisoner at Stalag XXA in Germany. It was sent in by his wife, Peggy Mitchell of Letchworth, Hertfordshire.

Appendices

Further Evacuations

Editor's note: The original 1990 edition of the book contained letters detailing memories of other evacuations during WWII. Although they are not about the Dunkirk rescue, they are no less important and so we have also included them in this new edition.

Although I did not take part in the evacuation at Dunkirk, the following story will show that I was very much part of the evacuation.

While the main British force was engaging the enemy in what turned out to be the evacuation of Dunkirk, a rearguard action was in fact being waged further south-west. The units engaged in this action consisted mainly of the 51st Highland Division and some of the Brigade of Guards. The enemy had thrown a considerable force against our units, thereby lightening the numbers being used against the main British force. Although defending gallantly, the German forces were too much for us and we were being pressed further and further westward. During this time we lost thousands of men, either killed or taken prisoner. Even the major general of our division was taken prisoner but, sad to relate, he died in a prisoner-of-war camp. Eventually we were pushed into a little town on the west coast which was called St-Valéry-en-Caux. By this time our resistance had broken down and it was then every man for himself.

Along with some other soldiers, we found ourselves at the outskirts of the town near to a cornfield. Beyond the cornfield was the sea and we decided to go into the cornfield and keep our heads down and go towards the sea. I can remember that the cornfield was ablaze with poppies and when going through it, I saw a cottage to the right of us. I crept over to it and knocked at the door.

An elderly Frenchman appeared and I said to him in French, 'The Germans are back there, come with us.' He looked at me and replied, 'It doesn't matter,' and closed the door. As I passed the cottage window I saw a large French loaf on the sill, probably left by the baker. As I hadn't eaten for many hours I took possession of the loaf! On coming out of the cornfield I found I was practically on the seashore. I teamed up with the other soldiers and there on the seashore we shared the bread.

We were still under heavy fire from the Germans, taking shelter wherever possible and not knowing what was going to happen next. However after a few hours a ship loomed up on the horizon, but we were not sure what nationality it was. However as it came nearer we recognised it was the British destroyer HMS *Boadicea*. We were seen waving on the beach and a small boat was despatched.

As many as possible were taken on board, soldiers, French coastguards and civilians and then we headed for the *Boadicea*. When we were all safely on board we set off down the coast to look for any more stragglers. We had not gone far, just off Dieppe, when we were attacked by nine Stuka bombers. One of them made a direct hit, completely blowing up the engine room and killing all the engine-room crew. We were now completely out of action but we tried to lighten the boat by dumping all the ammunition over the side. We were still as far away as ever from being saved, but a Channel mist came down and prevented the Stukas from getting low enough to do any more damage.

All hope was not lost, as a few hours afterwards another ship appeared. This was the HMS *Bulldog*, a sister ship of the *Boadicea*. We were taken in tow and without further incident we landed at Southsea.

I am not jealous, and I certainly mean no disrespect at all those who were at Dunkirk, but I always feel annoyed and saddened as year after year one hears of the accolades being presented to the heroes of Dunkirk, and of their pilgrimage to the Dunkirk beaches. I understand and respect that. But one never hears a word about Saint-Valèry, or the sacrifices made by thousands to help make 'Dunkirk' possible. At the end of the day we were all really one and the same. Dunkirk, or Saint-Valèry. It was on June 13th when we landed at Southsea, about a fortnight after Dunkirk, but at no time do I ever read anything in the press of our action.

Bob Sharp, Barking, Essex

When the *Lancastria* was sunk on Monday 17 June 1940 it was one of the major disasters of World War Two. It's almost unheard of, but it has nevertheless been described by some as 'the greatest maritime disaster of the war'. I was one of the men who were there. At that time I was a sapper in the Royal Engineers. But at the time, due to the evacuation at Dunkirk already being such a tragedy, Churchill thought the British public had already had enough and it was kept quiet.

But now to the story.

Dunkirk was finished around about the end of May and we were still trying to get out of France. We eventually ended up in St Nazaire on the north-west coast of France, having stolen cars and vehicles of all types to get there. We arrived on Sunday 16 June and the Germans were bombing us, machine-gunning us and the docks – we had one hell of a night. Next morning, at about eight o'clock, small ships started taking us out to *Lancastria* which was lying about ten miles off St Nazaire. By a quarter to four in the afternoon the ship was fully loaded. Then at four o'clock, just after we moved off, a plane dived on us as part of a general attack and put an aerial torpedo right through the funnel of the ship. It was a fluke, but within minutes she had heeled right over. I was terrified and, with others, we decided to jump off and swim for it.

We had nowhere else to go. But at least we were free, in the water – better than being trapped in the ship. There were hundreds of men dying around us, drowning, and catching hold of our clothes. I went overboard with my vest, my underpants and my socks on. I was picked up about three hours later. All I had on by then was my singlet. A French minesweeper picked me up, along with eighty others. They fed us well, gave us brandy and transferred us, in midwater, to the British ship the *John Holt* which eventually took us back to Plymouth. When we arrived, I had just a blanket around me and it took me three months to get my feet clean after walking in oil and things like this. I was frightened, I can tell. I was only twenty at the time but I still think I was one of the lucky ones!

The *Lancastria* was a pleasure-going liner, pre-war. A very good ship, but she was totally overcrowded. There

were about nine thousand troops on board, including civilians.

As it happened we had got away from the beaches just in time. There were prisoners taken of course. The captain of the *Lancastria* had received orders to move some six hours before he actually set sail. He said, 'No. There are thousands of British troops in those docks and I intend to take them off.' Of course then she was sunk. Aerial torpedoed.

There was generally a feeling of optimism at St Nazaire but when the boat was hit and we were in the water we were totally dejected! We'd got to the stage where we didn't care if we died. We had a feeling of 'well, this must be it'.

When the ship was hit I was down in the dining room deciding whether to have something to eat or go and have a bath in the other floor! Suddenly the corner of the ceiling came down and I thought well, I can eat, I can have a bath any time, but I've got to get off this damn thing and I was three decks down! The stairs were collapsing. It was every man for himself. I was walking over people. They were walking over me. Eventually I got to the top and she must have been listing at least thirty-five degrees by then. I said to these two friends of mine from Leicester, the three of us, to get hold of a rope from one of the lifeboats that didn't make it and we did and swung ourselves out into the sea and swam for it, or at least kept afloat. We were in the sea about three hours. We were in a terrible state. Frightened. Ready to die. Fear was the worst part of it and the cold, but fear was the worst.

But when we got back to Plymouth all we were given was forty-eight hours' leave. And then we were issued with tropical kit. Then put on the train at Plymouth and after an hour or so we noted we were heading north, to Scotland. There we were, in a compound and all the tropical kit was taken off us and we ended up in the Faroe Islands near Iceland and there we were for about a year.

We travelled there, finally, by ship. I was on top deck all the way.

I was too frightened to go down below. And it was raining too. It was all pretty traumatic. It took me about three months to get over because a thing like that, well one does relive it many many times.

Looking back, when I say there were nine thousand troops and civilians, it's a very rough estimate. Between seven and nine thousand. No one knows exactly because there were quite a number of French, Belgians, civilians of all types. But we do know that only about twelve hundred were saved. So something in the region of seven thousand five hundred people died within an hour. For most it was a quick death, probably within an hour.

And yet, you know, it seems as though it only happened three months ago. I can remember every detail. Something I shall take to the grave, I expect.

Oddly enough, when I meet former mates we don't discuss it. We just talk about the good times we used to have while we were in France but very rarely we talk about the ship. Very rare. I meet some of the boys every year. We have a small reunion. We go to Buxton in Derbyshire. One of the survivors, he owned a hotel there and we stayed for the weekend and had a get-together and the *Lancastria* is very rarely mentioned. Amazing, isn't it.

It does upset me a bit sometimes about Dunkirk when the *Lancastria* isn't mentioned because I think the country as a whole should be told exactly what happened because there were a lot of brave men on that boat as well as at Dunkirk, and as I've said about seven thousand five hundred died in less than an hour. A terrible thing really. And it did affect my outlook on life. For example, during the war when they wanted volunteers for frogmen I thought that, 'Well, if I can swim that far, I can pass the frogman's test,' and I became one of six. Six of us passed a test for frogmen and I worked on the invasion in 1944 on Pluto (Petrol Line Under The Ocean) and we were actually working under the sea.

And there's one thing more; I have a more philosophical outlook on life now!

Reg Brown, Bedworth, Warwickshire

I was a young wife and mother with four children at the time of Dunkirk. I had two daughters and two sons, and we lived in Hull, and at the time my husband Harry was in France.

I didn't receive any replies to my letters and I was still awaiting for replies, one for over six weeks, when one day a policeman came to my house, and I began to think the worst. He came and said my husband had asked him to call as he hadn't received any letters from me and was wondering if we were all all right. He told me that my husband was in hospital in Sutton, Surrey with head wounds and shell shock. He was taken off the beaches on a boat called HMT *Lancastria*, which was sunk when a plane came in and dropped a bomb down the funnel.

He was thrown into the water with hundreds of others and he couldn't swim, but he told me he was going down for the third time when suddenly he was plucked up out of the water. He doesn't even remember how it all happened.

I wasn't even informed of anything that had happened to him.

The letters I had sent to him were forwarded on to him weeks later, and as a result of his injuries he was discharged from the army on 7 August 1940.

He never even got a pension! He arrived home around 3.15 and I was so pleased to see him because he was home. But would you believe it, that very night we were bombed and lost just about everything. But life goes on.

Florence Wilson, Tuxford, Newark, Nottinghamshire

Losses at Dunkirk

TROOPS

Killed, wounded and taken prisoner . . 68,111

Evacuated 338,226

EQUIPMENT

Stores and ammunition . . . . 500,000 tons

Rifles . . . . 90,000 tons

Field guns . . . . 2,472 tons

Bren guns . . . . 8,000 tons

Anti-tank guns . . . . 400 tons

Vehicles . . . . 63,879 tons

Motorcycles . . . . 20,584 tons

ROYAL NAVY

Destroyers 6

Personnel carriers 8

Sloops 1

Minesweepers 5

Trawlers. 17

Hospital ships 1

Lesser Naval vessels. 188

TOTAL LOST 226

DETAILS OF TROOPS EVACUATED

Date	From the beaches	From the harbour	Total evacuated	Sum total
27 May		7669	7669	7669
28 May	5930	11874	17804	25473
29 May	13752	33558	47310	72783
30 May	29512	24311	53823	126606
31 May	22942	45072	68014	194620
1 June	17348	47081	64429	259049
2 June	6695	19561	26256	285305
3 June	1870	24876	26746	312051
4 June	622	25553	26175	338226
Grand Totals:	98671	239555	338226	

Acknowledgements

It will be clear to the reader as you have finished reading this book that the individuals who have written their stories and impressions have reconstructed one of the greatest dramas of all time. No one knew it at the time, but the miracle of Dunkirk was to change the world from what it would otherwise have become.

Our thanks go to the following:

All who actually took part in the evacuation and by their writings have given us a unique insight of what happened to ordinary soldiers and sailors.

All those others who saw them as they returned, or assisted in some way, because your memories have shown how 'those at home' saw events and were affected by them.

All those who wrote to us of their experiences. The response we received was marvellous and our great regret is that space prevented us using them all. Thank you for the articles, books, documents and so much help and assistance freely given to us.

Stephen Gamble for his assistance and general advice which was much appreciated.

The Dunkirk Veterans' Association and their members and officials for willing assistance and advice that made our job so much easier.

Those who are often forgotten but without whom the book could not have been produced – the typists. To Shirley Cartwright, Margaret Young and Judy Crawshaw of Hinckley & Bosworth Borough Council, our ever grateful thanks. Also the 'girls' in reprographics with the council – Brenda Moore and Diane Curtis for 'churning it all out'. And to Ann Higgins for doing all the posting work on what must have seemed thousands of letters – because there were. And finally we mustn't forget Jane Stew, secretary to Frank, who ground her teeth sometimes, but still saw it all through. Thank you very much.

Our thanks to you all. We hope you now go on to enjoy this book.

Frank and Joan Shaw

Index

Entries in *italics* indicate photographs.

Aalst, Belgium 86
abandonment of vehicles 7,
    20, 34, 51, 57–8, 59, 64,
    87, 96, 100, 149, 198,
    200, 225, 257, 271, 272,
    279, 285, 298, 306, 310,
    313
Abbeville, France viii, ix, 96
Abercynon, South Wales 84
Adams, Major 165
air attacks (bombing and
    strafing) 7, 8, 16, 17–19, 21,
    34, 35, 36, 37, 41, 50, 52,
    55, 58, 60, 65, 69, 70, 72,
    75, 79, 82, 87, 97, 100,
    102, 103, 105, 106, 113,
    117, 118, 122, 123, 126,
    128, 131, 133, 137, 141,
    142, 149, 153, 154, 155,
    163, 165, 166, 170, 171,
    176, 179, 185, 186, 187,
    199, 201, 204, 206, 207,
    210, 211, 212, 218, 225,
    236, 248, 262, 263, 273,
    276, 279, 280, 281, 288,
    295, 301, 305, 309, 314,
    319–20, 322, 323, 324,
    330, 339, 340–1
    anti-aircraft fire and 9, 51,
    60, 89, 97, 135, 140, 166,
    207, 271
    on Dunkirk 7, 8, 14, 16, 20,
    21, 35, 37, 49, 60, 70,
    82–3, 110–11, 118, 123,
    126, 136, 140, 142, 155,
    163, 178, 200, 214, 215,
    263–4, 276, 278, 281–2,
    295, 300, 311, 314, 320,
    325, 331 *see also* Dunkirk
    on French towns 26, 28, 34,
    37, 64, 105–6, 118, 122,
    138, 163, 175, 209, 225,
    262, 329, 330
    Heinkels and *see* Heinkel
    losses from 155
    mental reactions to 5, 11, 18,
    87, 115, 132, 148, 170,
    220, 243, 345
    Messerchmitts and *see*
    Messerschmitt
    noise of 17, 44, 51–2, 102,
    168, 194
    on railways 116, 151
    refugees and 12, 41, 87, 100,
    117, 174, 262
    on schools 117, 212
    on shipping 7, 18–19, 22, 79,
    85, 103, 114–15, 119, 133,
    137, 142–4, 153, 154, 168,
    179, 206, 210, 212, 263–4,
    266, 273, 280, 286, 310,
    312, 340–6
    Stukas and *see* Stukas
    vehicle convoys and 20, 70,

100, 128, 131, 155, 186, 204, 272

alcohol 7, 29, 36, 46, 121, 138, 238, 288, 289, 302, 305, 329, 330

Aldershot, Hampshire 24, 69, 164, 224

Aldridge, Walsall 11

Allied High Command viii, ix

ambulances 6, 7, 96, 150, 199, 211, 241, 242, 243, 263, 265, 295, 310

American troops 199, 202, 203

Amesbury, Wiltshire 80, 113

Amiens, France 33

ammunition xiii, 12, 44, 51, 70, 81, 86, 95, 124, 127, 131, 146, 155, 158, 164, 187, 190, 225, 233, 252, 269–70, 272, 286, 293, 294, 318, 319, 326, 339, 347

anti-aircraft fire 51, 60, 89, 97, 135, 166, 207, 271

anti-tank rifle 42, 117, 135, 144, 205, 257, 347

Ardennes Forest viii

Armentières, France 26, 41, 99, 118, 125, 137, 138, 162–3, 329, 330

Armstrong, Colonel 'Nipper' 233

ARP wardens 83

Arras, France 20, 86, 94, 95, 316

artillery/shellfire xi, xiii, 10, 14, 16, 25, 28, 32, 41, 43, 44, 49, 56, 67, 68, 70, 71, 72, 81, 87, 93, 96, 97–8, 107, 115, 117, 119, 125, 127, 129, 147, 153, 157, 171, 176, 185, 186, 187, 188, 189, 193, 194, 199, 201, 204, 210, 212, 214, 215–16, 217, 218, 222, 225, 227–8, 230, 237, 247, 254, 262, 266, 269–70, 271, 272, 273, 274, 277, 278, 280, 281, 282, 284, 285, 286, 288, 292–3, 294, 318, 323, 325, 329, 331

ammunition dumps 94, 95, 187, 269

anti-aircraft 97

British guns 32–3

at Calais 225

at Carvin 117

at Cassel 70–1

at Dunkirk 16, 17, 25, 28, 49, 50, 68, 107, 153, 157, 188, 189, 206, 210, 214, 215–16, 222, 227, 237, 273, 274, 285, 286, 292–3, 325, 331

French horse-drawn columns 6, 127, 257–8

gas attacks 67, 288

at La Panne 171, 210

mental reaction to (shell shock) 11, 87, 243, 345

noise of 129, 157, 176, 212, 273

at Roubaix 288

Royal Artillery *see* British Army units

Royal Navy and 294

shipping and 10, 67, 119

spiking of guns 230, 281

Ascot , Berkshire 119, 306–7

Ash Station, Surrey 24

Ashford, Kent 107

Atlantic convoys 181–2

Bailleul, France 165, 166

Baker, Lieutenant 151, 152

Barley, Sidney 261, *261*

Barnacle, The 306

Bath, Avon 137, 203, 253
Battle of Britain, 1940 286
Bazeley, Wynne 174
Bedford vehicles 12, 25, 57, 108
Belgian Army 9, 34, 129–30, 308
  BEF and 246, 293
  at Dunkirk 9, 145, 297
  line begins to crumble 122
  retreat to Dunkirk 257
  surrender of 34, 66, 86
Belgium 51, 121, 211, 213, 226, 245, 246, 253–4, 262, 277, 284–5, 290, 292, 297, 303, 307, 313, 316, 318
  abdication of King Leopold 86
  BEF arrival greeted with celebration in 33, 69, 253, 318
  BEF withdrawal from 20, 113–14, 117, 129–30, 155
  borders 38, 57, 66, 86, 95, 116, 155, 209, 214, 245, 262, 298, 317, 322
  German army invades vii, viii, 4, 33, 76–7, 81, 122, 124, 150, 165, 185, 284, 307
  Maginot Line and 81
  police 307
  POWs marched through 202
  refugees 77, 87, 215, 257, 297, 343
  surrender of 34, 66, 122
  see also under individual area or place name
Belle Vue Amusement Park, Manchester 119
Ben-my-Chree 171
Benn, Anthony Wedgewood 243
Bergues, France 96, 98, 304, 305

Berkshire 25, 40, 76, 115, 207, 317
Berlin, Germany 69
Béthune, France 217
Bewdley, Worcestershire 174
billets 4, 5, 12, 39, 47, 64, 108, 120, 154, 158, 209, 239, 252, 281, 292, 321–2, 324
Billingham, Cleveland 91
biplanes 257
Blackburn, Lancashire 154
Blackpool, Lancashire 98–9
Blandford, Dorset 124, 200, 250, 251, 302
Blitz 208
'blitzkreig' 150
Boadicea, HMS 339
Bofors gun 135, 320
Bolton, Lancashire 20, 201
Boston, Lincolnshire 329
Bournemouth, Dorset 251
Bovington Camp, Dorset 241
Bray-Dunes, France 48, 126, 167, 285, 288, 309, 310
Bren guns 71, 72–3, 117, 188, 195, 231, 238, 239, 240, 254–5, 271, 272, 286, 294, 347
Brentford, Middlesex 182
Brighton Queen, HMS 139
British Army units:
  2 Survey Regiment, Royal Artillery 56–7
  3rd British Infantry Division 210, 245, 246, 251, 288
  3rd Royal Tank Regiment 224
  4th Infantry Division 55
  5th Battalion, Royal West Kent Regiment 124–5
  5th Infantry Division 150
  5th Northants 326
  6th Green Howards 132
  7th Armoured Division 69

7th Battalion, Worcestershire Regiment 253–4

15th Field Park Company, Royal Engineers 209–10, 245

16th Field Regiment Royal Artillery 280–1

44th Home Counties Division 38

50th (Northumbrian) Division 25

50th Division, 523 Petrol Company 174

51st Highland Division 34, 182, 337

51st Lowland Division 47

53rd Field Royal Artillery 284

98th Field Regiment, Royal Artillery 252

98th Surrey and Sussex Yeomanry 48–9

141 Field Ambulance 150

145 Brigade, 48th Infantry Division 64

226 Field Company of the Royal Engineers 298

271 Battalion, 68th Field Regiment, Royal Artillery 32–3

B Company, 1/6th Battalion, Easy Surrey Regiment, The xiii

B Company, 5th Northamptonshire 154–5

Cheshire Territorial Army 84

Devon Heavy Regiment 211

Durham Light Infantry 144, 184

East Surrey Regiment 226

East Yorkshire Regiment 239

Grenadier Guards 36, 79, 95, 210, 213, 266, 305, 337

High Command vii–viii, 221

King's Own Scottish Borderers 146, 261

Lincoln Regiment 210

Loyal Regiment (North Lancashires) 64

Military Police 12, 13, 42, 59, 94, 166, 168, 173, 175, 247, 252, 325

Queen's Royal Regiment 137

RAOC Light Aid Detachment 'The LADS' 64, 66

Rifle Brigade 224, 226

Royal Army Medical Corps (RAMC) 15, 32, 66, 195, 276

Royal Army Service Corps (RASC) 4, 25, 86, 107–8, 118, 147, 200, 213, 252, 300, 313

Royal Artillery 32–3, 56–7, 97, 115, 204, 252, 266, 280–1, 284

Royal Berkshire Regiment 317–18

Royal Corps of Signals 99, 284

Royal Engineers 66, 67, 69, 95, 245, 249, 295, 298, 303, 324, 340

Royal Horse Artillery 153

Sherwood Foresters 288, 313–14

South Wales Borderers 303

Territorials 32, 46, 72, 84, 137, 228, 284, 298

Welsh Guards 95

West Yorkshire Regiment 198

British Expeditionary Force (BEF) ix, xiii, 11, 26, 35, 50, 61, 69, 102, 116, 146, 154, 165, 202, 224, 246, 252, 257, 285, 289–90, 293, 298, 313, 319

battles see under individual battle or place name

cheered into Belgium 33, 69, 253, 318
details of troops evacuated 348
lands in France 50
'Phoney War' and 217–18
retreat of 20, 26, 35, 38, 64, 77, 86, 102, 111, 117, 127, 131, 135, 151, 155, 165, 173, 174, 175, 186, 187, 201, 209–10, 214, 256, 262, 280–1, 318, 330, 331
sets out to France vii
surrounded/cut off viii, 154, 285, 289–90, 293
see also British Army units
Brittany, France 322
Brussels, Belgium xi, 33, 75, 117, 174, 307, 308
Buck, Private Jackie 229
Buckingham Palace 266
Builth Wells, Powys 307
Bulldog, HMS 339
Bullford 11
burials 63, 71, 79, 84, 100, 115, 160, 161, 195, 270, 293
Burntwood, Staffordshire 241, 243
Burrowite 305–6
Bushey Heath, Watford 61

Caerleon, Gwent 268
Calais, France viii, ix, 14, 35, 119, 224–6
Calcutta, HMS 316, 317
camouflage 26, 151
Canadian forces 152, 203–4
Cannock, Staffordshire 241, 243
Carvin, France 117, 323
Cassel, France 70–1, 96
casualty numbers 7, 9, 12, 25, 61, 71, 73, 103, 141, 217, 228, 236

Catterick, Yorkshire 331
cattle trucks 182, 184–5, 202
Chamberlain, Neville 75
Chant, Sergeant 68
Chatham, Kent 181, 277
Chelmsford, Essex 111
Cherbourg, France 116, 122
Chester, Cheshire 84
Chilham, Kent 284
Church Army 302
Churchill, Winston ix, 173, 224, 290–1, 340
civilian casualties 6, 12, 69, 131, 149, 217, 262
Clayton, Bradford 38
Codford St Mary 251
Codrington, HMS 137, 250
Collins, Sergeant S. C. 266
Colne, Lancashire 245
Connell, Henry 182
conscription 107, 121
convoys 307, 331
    ambulance 6, 190, 263, 282
    ambushed 158, 160
    Atlantic 181
    BEF 12, 25, 26, 27, 28
    German reinforcements 74, 95, 96
    NAAFI 12–13
Cookham, Hampshire 98
Cotton, Billy 31
County School for Girls, Ashford 92
Courtrai, Belgium 137, 304, 305
Crabb, Stanley 317
Crested Eagle 169
Crook, Co. Durham 296
Crowter, Corporal 232

D-Day, 1944 69, 86
Dagenham, Essex 84, 322
Danzig, Poland 202
Darlington, Durham 54, 56, 91

Deal, Kent 10
Dean, Corporal 'Dixie' 234
demobbing 5, 203
Dendre, River 304
Derby Royal Infirmary,
    Derbyshire 11
Derbyshire 11, 34
desertion 228
Devizes, Wiltshire 47
Devon 66, 131, 135, 211, 289,
    295
diaries 329–32
despatch riders 174, 176–7,
    288, 308
Distinguished Service Medal
    181
Distinguished Service Order
    233
doctors 220, 244, 282
dogfights 79, 87–8, 289
Doncaster, Yorkshire 331
Dorset 47–8, 83, 121, 124, 127,
    200
Douai, France 95, 298
Dover:
    billets at 154
    bombing of 37
    harbour 279, 312
    length of crossing from to
        119, 134, 141, 178
    lorry transport from 124
    number of ships at 90, 139
    press and photographers at
        88
    return of Allied soldiers to
        xiii, 14, 17, 18, 20, 22, 23,
        37, 47–8, 53, 65, 69, 82, 83,
        88, 90, 96, 102, 107, 119,
        124, 131, 134, 139, 141,
        154, 160, 164, 172, 177,
        178, 179–80, 213, 215,
        224, 241, 250, 253, 259,
        265, 275, 276, 277, 278,
        279, 280, 282, 302, 312

    smoke from Dunkirk visible
        at 278
    trains at 47–8, 65, 66, 83,
        107, 131, 224, 241, 250
    volunteer civilians aide
        homecoming of soldiers at
        160, 164, 253, 259
    white cliffs of 14, 102, 164,
        172, 259, 275
    wounded in 96
    WVS at 53, 65, 172, 215, 282
Dover Barracks 203
Dover Castle 154
Draper, Len 41
drownings 107, 143, 196, 205,
    266, 278, 341
'Dunkerque' (poem) xi–xiii
Dunkerque (French battleship)
    47
Dunkirk:
    beaches xi, 4, 5, 8, 9, 14, 15,
        20, 21, 35, 36, 39, 46, 49,
        51–2, 55, 59, 60, 67, 70, 78,
        85, 89, 100, 102, 106, 107,
        109, 113, 114, 115, 119,
        122, 123, 124, 126, 128,
        130, 132, 136, 138, 140,
        141, 145, 146, 147, 149,
        151, 152, 154, 155, 156,
        162, 163, 167, 168, 169,
        170, 171, 175, 176, 177,
        178, 180, 188, 189, 190,
        194, 195, 196, 197, 199,
        200, 205, 209, 210, 213,
        214–15, 216, 222, 233,
        234, 235, 236, 239, 247,
        248, 252, 258, 262, 263,
        264, 267, 273, 274, 275,
        277, 278, 279, 281, 286,
        287, 289, 290, 295, 299,
        300, 306, 309, 310, 311,
        312, 314, 316, 319, 321,
        322, 339, 340, 342, 345,
        348

details of troops evacuated
348
drownings at 107, 143, 196,
205, 266, 278, 341
dunes 7, 13, 36, 52, 58, 59,
67, 87, 101, 106, 109, 114,
126, 136, 146, 153, 154,
155, 157, 163, 167, 168,
176, 188, 190, 205, 206,
212, 216, 236, 252, 258,
272, 276, 279, 295, 306,
309, 310, 312, 314
as first great epic of the
Second World War vii
harbour area 35, 36, 78, 79,
81, 142, 222, 274, 275,
278, 280, 300, 310, 311,
312, 348
jetty 15, 16, 46, 55, 110, 111,
123, 147, 148, 149, 154,
178, 179, 200, 206, 210,
214, 252–3, 258, 259, 263,
320, 325
last man to leave 241
losses at 347–8
mole xii, 21, 29, 49, 52, 60,
65, 67, 68, 78, 79, 114,
118, 131, 136–7, 141–2,
171, 200, 237, 238, 239,
240, 263, 265, 266, 280,
295, 300, 301, 311, 325,
331
national euphoria in Britain
over ix
noise at 60, 73, 74, 88, 168,
169, 210, 286, 287, 295
oil storage tanks bombed 7,
14, 16, 49, 118, 200, 278,
295, 300
port 153, 269, 285
queues at 9, 49, 51–2, 68, 80,
82, 109, 110, 132, 136–7,
140, 163, 168, 169, 170–1,
189–90, 200, 222, 236,

237, 247, 248, 273, 274,
276, 291, 295, 300, 314
Royal Navy losses at 348
as a sad defeat 173
ships lost at 7, 9, 10, 15, 17,
18, 36, 52, 75, 78, 79, 129,
143, 153, 166, 169, 176,
188, 189, 212–13, 214, 222,
235, 258, 310, 311, 347–8
shore batteries 47
swimming to ships at 29, 50,
89, 102, 107, 112, 132,
143, 149, 154, 157, 178,
196, 197, 205, 206, 261,
264, 341, 344, 345
'Dunkirk Week' 23
dysentery 202

Earley, Berkshire 25
Earnshaw, Mr and Mrs 321–2
Eastern Front 202
Écourt-St-Quentin 252
Edwards, Thomas Selwyn 84
Egypt 69, 121, 174
Elizabeth the Queen Mother,
Queen 202, 283
Elsdon Grove, Bradford 165
Emett, Bob 227
English Channel 11, 14, 79
Essex 83, 84, 111, 265, 322,
340
Estaires, France 198
evacuations 62
'every man for himself' 9, 27,
136, 176, 188, 194, 313,
338, 342
Exeter, Devon 66, 253
Exeter, HMS 200
exhaustion 48, 77, 102, 121,
124, 151, 183, 211, 256,
260, 311

Faroe Islands 343
field guns 152, 155, 347

fifth-columnists 173, 258, 309
First World War, 1914–18 22, 207, 245
    British use of weapons from 32–3, 37
    familiarity of place names from 137, 147
    French civilian knowledge of English and 138
    Hill No. 60 198
    shell holes from used to shelter in 185
    veterans 144, 151, 309
Fitzroy, HMS 177–8, 181
Flint, Charlie 148
Folkestone, Kent 23, 160, 200, 211, 320
food/rations 94
    farms and 77, 87, 100, 166–7, 183, 256, 294, 330
    given as gifts on return to England 65, 69, 80, 93, 112, 116, 172, 211, 259, 268, 282, 293, 297, 302
    lack of food 7, 8, 43, 45, 49, 70, 75, 77, 81, 96, 117, 151, 169, 227, 233, 239, 300, 304, 330
    lack of water 8
    looting of shops 26
    NAAFI and 13, 34, 113, 128, 175
    provided on embarkation at Dunkirk 15, 103, 124, 240–1, 250
    Red Cross food parcels 76
    rum ration 191
    WVS provide 37, 53, 61, 66, 80, 101, 112, 158, 172, 215, 241, 282, 302, 312
France:
    battles in *see under individual battle name*
    BEF arrive in vii, 32, 33, 38, 43, 50, 137, 144, 184, 186, 201, 211, 213, 228, 261, 313
    D-Day and *see* D-Day
    explosion of German armies into vii–viii, 150
    fall of 75
    refugees *see* refugees
    see also French Army *and under individual area and place name*
Free French 283–4
French Army 35, 45, 59, 68, 69, 75, 97, 117, 152–3, 188, 201, 226, 237, 238, 262, 263, 272, 297, 300
    3rd French Infantry Regiment 284
    animosity between British Army and 167
    anti-tank guns 42
    artillery 6, 52, 257–8
    battleships 47, 142, 278
    cavalry 131, 152, 272
    defeat of 117
    at Dunkirk 9, 10, 35, 45, 50, 65, 66–7, 68, 75, 78, 97, 116, 127, 130, 145, 187, 188, 222, 225, 226, 237, 238, 263, 282, 299, 300, 308, 325–6
    fifth-columnists and 173, 258
    on the Maginot Line 201
    'medics' 34
    motorcyclists 173
    soldiers in hospital in England 283–4
    tanks 255
French Navy 341
'40 Hommes – 8 Chevaux' (forty men or eight horses) 116, 184
Froyennes, France 293

gangrene 16, 243
gas 12, 16, 67, 73, 100–1, 111,
    253, 281, 288, 293
gas cape 12, 111, 253
gas mask 12, 43, 253, 255, 288,
    293
Gedling, Nottinghamshire 275
Geneva Convention 19
George VI, King 251, 266
Geraldo 31
Geraardsbergen, Belgium 304
German Air Force *see* Luftwaffe
    and Stukas
German Army:
  airborne troops 173, 307
  artillery 67, 107, 147, 188,
    206, 215, 269, 274, 282
  Battle of Dunkirk and ix
  Calais, battle of 119, 224
  Eastern Front 202
  fifth-columnists and 173, 307,
    309
  gas attacks 288
  High Command vii
  invasion of Belgium viii, 4,
    33, 38, 48, 76–7, 124, 165,
    284, 307, 313
  invasion of Holland viii, 33,
    48, 124, 165
  Low Countries, invasion of
    vii, 48, 262
  Maginot Line, break through
    the 81
  morale of 74–5
  POWs, treatment of 31, 73–6,
    73, 88–9, 145, 158, 182,
    183, 184, 201, 202, 203,
    221, 228, 232, 238, 272,
    290, 291, 322, 325, 333,
    338, 342, 347
  rumours about 221–2
  snipers 326–9
  superior equipment of 33, 37,
    38

  tanks 29, 70, 117, 144, 145,
    158, 171, 226, 293
  underestimation of by British
    authorities 38
Germany:
  Allies in 51, 121
  POWs in 73, 75–6, 202, 333
  see also German Army *and*
    under individual place
    name
Gestapo 183, 184
Glen Avon 287
Gobberon 169
Godalming, Surrey 139
Goldsack, Corporal Percy 151,
    152
Gort, General 137–8, 144, 170
Gossamer, HMS 277–8
Grafton, HMS 61
Grantham, Lincolnshire 47, 48
Gravelines, France 215, 217
Gravesend, Kent 64
Great Doddington,
    Northamptonshire 215
Greece 104
Green, Private Bill 229, 232
Greenwood, Sapper Allan 104–5
Guildford, Surrey 23, 24

Halifax, Yorkshire 47, 320
Halifax, Canada 89
Halycon, HMS 311, 312
Harlech, Gwynedd 260
Hartley, Keith (Kev) 168
Harwich, Essex 277, 287
Hazebrouck, France 96
Headcorn, Kent 92, 93
Heinkel (German aircraft) 60,
    165
heroism xi, 332
  of British nurses 38
  defence of Calais and ix
  French and Belgian civilians
    treat BEF as heroes 70, 318

of French nuns 36
refugees change attitude towards British troops 70
returning British soldiers treated as heroes 61, 120, 192, 253, 259
unsung 339–40
Hilda 85
Hill No. 60, Flanders 198
Hinckley, Leicestershire 326
Hitchin, Hertfordshire 313
Hitler, Adolf 84, 116, 150, 251, 289
Hokaido, Japan 88
Holland 323
  German Army attacks through vii, viii, 33, 124, 165
  POWs force-marched through 182, 202
  shipping from 213, 301
Horrocks, General Sir Brian 53–6
horses 6, 44, 87, 114, 116, 131, 132, 152–3, 184, 225, 247, 257–8, 272, 294–5
hospital ships:
  bombed/sunk 7, 17, 36, 60, 114–15, 135, 286, 311, 312, 348
  troops taken into 14, 15, 16, 18, 36, 119, 221, 278
hospital trains 16, 83, 312
hospitals 11, 15, 16, 30, 62, 83, 153, 174, 211, 217–19, 241–5, 265, 282–4, 290, 345
Hounslow, Middlesex 277
House of Commons ix
Houtkerque, Belgium 64
howitzer 237, 272
Huddersfield, Yorkshire 320–1
Hull, Yorkshire 177, 345
humour 40, 131–2, 151

Hungerford, Berkshire 207
Hurricanes 326

Ijzer, Belgium 304, 305
India 101
injuries *see* wounded/injuries
Ipswich, Suffolk 47, 308
Isle of Man 119, 171, 172
Isle of Man 320
isolation camps 50
Italy 60, 69, 104, 121

Jackson, Edward 24–5
Japan 31, 88
John Holt 341
Johnson, General 55

Kelly, HMS 181
Kent 64, 92, 107, 251, 284, 296
Kettering, Northamptonshire 89, 162, 317
Kidderminster, Worcestershire 259
Kingston-upon-Thames, Surrey 91
Kirkby la Thorpe, Lincolnshire 56

La Panne, Belgium 132, 140, 236
  drownings at 157
  in flames xi
  lack of organisation at 67
  shells fall on 171
  ships sunk off 141
  troops on sand dunes 7–8, 13, 29, 51, 58–9, 67, 78, 141, 147, 153, 210, 235
  vehicles abandoned outside 147, 167, 175, 233, 247
  village of 55, 166, 167, 171
  wounded at 148
labour camps 202

Lady of Mann 172
Lancastria, HMT 340–4, 345–6
Lark Hill near Salisbury 104
Law, Mark 27
Lawrence, Sid 31
Le Bassée canal region, France 200, 254
Le Havre, France 90
leaflets, propaganda 70, 90, 170, 269
leave 5, 53, 101, 149, 164–5, 207, 208, 209, 211, 259, 261, 265, 302, 317–18, 343
Lee-Enfield rifles 37–8, 231
Leeds, West Yorkshire 150, 262
Leie, River 304
Leopold of Belgium, King 4, 86
Lewis gun 9, 56, 135, 140–1
Lichfield, Staffordshire 266
lifeboats 10, 18, 19, 139, 249, 253
Lille, France 25, 26, 57, 86, 127, 137, 158, 209, 245, 246, 262, 284–5, 298, 322
limpet mines 305–6
little/private boats 8, 24, 30, 36–7, 38, 46, 52–3, 55, 82, 89, 109, 110, 121, 139, 145, 157, 163, 168–9, 170, 171, 176, 177, 278–9, 290, 297, 339, 347
Lockerbie, Scotland 22
Lomme le Marais, France 162
Loughborough, Leicestershire 332
Louvain, Belgium 245, 303, 307
Low Countries 48, 116, 262
Lowestoft, Suffolk 295
Lübeck, Germany 202
Luftwaffe 8, 16, 17, 33, 42, 77, 87–8, 248, 271, 285, 286, 291, 295
Luxembourg vii, viii

Lyme Regis, Dorset 228
Lys, River 293
Lysander aircraft 138

machine-guns 6, 16, 19, 20, 22, 28, 33, 49, 60, 74, 77, 82, 87, 97, 102–3, 104, 105, 106, 109, 113, 126, 141, 143, 145, 146, 149, 153, 158, 159, 165, 170, 175, 178, 179, 186, 187, 188, 189, 194, 211, 227, 232, 236, 247, 252, 255, 262, 265, 273, 276, 279, 288, 292, 300, 301, 308, 319, 322, 340
Maginot Line viii, 38, 81, 201, 211, 289, 292
Maid of Orleans, The 275
Maidenhead, Berkshire 115
Malaya 88
Malcolm, HNS 181–2
Malo-les-Bains, France 65, 115
Malta 144
Manchester, Greater Manchester 119, 158, 200, 287
Manorbier, Wales 69
Mansfield Woodhouse, Nottinghamshire 217
Manxman 172
MARCO munitions factory 47
Margate, Kent 80, 144, 158, 192, 213, 296, 331
Marienburg labour camp, East Prussia 202
Market Harborough, Leicestershire 158
Marley, Sapper Sergeant 165
Massbach, Germany 184
Massey Shaw 297
medals/honours:
  Distinguished Service Medal 181

Distinguished Service Order 233
Dunkirk Medal 53–4, 56, 104, 181, 224
Military Medal 68, 266
Medway Queen 22, 79
Melton Mowbray, Leicestershire 48
mental effects of war:
  acts of cowardice brought on by terror 170
  'bomb happy' 132
  'cracked' 170
  doctors worked up to point of breakdown 220
  loss of nerve 18, 170
  nervous breakdown 148
  nightmares/bad dreams 5, 115
  shell shock 11, 87, 243, 345
  shooting of soldiers showing 170
Merchant Navy 160–2, 275
Merthyr Tydfil, Glamorgan 132
Messerschmitt (German aircraft) 97, 100, 210
Mexborough, Yorkshire 94
MI5 38
Middlesborough, North Yorkshire 134
Military Medal 68, 266
mines 53, 72, 85, 160, 181, 277, 278, 308, 342
minesweepers 85, 102, 139, 177, 191, 277, 311
Mitchell, Corporal William 333
Monmouth, Monmouthshire 302
Mona's Isle 119
Montgomery, General 55, 68, 210, 245, 251
morale 76, 132, 190, 264
Moroccan soldiers 24, 142
Morris, Frank 27

mortars 72, 211, 227, 230, 231, 292, 319, 323
motorcycles 36, 96, 107, 129, 130, 205, 247, 347
Mountbatten, Lord 181
Munro, Captain 67

NAAFI (Navy, Army and Air Force Institutes) 12–13, 34, 68, 113, 118, 151, 163, 164, 257, 258
Nash, Major 228, 229
Neave, Airey 225
Nederbrakel, Belgium 117
Nether Kellet, Lancashire 146
Newbury, Berkshire 76, 207
Newcastle-under-Lyme, Staffordshire 124
Newhaven, East Sussex 14, 15
Newport, Gwent 98, 268
Nieuwpoort, Belgium 156
Normandy landings, 1944 103, 217, 344
North Africa 63, 69, 121, 174
Northampton, Northamptonshire 275
Northamptonshire 89, 154, 198, 215, 317
Norton, Stourbridge 32
Nottingham, Nottinghamshire 14, 266
nurses vii, 30, 31, 38, 199, 217–19, 241–5, *244*, 282–4, *283*, 320

Oakham, Leicestershire 267
Oldham, Lancashire 104
Ostend, Belgium 252
Oudenaarde, Belgium 38, 125, 137, 154, 307

Page, Corporal 43, 44
Paignton, Devon 131, 135
Pangbourne, HMS 103–4

Panzers 117, 171, 293
Paris, France 77, 84, 87
Paris, SS 14, 15
Patton, General 184
Pegwell Bay, Kent 297
pen friends 260
Pen Mill station, Yeovil 120
pensions 161, 184, 346
Pepin, Peggy 162
Péronne, France 135
'Phoney War', 1939–40 vii,
    217, 245, 292
photographer, war 60
pillboxes 155
Pluto (Petrol Line Under the
    Ocean) 344
Plymouth, Devon 291, 341, 343
poetry xi–xiii, 3, 162, 332–3
Poland 75, 202
Poperinge, Belgium 118, 126,
    146, 214, 246, 285, 305, 307
Portsmouth, Hampshire 116,
    311
Post Office's London Telephone
    Service, Waterloo Bridge
    House 207
POWs (prisoners-of-war) 228,
    232, 238, 290, 322, 342
  conditions of 203
  deaths in camps of 338
  escape attempts 182–3
  exchange of 291
  German airmen taken 272
  German armoured advance
    and 145, 158
  Japanese 31, 88
  liberation of 184, 202
  number taken by Germans
    347
  prison camps 73, 75–6, 182,
    183–4, 202, 333, 338
  Red Cross and 75–6
  return of 89
  rumours concerning 221–2

  shootings of 202, 221–2
  Singapore 88
  slave labour and 88, 203
  suicide of 202
  surrender of 73–6
  transport of 75, 182, 202
  weather and 75
propaganda 70, 90, 160, 269
Purley on Thames, Reading 66
Pwllheli, Wales 83

Radford, Pilot Officer 185
RAF (Royal Air Force):
  bitterness towards 150
  dogfights 87–8
  fighter crashes 185
  German propaganda and 170
  lack of cover for Dunkirk
    evacuations 150, 194, 224,
    258–9, 286
  lorries 187
  outnumbered by German air
    force 37–8
Ramsgate, Kent 10–11, 23, 29,
    36, 40, 56, 60, 66, 115,
    197, 296, 306, 326
Reading, Berkshire 23, 24, 25,
    40, 54, 56, 66, 298, 302
Red Cross 30, 48, 60, 61, 75–6,
    79–80, 151, 312
Redcar, North Yorkshire 280,
    306
Redhill, Surrey 23, 152
refugees:
  as target for dive-bombers
    100, 117, 149, 155, 174,
    186, 215–16, 217, 257
  Belgian 77
  change in attitude towards
    Allied troops 70
  clog roads 12, 86, 87, 100,
    117, 145, 155, 225, 247,
    256, 257, 285, 294, 299,
    330

French 41, 77
retribution attacks on
  German soldiers 175
wounded 33, 34
Remembrance Day 32
reunions 344
Richmond, London 53
Rigby, Cyril 199, 200
Ripon, North Yorkshire 177
Rochdale, Lancashire 120, 160
Rommel, Field Marshal 201
Ross, Commander 277
Ross, Lieutenant 152
Rotherham, South Yorkshire
  282
Roubaix, France 203, 239, 245,
  288, 307
Rouen, France 184
Royal Eagle 126
Royal Military School of
  Music, Kneller Hall 5
Royal Navy 312, 348
  destroyers 7, 36, 46, 50, 55,
    60, 65, 88, 136, 139, 154,
    167, 181, 206, 210, 212,
    213, 222, 237, 249, 250,
    253, 275, 278, 279, 296,
    301, 315, 331, 339, 348
  Dunkirk evacuation and 53,
    82, 88, 111, 138, 143, 145,
    200, 202, 277–8, 294, 296,
    316, 348
  frigates 143
  guns 88
  hospital ships 7, 14, 15, 16,
    17, 18, 36, 60, 114–15, 119,
    135, 221, 278, 286, 311
  lesser naval vessels 348
  losses 36, 348
  minesweepers 85, 102, 139,
    177, 191, 277, 311
  motorboats 145
  personnel carriers 348
  sloops 348
  small craft 110
  trawlers 19, 20, 139, 142,
    177, 282, 348
  U-boat attacks and 32
  see also under individual
    vessel name
Rugby, Warwickshire 298
Rugeley, Staffordshire 243
rumours 57, 149, 169, 170,
  171, 221–2, 246, 258, 285
Rushden, Northamptonshire
  198

Sales, Private 228
Salisbury, Wiltshire 11, 66, 80,
  81, 104, 112, 113
Salisbury Royal Infirmary,
  Wiltshire 11
Saltash, HMS 143
Salvation Army 37, 302
Sanders, Alan 168, 172
Sanders, Dennis 168, 172
sappers 68, 104, 165, 235, 239,
  240, 246, 250, 340
Scotia, SS 143–4
Scotland 22, 91, 121, 343
Searchline 317
Seclin, France 209, 323
Second World War, 1939–45
  air war 7, 8, 16, 17–19, 21,
    34, 35, 36, 37, 41, 50, 52,
    55, 58, 60, 65, 69, 70, 72,
    75, 79, 82, 87, 97, 100,
    102, 103, 105, 106, 113,
    117, 118, 122, 123, 126,
    128, 131, 133, 137, 141,
    142, 149, 153, 154, 155,
    163, 165, 166, 170, 171,
    176, 179, 185, 186, 187,
    199, 201, 204, 206, 207,
    210, 211, 212, 218, 225,
    236, 248, 262, 263, 273,
    276, 279, 280, 281, 288,
    295, 301, 305, 309, 314,

319–20, 322, 323, 324, 330, 339, 340–1
Atlantic convoys 181–2
Battle of Britain 286
Blitz 208
'blitzkreig' 150
British Army see British Army units and British Expeditionary Force (BEF)
Calais, battle of viii, ix, 14, 35, 119, 224–6
D-Day, 1944 69, 86
Dunkirk see Dunkirk
Eastern Front 202
end of 6
fifth-columnists 173, 258, 309
French army see French army
gas attacks 12, 16, 67, 73, 100–1, 111, 253, 281, 288, 293
German army see German army
labour camps 202
Maginot Line viii, 38, 81, 201, 211, 289, 292
North Africa 63, 69, 121, 174
Pacific War 31, 88
'Phoney War', 1939–40 vii, 217, 245, 292
POWs 31, 73–6, 73, 88–9, 145, 158, 182, 183, 184, 201, 202, 203, 221, 228, 232, 238, 272, 290, 291, 322, 325, 333, 338, 342, 347
propaganda war 70, 90, 170, 269
refugees 12, 33, 34, 41, 70, 77, 86, 87, 100, 117, 145, 149, 155, 174, 175, 186, 215–16, 217, 225, 247, 256, 257, 285, 294, 299, 330
tank warfare viii, 27, 29, 33,

37, 49, 70, 73, 74, 97, 119, 135, 144, 158, 186, 202, 225, 226, 245, 255, 256, 257, 263, 272, 293, 303
Sedan, France 116
Selby, North Yorkshire 289
Semer, Suffolk 207
Semple, Bill 94, 97
Sheerness, Kent 47, 126
shell shock 11, 87, 243, 345
Shepton Mallet, Somerset 54, 149
Shipley, West Yorkshire 6
shrapnel 9, 15, 19, 31, 101, 103, 136, 254, 283
Singapore 88
Skillbeck, 'Chuck' 199–200
Skipjack, HMS 179–80, 311
smashing/sabotaging equipment 8, 12–13, 36, 40, 57, 71, 81, 100, 145, 167, 168, 188, 247
snipers 228–30, 326–9
Somerset 121, 149
Somme, France 201
South Eastern and Chatham Railway 22, 23
Southampton, Hampshire 24–5, 30, 89, 101, 111, 122, 201
Southend, Essex 47
Southsea, Hampshire 339, 340
South Shields, Tyne and Wear 192
Soviet Union 202
Spackman, Sergeant Clifford 62–4, 62
Spitfire 37
SS 97
St Albans, Hertfordshire 213
St Ives, Cornwall 292
St Malo, France 4
St Nazaire, France 90, 340–2
St Pol, France 105, 184
St Sylvestre-Cappel, France 27, 29

St Valéry-en-Caux, France
  338–40
Stafford 209
Stalag VIII B. 73, 75–6
Stalag XXA 333
Steele, R. G. 'Pip' 44
Steenvoorde, Belgium 64
Stephenson, Adrian 254
Stepney, London 321
stick grenade 228
Stoke-on-Trent, Staffordshire
  30, 226
Stone, Staffordshire 50
Strait of Dover 14, 17, 65
stretcher-parties 11, 15, 16, 21,
  22, 73, 83, 148, 150, 164,
  210, 220, 229, 274, 276,
  293, 320
Strontian, Acharacle 224
Stukas (German aircraft) 100,
  130, 155, 165, 225, 248,
  292
  Allied soldiers fire at with
    rifles 117
  attack civilians 117, 165,
    169–70
  attack Dunkirk mole 142
  attack ships at Dunkirk 114,
    300, 301
  attack ships in Channel 339
  attack soldiers on Dunkirk
    sand dunes 51–2, 276,
    319–20
  bail outs from 301
  bomb convoys 70, 96, 156
  Douai raids 95
  fear of attack from 142
  lack of RAF cover for attacks
    from 194
  leaflet drops 170
  length of bombardments 60
  Lewis gun used to attack 135
  number of 34, 113, 142
  pilots captured 301

'screamers' 44, 51–2, 102,
  168, 194
sheltering from 39, 43,
  299–300, 319–20
yellow nose of 102
suicide 202, 203
Sunderland, Tyne and Wear 144
Surrey 11, 24, 139, 152, 226,
  241, 282–3, 345
Sutton Emergency Hospital 11
swimming to ships, Dunkirk
  29, 50, 89, 102, 107, 112,
  132, 143, 149, 154, 157,
  178, 196, 197, 205, 206,
  261, 264, 341, 344, 345

tank warfare 303
  Abbeville area viii
  anti-tank guns 42, 117, 135,
    144, 205, 347
  anti-tank rifle 144, 257
  arrival of German armour at
    St Sylvestre-Cappel 29
  battles see under individual
    battle or area name
  breakdown of British tanks
    225
  British ambushed by German
    tanks 158
  British anti-aircraft guns and
    97
  Calais battle and 224, 225,
    226
  First World War tanks used
    by British 37
  German air attacks on Allied
    tanks 33
  Le Bassée canal region,
    France 255–6
  light tanks 272
  new concept of viii
  Panzer tanks 117, 171, 293
  regiments see British army
    units and German army 202

tank traps 245
tanks put beyond use 225, 272
Taylor, Curly 40
.303 rifle 27, 67, 144, 205
Thorrington, Essex 265
Tidworthm Wiltshire 207, 313
Tidworth Military Hospital, Wiltshire 11
Tonbridge, Kent 23
torpedoes 32, 61, 223, 278, 315, 341, 342
Tourcoing, France 155
Tournai, France 34, 256, 293
Trent Valley 241, 243
troop trains 23–4, 60, 69, 112, 120
Tweseldown, Hampshire 119
Tynwald 171
Tyrie, Fraserburgh 184

U-boats 32, 169, 278
Union Jack Club, Waterloo Road, London 208
Upper Silesia 75

Vanquisher, HMS 50
Veurne, Belgium 226
Vimy, France 20
Vimy Ridge, France 96, 185
Vitry-en Artois aerodrome, France 51

Wakeful, HMS 169, 278, 315, 317
War Office, British 62
Ward, Tony 179–81
Warner, Lieutenant 64, 66
Warwick, Warwickshire 120
Waterloo, London 207–9
Waterloo, Belgium 69–70, 209
Watson, Commander 103, 105
'We're going to hang out the washing on the Siegfried

Line' (song) vii, 74
weather 17, 43, 59, 64, 65, 75, 87, 116, 118, 125, 141, 152, 169, 185, 187, 208, 216, 284, 292, 331
Webster, Captain 252
Welwyn Garden City, Hertfordshire 211
Westende, Belgium 252
Westminster Abbey, London 54
Weybridge, Surrey 241
Weymouth, Dorset 121, 128
Wez-Velvain, Belgium 253–4
Whitley Bay, Tyne and Wear 101
Wilson, Harry 345–6, *345*
Wiltshire 61, 80, 81, 113, 164, 251, 313, 326
Winchelsea, HMS 213, 214, 253
wireless communication 18, 152, 284, 329
Wisbech, Cambridgeshire 99
Wollaton Park, Nottingham 14
Wolsey, HMS 65, 206
Woodchurch, Kent 251
Worthing, SS 17
wounded/injuries 31, 33, 34, 35, 82–4, 96, 101, 114, 119, 123, 135, 136, 140, 147, 148, 158, 159, 178, 180, 182, 199, 203, 210, 215, 217–19, 221, 225, 228, 235, 241–3, 244, 254, 263, 266, 267, 269, 273, 274, 276–7, 278, 290, 291, 293, 294, 295, 307, 311, 321, 322, 345, 346, 347
  ambulance trains 15, 16, 30, 265
  at Calais 14
  courage of 28
  doctors and 220, 244, 282
  at Dunkirk 21, 35, 82, 136,

178, 210, 273, 274, 276, 278, 295, 311
gangrene 16, 243
horses 6
hospital ships 7, 14, 15, 16, 17, 18, 36, 60, 114–15, 119, 135, 221, 278, 286, 311, 312, 348
hospital trains 16, 83, 312
hospitals 11, 15, 16, 30, 62, 83, 153, 174, 211, 217–19, 241–5, 265, 282–4, 290, 345
at La Panne 7–8
medical centres and 7–8
nature of wounds 31
numbers of 119, 123, 347
nurses and vii, 30, 31, 38, 199, 217–19, 241–5, 244, 282–4, *283*, 320
prisoners and 74, 291
refugees 33
return home to England of 10–11, 14
on ships 10–11, 82–4, 135, 263–4
stretcher-parties 11, 15, 16,

21, 22, 73, 83, 148, 150, 164, 210, 220, 229, 274, 276, 293, 320
Wrexham, Clwyd 86
Wright, Lance Corporal 96–7
WVS (Women's Voluntary Service):
ambulance teams run by 241
give 'wonderful reception' to returning BEF soldiers 37
lost property and 66
postcards collected and posted by 80
provide returning soldiers with food and tea 53, 61, 80, 101, 158, 172, 215, 282, 302, 312
relay messages to families of returning soldiers 112

Yeovil, Somerset 53, 120, 121, 207
Yewdale, SS 9, 10
Young, Joan M. 76
Ypres, Belgium 20, 38, 98, 307

Zonnebeke, Belgium 38

Index of Contributors

Entries in *italics* indicate photographs.

Bambury, James A. 48–50, *49*
Bamford, Ken 11–14, *13*
Bazeley, E. G. R. (Reg) 165–74, *169*
Beard, Cyril L. 56–61, *58*
Bishop, Brian 20–2, *21*
Blackburn, Reginald 94–8, *95*
Blakeburn, Arthur 139–44
Bowers, George 25–30, *27*
Brown, Gladys 47–8, *48*
Brown, Reg 340–5, *342*
Brown, Robert 102–4
Burbidge, Bill 154–8, *156*
Burrow, Albert 'Bunny' 113–15, *115*
Butcher, Peter W. 213–15, *214*
Butterfield, Lily 3–6, *5*

Cannon, Reginald 177–82
Carter, John W. 253–9, *255*
Cassell, William 277–80, *279*
Castle, Graham 150–2
Chalker, Harold J. 124–7, *126*
Clapham, Fred 184–92, *186*
Clarke, Alfred 'Nobby' 174–7, *175*
Cobley, Dick 115–20, *118*
Collins, Mary 120–1
Collins, Mrs P. M. 265–6, *265*
Cope, Mary 30–2, *32*
Critchell, George 64–6, *65*

Davies, Arthur 132–4, *133*
Davies, Ivor 84–6, *85*
Davison, Ron xiii, 226–41, *234*
Dilley, Stanley C. 211–13, *212*

Earnshaw, Raymond 209–11, *211*
Edwards, Lawrence 217–24, *220*
Etherington, Joyce 243–5, *244*

Flaherty, Bill 131–2, *131*
Foard, Ernest 66–9, *68*

Gingell, Wilfred A. 252–3, *252*
Grant, Verna 104–7, *105*
Greenhow, Mrs P. 111–13
Gunn, Arthur Thomas 6–11, *8*

Hall, Jim 322–6, *324*
Hamer, Mary 259–60
Hammond, Norman 135–7, *136*
Hammond, Thomas 'Darkie' 262–5
Handley, Mr L. 144–6
Harfitt, Veronica 80–1
Hatchman, Ted 317–22, *319*
Hellings, Douglas 50–3, *52*
Hewett, Jack 22–5, *24*
Hine, Anne 98–9, *98*
Hogg, Kenneth 162–5, *164*
Homan, Clifford 192–8, *193*

Jacklin, Alice 261–2
Jewiss, Pauline 62–4, *63*
Jones, Ernest 198–201, *199*
Jones, John 303–7, *305*
Jones, Thomas William 32–8, *37*

Kerley, William Leslie (Digger) 329–32, *330*
Kingsley, Peter P. 298–303, *300*
Kite, Fred 224–6, *225*

Lane, Dora 241–3, *242*
Launders, Joan 92–4
Lee, Frank 14–20, *16*
Legg, Richard 201–3, *202*
Long, Ernest G. 76–80, *78*

Marshall, Wyndham G. 280–2
Martin, Alex 284–7, *286*
Martin, Eric 296–8, *297*
Martin, Ken 203–7, *205*
McDonald, Percy W. 107–11, *108*
McNicholas, Cecilia 215–17, *217*
Mitchell, Corporal William 332–3, *333*
Montague, Thelma 266–7, *267*
Morgan, Joan 267–8, *268*
Mortimer, Ted 269–75, *273*
Mott, Ronald H. W. 137–9, *139*
Mutch, Fred 127–31, *129*

Naylor, Ken 245–51, *249*
Newbould, E. 146–50, *147*

Noble, Claude 'Mush' 288–9, *288*

Page, Frederick 40–7, *45*
Parry, Rex 207–9, *208*
Paton, Myrtle 282–4, *283*
Patrick, Stanley 313–17, *314*
Pepin, Peggy 160–2, *161*
Porter, J. W. 81–4
Pusey, Henry 275–7, *276*

Rabbets, Edgar 326–9, *327*
Raynsford, Bob 38–40, *40*
Robertson, Douglas 'Titch' 182–4

Sadler, Eileen F. 289–92
Sharp, Bob 337–40, *339*
Shearman, Frank 86–9, *88*
Smart, Roy H. 53–6
Stribley, Leon G. 307–13

Tatlow, Lieutenant Alan xi–xiii
Turner, Alex 292–6, *294*

Vincent, William B. 99–101, *101*

Walker, Jim 89–91, *91*
Williams, Charles 152–4, *153*
Wilson, Florence 345–6
Worswick, Arthur 158–60
Wright, Wilfred 121–4, *123*

Young, Joan M. 76
Young, Rowland J. S. 69–76, *73*